"I love pastors. I am humbled by the fact that pastors often come to me for advice and wisdom. Now I have a resource that answers so many of their questions. This book is fantastic! There is no doubt that it will be on my shelf as a reference for years to come. Great work Gary McIntosh and Charles Arn!"

Thom S. Rainer, president and CEO, LifeWay Christian Resources

"Drawing on their combined church leadership wisdom, Gary McIntosh and Charles Arn have created an incredible reference guide that reflects their passion for helping local churches fulfill the Great Commission. *What Every Pastor Should Know* is aptly named; the practical information in these pages is essential knowledge for those of us who want to lead growing, effective churches."

Nelson Searcy, lead pastor, The Journey Church; founder, www.ChurchLeaderInsights.com

"*What Every Pastor Should Know* is an invaluable reference book. Its value lies in being well researched, comprehensive, specific, and practical. It is also 'user friendly' in listing so many guidelines and rules to help church leaders keep on course and not become sidetracked."

Eddie Gibbs, Professor Emeritus, Fuller Seminary

"A wealth of insights for pastors on the day-to-day issues of leading an effective church."

Ed Stetzer, author of *Subversive Kingdom*

"I am thrilled that Gary McIntosh and Charles Arn have prepared this book. Both of these writers have an excellent history of research as well as a heart commitment to the church and the ministry of Jesus Christ. When they write *What Every Pastor Should Know*, they mean it, and every pastor should read this book to find out what they must know."

Elmer Towns, cofounder, Liberty University

WHAT EVERY
PASTOR
SHOULD KNOW

WHAT EVERY
PASTOR
SHOULD KNOW

101 Indispensable Rules of Thumb
for Leading Your Church

GARY L. McINTOSH AND CHARLES ARN

BakerBooks
a division of Baker Publishing Group
Grand Rapids, Michigan

Published by Baker Books
a division of Baker Publishing Group
P.O. Box 6287, Grand Rapids, MI 49516-6287
www.bakerbooks.com

Printed in the United States of America

Library of Congress Cataloging-in-Publication Data is on file at the Library of Congress, Washington, DC.

ISBN 978-0-8010-1435-2

13   14   15   16   17   18   19   7   6   5   4   3   2   1

Contents

12. Ministry Rules for Finances   200

13. Ministry Rules for Change   216

14. Ministry Rules for Revitalization   232

15. Ministry Rules for Demographics   252

Introduction

Rules, Laws, and Ratios

"How many visitors do we need to grow?" Jenny asked to no one in particular, as she slid into an overstuffed chair in the Petersons' living room for the church's quarterly leadership gathering.

"Well, technically, just one," Mike responded while balancing his steaming cup of coffee.

"But according to our attendance records, last year we had over seventy visitors . . . and our worship attendance is down. So it seems like even seventy isn't enough."

"I guess it depends on how many of them stay," Andy remarked as he joined the conversation.

"And how many of our own members stop coming," Sylvia commented with an edge of disgust in her voice.

"Since we're pondering imponderable questions, I've got one," Andy said. "I'm trying to figure out how many workers we're going to need this fall in the nursery. Any suggestions?"

"I think one should be plenty," Mike responded. "Of course I'm not a young mom so I'm not sure what they would say. And if we're bringing up questions about doing church, I've been wondering about how our budget should be broken down. For example, how much should we be spending for salaries, debt reduction, educational materials, mortgage, and outreach? With all this belt tightening, our finance committee will be rethinking our expenditures, and I'd like some guidelines on this."

Listening to all these questions, the pastor couldn't help but feel a twinge of anxiety in the pit of his stomach. He wished he knew the answers, but he wasn't sure either.

Questions like these are similar to ones we have heard from pastors and other church leaders in our years of consulting. The specific people and situations may vary, but there is one basic question: Are there standard guidelines—or rules—for effective church ministry? The concerns, like church ministry, itself, cover a wide breadth of topics:

How many staff members does our church need?

How much should we be spending on our mortgage?

How many visitors do we need to grow?

How many people will our auditorium actually hold before attendance plateaus?

How closely must we reflect our community for growth to occur?

For a number of years church leaders have analyzed, observed, and collected standard ways of measuring various aspects of church ministry. While many helpful guidelines are available, they are spread out in articles, books, and research papers too numerous for most church leaders to read, let alone remember or find when needed.

Thus we've written *What Every Pastor Should Know* in an effort to consolidate a number of these rules, ratios, and guidelines. Between us, we have led or contributed to more than eleven hundred national and local church seminars, conducted more than five hundred church consultations, and researched and written several dozen books on the broad topics related to congregational health, growth, and ministry. This book reflects those years of experience in an effort to present bite-sized insights and rules of thumb to church leaders on the go.

Think of this book as a reference to keep near your desk, providing you with basic guidelines for a fruitful ministry. Granted there are significant differences among churches, including their community, age, location on the institutional life cycle, denominational affiliation, and a host of other factors. These all contribute to the dynamic mix that makes for a healthy church. Thus while the rules of thumb in this book are not guaranteed to work in every situation, we believe they are generally reliable for most churches.

We don't claim that these are the *only* rules of thumb that exist. In fact, we encourage you to send us rules of thumb that have been helpful in your ministry. We may include them (with credit to you) in another volume.

If you're seeking an answer to a specific question or ministry area, turn to the contents where the rules are listed under each chapter title. We've tried to group the rules and guidelines into major categories, such as facilities, evangelism, education, and so on. Each category or chapter has a half dozen or so recommendations we think apply to most churches. Each rule includes a statement of the rule, followed by an introduction, an explanation, and then some practical ideas on how to apply the rule. If you don't have any particular questions in mind, it will be helpful simply to browse through the different rules and consider whether your church is (or could be) applying them. As you look at your church through the lens of these rules, you'll discover good ideas to improve your ministry.

Helping local churches fulfill the Great Commission is our passion. We hope this book proves to be a practical resource as you seek to make disciples in response to the call and example of Jesus Christ.

1

Ministry Rules for Evangelism and Outreach

The focus of this first chapter is evangelism and outreach because these topics are so important. Churches that do not focus on these ministries will die in just a few generations. Hoping and even praying that the harvest will be brought in on its own is simply wishful thinking. Yet many churches seem to base their activities on this naïve expectation. Howard Snyder observes, and we agree: "Evangelism is the first priority of the church's ministry. . . . The church that fails to evangelize is both biblically unfaithful and strategically shortsighted."[1]

It is not just survival that should motivate a church to prioritize evangelism and outreach. It is the very call of Jesus—the head of the church—who concluded his earthly ministry with the words: "Go out and train everyone you meet, far and near, in this way of life, marking them by baptism in the threefold name: Father, Son, and Holy Spirit" (Matt. 28:19 Message).

In our experience, churches that prioritize evangelism and outreach in their prayers, in their member deployment, in their budget, in their staffing, and in their leadership training find that God blesses their endeavors with an abundant harvest. We know there is more to making disciples than just evangelism (thus the need for the remaining chapters of the book), but many churches that are not experiencing the potential harvest that is all around them are focusing on everything *but* evangelism.

So here are some guidelines for putting evangelism back on the to-do list for your church.

#1 THE GREAT COMMISSION CONSCIENCE RULE

At least three of every five elected church officers should have a "Great Commission conscience."

■ Introduction

Is your church inward-focused or outward-focused? An inward-focused church spends its time, money, and people resources on self-centered activities. An outward-focused church invests its resources in others. An inward-focused church tends to focus on the past, an outward-focused church on the future. Inward-focused churches are motivated to perpetuate the institution; outward-focused churches are motivated to pursue a vision. Inward-focused churches serve the core constituency; outward-focused churches serve the community. Inward-focused churches use money to preserve the present; outward-focused churches use money to invest in the future. One good way to measure whether you are an inward- or outward-focused church is to measure your "Great Commission conscience."

■ Explanation

What is a Great Commission conscience? It is an attitude that permeates the thinking and the decision-making process of a church. It is an attitude that sees people outside of Christ as lost and rejoices when new people join the church, especially if they are new believers. This attitude means disciple making is a priority and resonates with the Great Commission found in its various forms throughout Scripture. It is an attitude that sees missions as both "over there" and "right here." It is an attitude that motivates both corporate and personal action in prayer, giving, and service for Great Commission results.

What is the Great Commission conscience that is necessary for effective outreach? Actually, there are two. The first is the *lay leader* Great Commission conscience: 60 percent. In other words, a church should have at least three of every five lay leaders (a voting majority) with such a conscience. The second is the *church membership* Great Commission conscience: 20 percent. That is, at least one of every five members of the church body has a similar Great Commission conscience. But how do you determine the Great Commission conscience of either? Simple. You ask them.

Here are ten statements concerning evangelism. If a leader or member of the congregation agrees with at least seven of the ten, it is an indication of a reasonably strong Great Commission conscience.

1. I see the primary purpose of our church as responding to the Great Commission.
2. I have participated in an outreach training event in the last year.
3. I have invited an unchurched friend or relative to a church event in the last six months.
4. I would support a motion to designate at least 10 percent of our church budget to outreach events and training activities.
5. I would prefer that the pastor call on nonmembers more often than on members.
6. I would be willing to take a new member or visitor home for dinner once every six months.
7. I have intentionally introduced myself to a new member or visitor in the past month.
8. I have talked with an unchurched person about my faith in the past three months.
9. I have prayed for a specific unchurched person in the past month.
10. I would be willing to be a pioneer in a new group or new church fellowship to help reach new people.

First, ask your church leaders (Sunday school teachers, small group leaders, deacons, ushers, elders, and others—anyone with a role or task responsibility in your church) to respond to these statements. Once you have collected the (anonymous) responses, determine what percentage of these people answered yes to seven or more questions. (It doesn't need to be the same seven questions.) If more than 60 percent of the total gave an affirmative answer to seven or more questions, you have leaders with a Great Commission conscience.

Next (if you're brave), some Sunday morning, ask your congregation to respond to the same ten statements. You're still looking for the percentage who respond yes to seven or more of the questions. If 20 percent or more respond favorably, you have a congregation with a Great Commission conscience. Research shows that when a group has a minimum of 20 percent who support a particular idea, this is the minimum number (or percentage) necessary to move the entire group forward. Less than 20 percent makes it an increasingly uphill struggle.

■ What You Can Do about It

If you determine that your leaders and congregation don't have a Great Commission conscience, what do you do? Here are a few ideas:

- Talk about it at your leadership meetings. It shouldn't be an indicting or judgmental discussion. It should simply be a discussion starter on some important issues, namely, are we, as leaders, really committed to the Great Commission of making disciples? If so, how can we tell? Does the budget confirm our commitment? (See #74, The Evangelism Budget Rule.)

- Review the purpose and mission of your church. Is there a formal statement that describes your purpose? Do the church's activities, staff, budget, and program reflect the pursuit of this purpose or are they generally unrelated to it?
- Talk with the church board about how to build a stronger Great Commission conscience in the church.
- Review the other rules and recommendations in this book and discuss which of them might be applicable in your situation and how they could be implemented.
- Preach on the topic of the Great Commission and the mission of the church. Have small group leaders focus on this topic. Try a churchwide study of the book of Acts and its implications for your church.

"For the Son of Man came to seek and to save the lost," said Christ, referring to himself (Luke 19:10 ESV). There is clear evidence that, when people grasp this passion, their churches come alive, reach people, and change lives. If your church has a Great Commission passion, God will bless most any efforts you make. Without that passion, it is unlikely that much of anything you do will be blessed.

#2 THE RECEPTIVITY RULE

For the most effective outreach, focus on receptive people.

■ Introduction

There is a principle found throughout Scripture that when applied will help every church better invest its resources for effectively spreading the gospel and reaching people for Christ. The principle is: Focus on receptive people.

■ Explanation

Not everyone is equally open and receptive to the good news of God's love expressed through Jesus Christ. Some people welcome the story with great joy and an open heart; others respond with disdain and a closed mind. While there is not much we can do to force open closed minds (only God can do that), there is much we can do when God connects us with people who have open hearts. The principle of focusing on receptive people can be found in a number of places throughout Scripture. Here are some of them:

1. *Sending the seventy-two* (Luke 10:2–12). Here Jesus dispatches seventy-two followers on a mission to preach in those places that were open and receptive.
2. *Parable of the growing seed* (Mark 4:26–29). Jesus spoke often of the harvest and talked about the right timing to bring in the harvest.
3. *Sending the Twelve* (Matthew 10). Jesus commissioned his followers to go into any neighboring towns and villages that would listen and proclaim that the kingdom of heaven had come.
4. *Parable of the sower* (Luke 8:1–15). Many of Jesus's parables represented the message of the kingdom of God and the people who were exposed to it. Some of the seed fell on receptive ground, while other seed fell on less responsive places.
5. *The Macedonian call* (Acts 16:6–10). While Paul and his team planned to go to Phrygia, Galatia, and Bithynia, the Holy Spirit providentially directed them to a more receptive field in Macedonia.

The Receptivity-Resistance Axis is a helpful tool to understand how different people will be more or less open to following Christ and becoming his disciples at a given point in time.

Receptivity-Resistance Axis

←——————————————————————————————→

Receptive   Resistant

Every non-Christian can be located somewhere on this Receptivity-Resistance Axis. The continuum represents a person's openness (receptivity) to following Christ. Not only does this axis help us see that people are at different places in their readiness to respond to the gospel, it rightly suggests that people move back and forth—from receptivity to resistance to receptivity—throughout their lifetime. A person who is resistant to the gospel today may, through a series of unanticipated circumstances, become very receptive several months from now. One of the most important causes for people moving back and forth on the Receptivity-Resistance Axis is a life-transition event. A transition event is defined as "a span of time in which an individual's or family's normal everyday behavior patterns are disrupted by some irregular event that requires an unfamiliar response."[2]

Transition events greatly affect a person's receptivity and openness to the Christian message. As a rule, the more significant the transition event, the more immediate the move toward receptivity. In contrast, the more stable and unchanging a person's life situation is, the more resistant he or she will be to changing spiritual values.

■ What You Can Do about It

The Holmes-Rahe Social Readjustment Scale,[3] often simply called a stress scale, provides a helpful way to identify transition events in a person's life. These events may be indicators of a person's openness or receptivity to religious conversion. (The number on the right is an indicator of the relative severity of the stress-producing event, on a scale of 1 to 100.)

Holmes-Rahe Stress Scale

Death of spouse	100
Divorce	73
Marital separation	65
Death of close family member	63
Jail term	63
Severe personal injury or illness	53
Marriage	50
Fired from work	47
Marital reconciliation	45
Retirement	45
Change in family member's health	44
Pregnancy	40
Sex difficulties	39
Addition to family	39
Business readjustment	39
Change in financial status	38
Death of close friend	37
Change in number of marital arguments	35
Mortgage or loan over $250,000	31
Foreclosure on mortgage	30
Change in work responsibilities	29
Son or daughter leaves home	29
Trouble with in-laws	29
Outstanding personal achievement	28
Spouse starts work	26
Start or finish school	26
Change in living conditions	25
Revision of personal habits	24
Trouble with boss	23
Change in work hours/conditions	20
Change in residence	20
Change in recreational habits	19
Change in social activities	18
Mortgage or loan under $250,000	18
Easter season	17
Change in sleeping habits	16
Change in number of family gatherings	15
Vacation	13
Christmas	12
Minor violation of the law	11

When two or more of these events happen around the same time, the effect on the person is compounded. For example, a person who has experienced major physical problems (53) and is recently retired (45) would be more receptive than if either event had occurred separately.

Timing of the event is also a factor in determining receptivity. Events that have occurred more recently will have a greater effect on a person's receptivity. The more distant the event, the less influential it is in determining a person's present receptivity.

The scale below can be used to identify a person's receptivity, based on the transition event values in his or her recent life history. In calculating the values on the stress scale, use 100 percent of the number if the event occurred in the person's life within the past eighteen months. Use half the value if it occurred between eighteen and thirty-six months ago. Do not calculate a value if the event occurred more than three years ago.

Determining Spiritual Receptivity

51+	39–50	31–38	0–30
◀────			────▶
very high	high	moderate	low

Present the idea of receptivity in a small group or adult Bible class. The topic itself makes for a fascinating discussion. Then ask people in the group to think of several people they know in their social network. Have them add the total number of points from the Holmes-Rahe Stress Scale, and then calculate (based on the instructions above) where they would be on the Determining Spiritual Receptivity scale. Obviously, a conversation such as this would lead to other issues, such as how individuals and the church can be responsive to particular events that create receptivity in a person's life. It's a good conversation to have.

 THE ENTRY EVENT RULE

Offer at least nine entry events per year for effective community outreach.

■ Introduction

What pastor has not encouraged members to bring a friend to church next Sunday? And research tells us that friends bringing friends is the primary way churches grow. But in plateaued and declining congregations, most people don't invite friends to the church service on Sunday morning. Generally it's because members are unsure whether their unchurched friends will find the experience of interest or relevant to their life. And the risk of inviting a friend is not seen as worth the benefit. So how can you see more church members inviting more friends and relatives to church events?

■ Explanation

The remedy to the problem of members not inviting friends may seem counterintuitive. The answer is to offer more events. You can support your church members' disciple-making endeavors by increasing the number of events to which they can comfortably invite friends.

The key word is "comfortably." Let's be honest. For most church members, it's uncomfortable to invite a friend or neighbor to a Sunday church service. It just seems too intrusive into the friend's life and creates an awkward situation if the friend says no. Many members feel it's likely to strain the relationship. Often it feels as if the member is using the relationship for the benefit of the church.

But when the church can provide events that are more likely to be interesting to the unchurched friend or family, then the assumption behind the invitation changes. Now the friend is the beneficiary. Consider the difference between an invitation to a neighbor family with two elementary-age kids to church, compared to an invitation to the same family to a Halloween party at the church. There are several benefits in promoting the latter. First, if the church member has never invited an unchurched person or family to church, inviting them to *anything* at church is going to take a monumental effort. But an invitation to a Halloween party is a much easier first step for the member. It's like a baby taking its first step—it's going to be small and tentative. But it's the first step toward more steps in the future. Kids who have fun at a Halloween party are more likely to want to return to other church-related events. And the parents are more likely to want to bring them.

These kinds of church-sponsored activities are called "entry events." An entry event is a high-visibility, usually one-time activity or event, sponsored by the church and designed to be of interest to both churched and non-churched in the community. The goal of an effective entry event is to see a large number of unchurched adults and/or families attend the event with the idea of developing those contacts into deeper relationships over time, perhaps through an ongoing group or activity. (See #4, The Side-Door Ministry Rule.)

Here are a few examples of entry events to which members are likely to invite unchurched friends, neighbors, and relatives:

Holidays/Seasonal
- Valentine's Day father/daughter banquet
- Christmas pageant

- Halloween/harvest festival
- Fourth of July celebration
- Memorial Day picnic and parade

Sports
- Super Bowl Sunday
- Trip to local sports game
- Local Christian sports celebrity speaker

Family/Parenting Issues
- Discipline for Your Child seminar
- Guest speakers on relevant topics
- Beginning a Blended Family seminar
- Potty Training Your Youngster workshop

Marital Issues
- Getting Started in Your Marriage seminar
- Handling Divorce seminar
- Guest speakers on relevant topics

Special Interests
- Visit to local points of interest
- Picnic
- Welcome to the Neighborhood orientation
- Tax planning
- Parent/kid hike

Kids' Events
- Taffy pull
- Ice cream social
- Pet show and races
- Swimming party
- Pinewood Derby race

■ What You Can Do about It

Holding successful, high-visibility entry events is not only fun, it contributes an awareness of your church in the community and raises the corporate self-esteem of the congregation. But keep in mind that successful entry events should be judged on the number of *unchurched* people who attend, not the number of church members.

Here are six recommendations for planning and conducting a successful entry event:

1. *Involve both church members and nonmembers in defining, planning, and conducting the event.* When people work together on a common task, relationships develop naturally. Even the planning of the event is a great way to involve non-churched friends and relatives.
2. *Publicize the event.* Distribute well-designed brochures and posters to get the word out about the big event. Provide a half-dozen copies of the brochure to each church member to give out to friends and relatives.
3. *Conduct the event in an appropriate location.* Think about whether you really want to hold your entry event on your church property. The chances are good that people not used to being on a church campus will be intimidated with the prospect of attending and might actually choose to avoid the event altogether if the location is a psychological barrier.
4. *The event should address a felt need.* The unchurched person's decision to attend your entry event will be based on his or her perception of the cost versus the benefit; the price versus the promise. Make sure the benefit of attending is worth the risk people are being asked to take.
5. *Opportunities for further involvement are communicated.* An entry event can be an extravagant waste of time and money if it doesn't lead to subsequent connections with many who attend. Think through the logical (and easy) next steps first-time contacts can take to continue a relationship with your church. Then make sure you communicate those steps.
6. *Names and contact information of attendees are obtained.* It will be up to your church to take the next step in nurturing a relationship with these new contacts. Name and email addresses are the easiest (and psychologically safest) way for attendees to give you their information. Offer to send them announcements of future events.

#4 THE SIDE-DOOR MINISTRY RULE

Churches should build a minimum of two side doors every year.

■ Introduction

The front doors of America's churches are closing. Traditionally people have come through the church's "front doors" to visit its worship service, education classes, or special events. The primary way that most churches identify their prospective members is through visitors to these activities. However, in the past twenty years not only has the *number* of visitors been declining but also the *percentage* of visitors in relation to a church's total attendance has declined. To survive, let alone thrive, churches need to build "side doors" to create connections with the people in their community who will find faith.

■ Explanation

What are "side doors" for the church? Here is a definition:

> *Side door.* A church-sponsored program, group, or activity in which a nonmember can become comfortably involved on a regular basis. It is an ongoing function in which a nonmember can develop meaningful and valued relationships with people in the church.[4]

The purpose of a side-door group or activity is to provide an opportunity for participants (church members and nonmembers) to develop friendships around something important they share in common. And relationships are the key to effective evangelism. It is through relationships that the gospel has primarily spread throughout the centuries, as well as today.

Here are just a few examples of actual side doors through which church members and nonmembers are developing friendships around common interests. Side doors have been created by churches for people who

ride motorcycles	want to get in better physical condition
have children in the military	wish to help homeless families
own RVs	play softball
are recent widowers	are interested in end-times
are newlyweds	have a bedridden parent
enjoy reading books	are raising grandchildren
are unemployed	are moms with teenage daughters
suffer from chronic pain	need help managing their finances
have husbands in jail	enjoy scrapbooking
are nominal Jews	are children in blended families
have spouses who are not believers	have children with a learning disability
are fishermen	are married to men who travel frequently
are single mothers	

enjoy radio-controlled airplanes	are divorced with no children
are pregnant	have a family member diagnosed
are affected by homosexuality	with cancer
struggle with chemical dependency	are single dads
are empty nesters	enjoy scuba diving
enjoy camping	are hearing impaired

And that's just a start!

About 10 percent of the churches in the United States are side-door churches in which "most of the new people who connect with the church made first contact through a ministry other than the worship service."[5] We also know that approximately 14 percent of churches in the United States are experiencing growth in their worship attendance. While we have not tried to correlate these two numbers, it would not be surprising to find a strong relationship between side-door churches and growing churches. Rev. Craig Williford, recalling his experience in leading two growing churches, says, "Our weekend services were very vital. But the side-door ministries produced more evangelism and brought far more people into our church."[6]

But why are side doors necessary today for churches to reach out and evangelize effectively? It is because the longer a person has been a Christian, the fewer friends he or she has who are *not* Christians. Eventually many long-term Christians have no real friends outside their church or faith. Put another way, the outreach potential (and thus the growth potential) of a church that is comprised of mostly long-term Christians is quite limited compared to a church with many new believers. If your church is made up mostly of people who have been Christians for more than five years, you need to create some side doors where people can develop new friendships with people outside the church. A good rule of thumb is to create at least two side doors per year.

■ What You Can Do about It

So how does a church begin creating side doors—new groups, new classes, new activities—where members and nonmembers can build friendships? First, realize that side doors form around people's passions—topics or experiences that people care deeply about. Successful side doors connect people who share a common passion. Here are some guidelines for creating new side doors:

- *Find the passion.* Everyone in your church cares deeply about something—sometimes it's a number of things. Generally such passion falls into one of two categories: recreational or developmental. The first relates to how people like to spend their free time, which can range from making apple pies to studying zoology. The second category, developmental, relates to major life issues, which usually center around health, finances, relationships, or employment.

- *Hold an "exploratory" meeting.* Invite three or more people who share the same passion to a brainstorming session to discuss the idea of your church starting a new ministry for people who share the passion. Include an announcement in the church bulletin inviting interested worshipers to the meeting. Explain that participants in the meeting are not being asked to get involved in the project, just to share their ideas and brainstorm possibilities for a new ministry. Gather the group, perhaps over a meal, and explore the possibilities of your church starting such a ministry. Explain that one of the purposes of the ministry is to build friendships with nonmembers through connecting around a common interest. Let the meeting take its course and see what kind of interest is generated. If there is any enthusiasm, take the next step.

- *Research other churches.* Probably there are churches that have already developed a creative ministry in the area you are considering. If the brainstorming group is interested and willing, ask individuals to go online and search out any other churches that might have a ministry for people with that particular interest. Then compare notes with others who have done similar research.

- *Dream.* At your next brainstorming meeting, discuss what such a ministry might look like in your church five years from today. Assess the enthusiasm of the group in taking the next step to explore a new ministry. Don't expect 100 percent success in all exploratory gatherings. If there aren't at least three people with the desire to help start a new ministry, put the idea on the back burner. You're looking for a spark of enthusiasm that might catch hold of a group of dreamers in your church.

- *Make a time line.* If there are at least three people willing to help birth a new side-door ministry in your church, work on a time line with dates and events for the next year. Agree that in one year the progress will be evaluated on this new ministry idea. And discuss how the church can be most supportive in this new initiative.

There is, of course, much involved in creating a fully functioning side-door ministry.[7] But a majority of effective, growing churches today have a wonderful variety of such ministries that grew out of the passion of one or more members and have become well-traveled pathways to life in Christ and the church.

#5 THE UNCHURCHED FRIENDS RULE

For the church to grow, each worshiper should have an average of nine or more unchurched friends or family members.

■ Introduction

Research demonstrates that the most effective way to reach new people for Christ and the church is through the social networks of members' family and friends. This means that, for a church to reach out effectively into its community, members must be in regular contact with unchurched friends and family members.

■ Explanation

There is a direct relationship between the number of unchurched friends and family your average church member has and your church's potential for growth or decline. The basic rule of thumb is that if the people in a church have an average of three or fewer non-churched friends and family members living in your ministry area, the church will most likely decline. If the average is around six, the church will likely be plateaued. But if the average number of non-churched friends and family members is nine or more, then the church is very likely to be growing.

New churches are often silently empowered by the implications of this rule due to the large social networks that attendees have with non-churched people in the community. These new churches tend to reach people through conversion growth, and new believers in younger churches typically know twelve or more people who are outside a local church. As a church ages, however, members tend to spend more of their discretionary time in church-related activities and with church-related people, thus gradually losing contact with people outside the life of the church ministry. Over time, with fewer contacts, there is decreasing potential for effective outreach to occur.

■ What You Can Do about It

Activating outreach through the social networks of present members and worshipers is key for effective evangelism in a local church. Pastors can help their regular attendees discover their networks by using the following strategy:

1. Design a sermon series on a theme, such as "Making Friends for Jesus." A six-part series seems to work the best since it is long enough to cover the subject but short enough not to lose people's interest. Use passages that show how others invited friends and family members to find Jesus. John 1:35–51 tells how Andrew brought his brother Peter to Christ, and Philip brought his friend Nathanael. Acts 16:11–40 tells two delightful stories of how Lydia and her family were led to Christ and how Paul and Silas brought the Philippian jailer and his family to faith.

2. In the final sermon of the series, ask attendees to make a list of all their non-churched friends and family members. One way is to distribute two

3x5" cards to everyone in attendance. Ask them to make two identical lists of friends, neighbors, and associates who live within a ten- or twenty-mile radius of the church and are not currently active in a church. Then challenge the congregation to commit to praying for the people on their list at least once each week for the coming year. As a sign of their commitment to pray, ask attendees to place the other card in the offering plate as it goes by. Be sure to tell them you will not contact the people on their list but that you want to know how many people your church will be praying for in the coming year. Collect the cards, asking those in attendance to keep the other card in their Bible, purse, or a place where they will see it and remember to pray.

3. After collecting the cards, add up the total number of people listed and divide by the number of cards you receive. This will tell you the average number of non-churched friends and family members of your people. Compare this to the rule above to evaluate the effect of members' existing social networks on the growth potential of your church.

4. The Sunday following this activity, announce the total number of people your church will be praying for in the coming year. Then on a regular basis (perhaps once a month), remind the congregation of their prayer commitment.

5. Once each quarter, the church should host an event appropriate for your people to invite one or more of those they are remembering in prayer. These could include a Christmas Eve candlelight service, Easter sunrise service, alternative Halloween gathering, summer outing (camping, swimming, picnics, for example). Throughout the year, if and when friends and family come to Christ and your church, celebrate the occasions with the entire church body!

#6 THE EVANGELISM TRAINING RULE

Churches that are effective in reaching their community train at least 10 percent of their people in friendship evangelism each year.

■ Introduction

Encouraging—and equipping—people to connect with non-churched friends and relatives is just the beginning of effective evangelistic outreach in a church. But it is a very important beginning and the right place to start. Churches that are successful in reaching new people for Christ focus on training a minimum of 10 percent of their people each year in friendship evangelism.

■ Explanation

It takes time to build the "evangelistic consciousness" of a congregation. This is particularly true when a church has seen little or no conversion growth in the past several years. While church leaders may desire to train many people quickly, the fact is in most churches people are not ready to participate in a new evangelistic program.

Because of this it is important to begin slowly by focusing on around 10 percent of your adults. This is about the number who will be open to nurturing more meaningful relationships with their non-Christian friends and relatives. By starting with this receptive 10 percent, your evangelistic emphasis will get off to a good start. The next year other adults will have heard about the good experiences from the first year's training and be open to taking part.

Since new members and new believers tend to have more unchurched contacts than do long-term members, invite newcomers to join in the training the second year. Newcomers also have an excitement about the church and want to spread the word in any way possible. By recruiting and training new people, you will see the evangelistic outreach of your church grow quickly.

When a church has annually trained 10 percent of its members for five years, it reaches a turning point—half of the congregation has now completed the training. A new attitude and sensitivity toward newcomers becomes evident throughout the congregation. And as the church continues to train 10 percent per year, dramatic new life and enthusiasm take root as a growing majority of members become interested in reaching new people for Jesus.

There are many good books and study guides available for evangelism training. We recommend keeping the course a regular part of the educational process in your church. And don't forget to include it in the new members classes.

■ What You Can Do about It

Here are some important things to consider as you plan your evangelism training. First, realize that there is much baggage out there about the "E" word. Somehow along the way, the word *evangelism* came to be associated with knocking on strangers' doors, passing out tracts on street corners, and generally participating in activities that induce sweaty palms, stomach butterflies, and too-tight collars. If you expect to have people in your church sign up for evangelism training, realize there are many misconceptions.

Using the word *evangelism* is not a hill you need to climb. The very word is likely to inhibit your goal. In fact, as much as it may surprise you, the word *evangelism* is nowhere to be found in the Bible. (The word *evangelist* is found only twice, once in Acts 21:8, referring to Philip who seems to have a specific function or role as an evangelist, and in Ephesians 4:11, referring to a particular spiritual gift that has been given to a limited number of members of the body of Christ.)

At the same time, the call to spread the Good News permeates Scripture. Christ made clear this priority: "Go into all the world and proclaim the gospel to the whole creation" (Mark 16:15 ESV). Just because you don't find the word in Scripture doesn't mean we're not called to make disciples. In fact, to make disciples is the ultimate marching order from Christ to his followers. It's just that the word *evangelism* is not the flag under which this process must fly.

We should realize the traditional methods in which many of us have been trained to "do evangelism" are not necessarily the only ways—or even the best ways—to make disciples. Here is a brief description of three different approaches to the evangelistic process:

1. *Teacher-Student Approach*. This approach views evangelism as a one-way transmission of information from a sender to a receiver. The assumption is that people will give the correct response when given the correct information. If the receiver does not do what is expected, it is because the sender did not transmit the information in the correct manner.

2. *Salesperson-Customer Approach*. This approach views evangelism as a process of manipulation. The message might be an emotional appeal or it might be leading a person through a set of carefully prepared questions. The techniques of high-pressure salesmanship are based on this model of communication.

3. *Friend-Friend Approach*. This third approach views evangelism as a two-way interaction between equals. It is based on the recognition that no two people see things in exactly the same way and is an effort to look at things from the perspective of the receiver. This model does not rule out a desire to share one's convictions but the desire is motivated by an interest in the other person and believing he or she would want to hear our conviction.

Which of these three approaches do you think come to mind when most people hear the word *evangelism*? If you said the second, you're right. However, research indicates that 81 percent of the people who make a decision for Christ because of the Salesperson-Customer approach drop out of church involvement within a year.[8]

Here's another interesting, but not surprising, result from the research: The third approach is by far the most effective in making disciples—new believers and active members of a local church. Of those who make a commitment to Christ through this approach, 78 percent stay active and involved.

So the *approach* to the process of disciple making is important. But obviously the content is as well. Here are four simple yet profound questions that your evangelism training should help church members answer:

1. How has being a Christian made a difference in my life?
2. What does it mean to be a Christian (in words understandable to a non-Christian)?
3. Why would I want my friend to be a Christian and member of my church?
4. How does a person become a Christian (in words understandable to a non-Christian)?

We recommend you spend several weeks in your training on each question—discussing, researching, sharing ideas, role playing, and reflecting on it. When your people feel comfortable with their answers, they will be better equipped to share their faith in a natural, "friend to friend" manner.

#7 THE NUMBER OF CONVERSIONS RULE

Churches that train members to reach out to unchurched friends and relatives see about 12 percent of these contacts come to Christ.

■ Introduction

New people will be reached for Christ as a church regularly trains its people and encourages evangelistic conversations with the non-churched. In most situations, these churches will see around 12 percent of their evangelistic contacts make a profession of faith over a five-year period.

■ Explanation

Effective evangelism happens when churches intentionally train, encourage, and resource their regular attendees to connect with their non-churched friends and family members. This takes place in three distinct steps:

1. A regular, ongoing evangelistic training class or small group is conducted that involves at least 10 percent of a congregation. The class/group focuses on practical ways to build friendships with those who are outside of Christ but within the natural networks of those who are already in the church.
2. Each participant lists the names of people he or she knows and commits to praying for and building a relationship with them during the coming twelve months.

3. Throughout the year, the church offers a minimum of four "seeker events" that focus directly on connecting newcomers to Christ and his church. As each event is offered, those who have been praying and building relationships with people outside the church try to bring them to the events.

When such a process occurs on a regular basis, about 12 percent of those non-churched friends and relatives will make a commitment to Christ and his church. Here is an example:

Number of church members trained	12
Average non-churched friends/family per member	8
Total number of people on prayer lists	96
Approximate percentage of people who come to faith	12%
Number of people who come to faith	12

■ What You Can Do about It

Here are a few suggestions to empower effective evangelism in your church:

1. Ask yourself, Do we have an intentional plan to train, encourage, and resource our current attendees to build relationships with their friends and family members? Churches with an intentional plan always do better than those without a plan.

2. Have your attendees make a list of their friends and family members whom they would love to see as part of the church. (See #5, The Unchurched Friends Rule.)

3. From these lists determine the total number of friends and family members identified, and multiply that number by 12 percent. This will give you an idea of how many potential new believers you may have in the following twelve months if there is a special love and prayer emphasis on these people.

4. If this number of people come to faith and your church in the coming year, what do you need to do now to prepare for them? For example, if you could potentially have twenty-four new believers join your church this year, how will you assimilate them into the family? Do you need a new adult Sunday school class? How about several new small groups?

By beginning a new class, small group, or welcoming process *before* these people come to Christ, you are acting on faith that God will bless the prayers of your attendees, as well as their invitations and conversations, by bringing new people to Christ and your church.

2

Ministry Rules for Visitors

A newcomer's assimilation into your church begins long before he or she joins your church or even becomes a regular attender. Newcomer integration begins with the visitor's very first contact with your church. The welcome that newcomers receive will have a great deal to do with whether they come back a second time. So if you want to see visitors become regular attenders, one of your first priorities is for the church to extend a warm, friendly, and genuine welcome to first-time guests—a welcome that says, "We're glad you're here and we would love to see you again." In this chapter we will share some tips and rules that will increase the likelihood of first-time visitors becoming longtime members.

#8 THE VISITOR LABEL RULE

Don't call your visitors "visitors."

■ Introduction

Let's play a word-association game. Your first word: *visitor*. What comes to mind? Here are some ideas that occurred to us: uncertain, curious, unfamiliar, anxious, uncomfortable. The whole assumption behind the word is that the person has little or no experience in the new situation. The person is *visiting* and thus doesn't really know what to expect. Being a visitor—in most situations—can be a rather uncomfortable experience.

Here's another word: *guest*. First impressions? Ours include important, re-spected, invited, welcome, honored, getting attention. Much more positive im-ages, aren't they?

Now think about the words used in your church to describe newcomers who attend for the first or second time. What do you call them publicly and privately? Does *visitor* or *guest* best describe how you feel about them? And which word do you think best describes how they feel themselves?

■ Explanation

The word *visitor* is defined as "a person who resides temporarily; one who goes or comes to inspect; one who makes a short stay at a place for a particular pur-pose." The word implies previous distance from an experience or event or people.

Why not begin referring to your visitors as *guests*, defined as "a person wel-comed into one's home; a person to whom hospitality is extended; a person held in honor who is due special courtesies." While the word still suggests "newcomer," it implies that this newcomer has a much more important place. Changing your vocabulary may not change how your newcomers feel about their experience, but it may very well change the way your members feel about the newcomers. And that *will* change the way newcomers feel about their experience.

Think about your own situation. When you have guests over to your house, how do you treat them? You probably meet them at the door, greet them warmly, and express genuine pleasure at the honor of their presence. When you think about it, it *is* a compliment that guests have come to your home. Probably you feel honored that they would choose to spend several hours with you when they could easily be doing something else. You offer to take their coat and bring them something to eat or drink. You introduce them to others in the room with whom they might have something in common. You prime the conversation with bits of information that might interest them. While they are in your home, you pay at-tention to whether your guests are comfortable. Periodically you engage them in conversation and attempt to show, through your actions, that you are glad they came. At the end of your gathering, how do you treat guests? Do you let them slip out the door unnoticed without saying good-bye? Of course not. You find their coats. You thank them for coming. Perhaps you walk them to their car and wave as they drive off, hoping they had a good time.

So how do you treat those who attend your church for the first time? Unfortu-nately most church newcomers are not treated as guests.

■ What You Can Do about It

Introduce the term *guests* into the vocabulary of your church leaders as you discuss those who are attending for the first (or second or third) time. It is surprising how our language affects our perception of others, which in turn affects our behavior toward them. Calling newcomers guests rather than visitors is a first step toward extending to them the honor and importance they deserve. The pastor of a large church in Oklahoma City became so convinced of the importance of just this little change in language that he decided to fine his staff five dollars anytime they used the word *visitor* in their staff meetings. We never heard how the experiment worked but we suspect it encouraged church leaders to be more conscious of their vocabulary.

Let's take this idea a little further. In addition to calling newcomers guests, why not make another change in your vocabulary? Many churches have greeters who stand at the doorway of the church and extend a smile and "good morning" to those entering the building. Here's the dictionary's definition of the word *greeter*: "one who meets or extends welcome in a specified manner; one who gives a formal salutation at a meeting." But if we're serious about entertaining newcomers in God's house, what might we better call those of us who have a responsibility for welcoming these guests? "Hosts," of course! Here is the definition: "one who receives or entertains socially; one who opens his or her home for a special event; one who takes particular care and concern that guests are well accommodated." If you are serious about welcoming the guests who come to God's house, here are a few ideas on how and where you might be good hosts:

- *Parking lot hosts.* Why wait for guests to come to you; why not go to them? Some church buildings can be quite confusing for a newcomer to even find the front door. (That's assuming the front door is the appropriate place to enter the building, which is not always the case.) Meet your guests soon after they get out of their car. If you have a visitors parking section, pay special attention to who parks there (although we're not convinced a separate parking area for visitors is really a good idea, since most visitors prefer to remain anonymous and don't park there anyway). If it's raining, parking hosts should have a large golf umbrella to hold over guests as they walk to the building. Escorting guests to the building is an excellent time to learn more about them, whether they need help with kids or babies, whether they're new in town, and so on. Then, on reaching the front door, the parking lot hosts should "hand off" their guests to the lobby hosts.

- *Lobby hosts.* The lobby (foyer, vestibule, narthex) is where most churches station their "greeters." Often the problems with greeters are that their feet seem to be nailed to the floor, a smile glued to their face, and their vocabulary limited to "good morning." A lobby host, on the other hand, is a person who can move around to make guests feel comfortable. One guest family might encounter a lobby host who escorts the mother to the children's department and explains the process of dropping off and picking up her kids. Another lobby host might introduce the guest to someone in the church who lives in the same neighborhood or might have a similar job. Still another host encounter might be the invitation to meet after the service at the refreshment table to introduce the guest to the pastor.

- *Service hosts.* These are people who are actually *inside* the worship center. If your worship center is a bustle of activity before the service begins, some people with the "gift of gab" can simply mingle with others in a casual way. Service hosts are looking particularly for guests or people they don't recognize and taking the initiative to introduce themselves. If guests are seated by themselves, good social etiquette is to introduce someone from the church to the newcomers (a "social handoff"). It's a great time to answer any questions guests might have and do a little honest bragging about the church.

- *Coffee hosts.* The time set aside for coffee in the Sunday morning schedule can be one of the most effective—or destructive—ways to extend a welcome to guests. If guests come alone, they will probably not make it to the coffee table after the service; it's just too awkward. A visiting couple may make a brief stop at the refreshment table. But if no one engages them in conversation, they won't stay long. Coffee hosts hang out in the immediate vicinity and are on the lookout for newcomers standing alone. Their task is to engage these guests in conversation and not leave them until they have handed them off to someone else in the area.

- *Many hosts.* Spread the hosting responsibilities among many people throughout the year. This allows more members to be involved in welcoming newcomers. And experience has shown that when members perform their hosting duty on their assigned days, they are increasingly friendly with guests even on the days they are off duty.

Some long-term members contend that their church is naturally friendly and that making plans to welcome guests makes the welcome artificial rather than natural. But when we have asked visitors or guests about how they felt when attending a church with an intentional welcome strategy, they had only high praise for how welcomed those churches made them feel. An intentional strategy means that you care enough about newcomers that you have a plan to be sure they feel truly welcomed. And an effective welcome is one of the best ways to assure that your guests return.

#9 THE TEN MINUTE RULE

The ten minutes immediately following the worship service are the most important minutes in your guests' visit.

■ Introduction

You don't have a second chance for a good first impression. And this is especially true when it comes to first-time visitors at your church. The first impression guests leave with determines whether they will be back. So what is it that goes into a good first impression? Or for that matter, a bad one?

We interviewed a number of people who had recently visited a church for the first time. We asked them what made the biggest impression on them and what effect it had on their decision to return the following week. Can you guess the number one (by far) issue that impressed (or depressed) visitors? It was *the friendliness of the people*.

Over and over again this was mentioned. Regardless of denominational affiliation, attractiveness of the facilities, eloquence of the preacher, breadth of the program, or quality of the music, visitors seem to be most impressed with friendliness.

■ Explanation

How do visitors determine the friendliness of a church? We wanted to know, so we asked our interviewees. Their response was simple, yet insightful. Visitors determine the friendliness of a church—of your church—by *the number of people who talk with them!* That's it. Simple but significant! Here are two visitor formulas you'll want to remember:

Many conversations = friendly church

Few or no conversations = unfriendly church

We asked our visitor-subjects one more question: "*When* did you conclude that the church you visited was—or was not—a friendly church?" This is when we learned the answer that is stated in the above rule. More than any other, the critical time for making a friendly impression is the ten minutes right after the last prayer is prayed or the last song is sung. It's when "the game is over and the rules are off" (as one young man put it). What he meant was that people don't have to do anything after the service except be themselves. Some talk to friends. Others hurry out to pick up children or get to a nearby restaurant. And a few, apparently, stop to talk with the visitors. That made a big impression when it (infrequently) happened.

Consider the experience as perceived by newcomers. Entering the worship center is experienced as a sort of individual act, since people do it more or less separately. Leaving, however, is a group experience, since it happens together. This can be the loneliest moment of all if everyone else is greeting friends as the visitor walks up the aisle in a pocket of isolated silence.

Here are a few other reasons we were told that the last ten minutes are so important to visitors:

"It's the last thing I experienced and the most vivid memory I drove away with."

"It confirmed the experience I had had before and during the service."

"It told me a lot about the priorities of that church."

"When no one talked to me after the service, it made a mockery of the 'friend-ship time' during the service when we were supposed to greet the people next to us."

■ What You Can Do about It

Throughout the year, encourage members to take the initiative after the service and greet anyone they do not recognize or anyone who appears to be alone. Almost everyone can say hello and carry on a conversation with a newcomer as they walk out of the worship center together.

Here's a good idea we picked up from a pastor several years ago—*after-service hosts*. This is a group of four to five people (for a congregation of around two hundred) who are on the lookout for people who seem to be new or who are standing alone. Their job is simply to initiate a conversation, perhaps invite the person to the coffee hour, offer to show him or her around the church facilities, and introduce the person to the pastor. In the overall visitor strategy, after-service hosts can perform a vital function.

A church newsletter carried an article about a man who visited eighteen churches on consecutive Sundays to discover how friendly the churches were to newcom-ers. For each visit the man followed the same pattern. He sat near the front so he would exit the length of the sanctuary and he rated the church for its friendliness. He devised the following rating scale:

A smile of welcome—10 points

A word of greeting—10 points

Exchange of names—100 points

Invitation to return—200 points

Introduction to another member—1,000 points

An invitation to meet the pastor—2,000 points

In eleven of the eighteen churches he visited, less than one hundred points were scored; in five churches less than twenty.

Here are a few other ideas that churches use to create an environment where visitors feel welcome:

- *Three minute rule.* The pastor concludes the service with a reminder to the congregation of their "three minute rule." For newcomers, the pastor reviews the rules: "No one is allowed to speak to anyone they know for the first three minutes after the conclusion of the service. Worshipers can (a) sit quietly in their seat for three minutes and meditate on the service, (b) walk silently out of the worship center, or (c) talk with someone they don't know." Most people choose the third.

- *Greeting time at the end of the service.* It's common for churches to include a time of greeting during the service. This is nice but not particularly helpful in terms of welcoming newcomers. Most people simply turn to the persons next to them, smile, shake their hands, say good morning, and then go on. Some creative churches have moved the greeting time to the last event of the service. The pastor may give the final prayer, then encourage people to greet their neighbor. This makes it easier to have a conversation that isn't abruptly cut short by the next event in the service.

- *Your favorite flower.* Some churches give even more encouragement in the post-service conversation by suggesting a discussion question to ask the person next to them, such as, What is your favorite flower and why? What is your favorite food? Where were you born? or some other ice-breaking question that will facilitate a more extended conversation.

#10 THE GUESTS TO GROW BY RULE

A church needs the same number of guests each year as its average worship attendance in order to grow.

■ Introduction

Visitors represent 100 percent of your church's growth potential. You may have beautiful facilities, exceptional music, inspired preaching. You could hold numerous community outreach events, contribute hundreds of hours in community service, make thousands of phone calls to neighbors. But eventually you need visitors. No visitors—no growth. No growth—no church. So how many visitors or guests do you need to grow? It's easy to calculate. Regardless of your church's size or location, you need as many first-time guests per year as your average weekly worship attendance.

■ Explanation

Let's look at a hypothetical church of one hundred worshipers and make two assumptions that hold true in many congregations around the country: the church keeps an average of 15 percent of its first-time guests and it has an annual loss of 10 percent of its attendees through death, transfer, and dropouts. To grow slightly in one year, this church needs one hundred first-time guests throughout the year. Here's why:

Beginning worship attendance	100
Annual loss (10%)	-10
Subtotal	90 worshipers
Retention rate (15% of 100 guests)	+15
Total net attendance	105 worshipers (5% growth)

The same formula holds true for a church of 1,500 worshipers and would look like this:

Beginning worship attendance	1,500
Annual loss (10%)	-150
Subtotal	1,350 worshipers
Retention rate (15% of 1,500 guests)	+ 225
Total net attendance	1,575 worshipers (5% growth)

In both examples the churches need the same number of first-time guests in one year as their annual average worship attendance to see a 5 percent net increase.

In reality larger churches need slightly more guests due to the fact that they experience a higher rate of attrition than smaller churches. Here are three typical examples of "back door" rates, depending on church size.

Average Yearly Attrition

	Small Church 100 Worshipers	Medium Church 400 Worshipers	Large Church 1,500 Worshipers
Transfer out	-3 (3%)	-20 (5%)	-105 (7%)
Death	-1 (1%)	-4 (1%)	-15 (1%)
Reversion	-3 (3%)	-16 (4%)	-90 (6%)
Total %	-7 (7%)	-40 (10%)	-210 (14%)

Because of these higher attrition rates, larger churches actually need a higher percentage of guests to grow at the same rate.

	Small Church	Medium Church	Large Church
Guests to remain steady	40 yearly (.75 weekly)	275 yearly (5 weekly)	1,450 yearly (28 weekly)
Guests to grow	75 yearly (1.5 weekly)	400 yearly (7.7 weekly)	1,900 yearly (36.5 weekly)

■ What You Can Do about It

There are two ways to bring guests to your church:

1. A personal invitation
2. A public announcement

From experience we know the percentage of invitees who will respond to each:

Type of Communication	Positive Response Rate
Personal Invitation	10–25%
Public Announcement	.25–2%

A personal invitation is an individual request from one person to another (face-to-face, email, phone), and *assumes the two individuals already know each other.* A public announcement includes newspaper ads, direct mail, radio or television spots, telemarketing, posters, door hangers, and the like.

With this information you can actually set goals for the number of visitors you desire and project the results of your invitation strategy. Suppose you want to see one hundred new people attend your church in the coming year (two per Sunday). There are different combinations of the two invitation styles that will result in one hundred new people. These examples assume a 15 percent response rate to personal invitations and a .75 percent response to public announcements.

Reason for Attending	Projected Response	Example 1 Number of Invitations	Number of Responses	Example 2 Number of Invitations	Number of Responses	Example 3 Number of Invitations	Number of Responses
Personal Invitation	15%	333	50	500	75	167	25
Public Advertising	.75%	6,700	50	3,350	25	10,000	75
Total		7,033	100	3,850	100	10,167	100

An "Insider's Tip"

Our "insider's tip" is this: as you consider a strategy to increase visitor flow in your church, place the greater investment in personal invitations for the following reasons:

- Visitor "retention rate" (visitors who stay) is higher among those invited by a friend than those who come because of a public announcement.
- When visitors who were invited by a friend become active, they will more often invite their friends since they assume that this is the norm.

- Personal invitations are active and involve church members in the process of outreach. Public announcements are passive.
- Higher morale and enthusiasm occur when unchurched friends and family members begin to attend.
- Visitors who begin attending through personal invitation are less likely to drop out in the critical first year.
- Personal invitations are more cost-effective (i.e., cheaper).

Personal Invitation Ideas

Set a goal for at least 20 percent of your worshiping congregation to invite a friend or relative to a church-sponsored event in the coming year. Here are a few ideas for how to realize this goal:

- Preach several sermons on how the gospel has spread since the first century—through "households" of friends, neighbors, and relatives. (The Greek word for household is *oikos*.) Talk about the modern application of this timeless process.
- Be aware that attendees will be more comfortable inviting a friend or neighbor to some event *other than* a Sunday service. Identify and promote activities on your church calendar to which a member would be comfortable inviting a friend.
- Develop and print a nice flyer on each of these events. Give three copies to each person in your church and encourage them to give a flyer to one or more people in their network.
- Build an "invitation consciousness." Throughout the year plan periodic interviews in your service with a person who actually invited a friend to a church event, discussing how it went.

Public Announcement Ideas

While personal invitations are the most fruitful and cost-effective for increasing your visitors, public announcements have their place. The process should be both-and rather than either-or.

As you formulate your public announcement strategy, remember two basic principles:

1. *Say it more than one time.* There is one principle that works above all others: Redundancy. Redundancy. Redundancy. Redundancy. Redundancy. Studies of retention tell us that people will hear the same message up to seven times and yet hear something new each time.

2. *Say it more than one way*. The more of our senses that receive a message, the more likely we are to remember it. Those who only *hear* a message will remember less than those who hear it, see it, and touch it. Use a *variety* of media to communicate with your target audience.

Rather than simply using a "yellow pages" list of names, focus your public invitations on people groups who will be the most receptive. In order of receptivity, they are:

- friends and relatives of your existing members
- visitors who have not become active
- participants in special ministries who are not active
- inactive members
- Christmas and Easter visitors
- wedding and funeral connections
- VBS families
- people in life transitions

Here are some suggestions for various media to use in your public invitations:

Direct Mail

- Use a stamp rather than metered or bulk rate indicia.
- Hand address the envelope.
- Use an envelope, letter, and flyer—not just a flyer.
- Write the copy in a personable, readable, honest style.
- Mail to the same people more than once.
- Send a last minute postcard to arrive the week before the event.

Telephone

- Plan to make a total of several thousand calls since you normally will get only 1 percent response.
- Prepare a written script and train the callers.
- Make the calls from a phone bank over a two-week period.
- Your goal in the phone call is to identify people who are willing to have their name added to your mailing list, not necessarily to get a commitment to attend the event.

Newspaper Ads

- Focus on and write for a specific target audience.
- Highlight relationships and people, not programs and institutions.

- No more than 40 percent of the ad should be copy; most of the ad should be title, picture, or white space.
- Advertise on Wednesday for any events the following Sunday.
- Place the ad where your target audience will be reading; avoid the church page.
- Develop a series of weekly ads with the same format but variations in message.
- Use the local paper, not the metropolitan paper.
- Articles (written by newspaper staff reporters) are more valuable than paid ads; make friends with the religion and community events editors.

Radio and Television

- Get information from the radio and TV stations on their audience profiles; use only stations and/or programs that reach your target audience.
- Hire a professional advertising agency to develop the spots.
- Identify and focus on your specific target audience.
- Offer a free "premium" related to your target audience to get the listener on your mailing list.
- Don't expect listeners to remember a seven-digit phone number.

#11 THE SECOND-TIME RULE

Give higher priority to second-time guests than to first-timers, and to third-time guests than to second-timers.

■ Introduction

Ten years ago my family and I (Charles) moved into a new home and neighborhood and used the summer to search for a new church home. In eight of the ten churches we visited, I filled out a visitor card or signed a guest register. (Two churches had no way for visitors to identify themselves, which says something about their priorities.) Six of the eight churches sent our family a "thank-you for visiting" letter, and two of the churches had a representative phone the following week.

My family especially enjoyed three of the churches and decided to go back for another visit. Again I completed the visitor information, and the following week, checked the mailbox for a follow-up contact. Monday . . . Tuesday . . . Wednesday . . . no letter . . . Thursday . . . Friday . . . Saturday . . . nothing. No card. No phone call. No contact of any sort.

We returned to the same three churches for a third visit in our search for a church home. Visitor information? Completed. Left with the church? Check. Received a follow-up contact the next week? Not a word.

■ Explanation

Do you have a way to let your first-time guests know that you are glad they came, perhaps a letter, a phone call, or a postcard? Hopefully you do. But what about your *second-time* visitors, the ones who liked the experience enough to come back? By their presence, they are telling you, "We're interested in your church."

And what about those who visit your church a third time? They are telling you, "I'm *really, really* interested in your church!" Do you even know who they are? Do you do anything about it?

It should seem obvious that people who visit a church are more likely to join than those who don't visit. That's the reason most churches have a follow-up process for first-time visitors. But why do we often miss an equally obvious conclusion that people who visit twice are more likely to join than those who visit just once? And when people visit three times, they are more likely to join than those who visit twice?

A few years ago we were part of a research study on the topic of visitor retention. We asked participating churches to go back into their records two to three years and select a continuous six-week period (such as September 1–October 15 or January 1–February 15). Then we asked the churches to examine their data and identify all those people who had visited one time during that six-week period, anyone who had visited twice, and finally the people who had visited three times during those six weeks. Then we asked the churches to jump forward one year and identify which of those visitors were now regular attenders. We divided the churches into two categories: those growing in worship attendance and those not. Here were the percentages of visitors who were in the church one year later, based on how many times they had visited in the six-week period.

Percentage of Visitors Who Stayed

Visits in Six Weeks	Nongrowing Churches	Growing Churches
1 visit	9%	21%
2 visits	17%	38%
3 visits	36%	57%

There are some important insights from this study:

- The typical American church sees 9 percent of first-time visitors (or about one in ten) become part of their congregation. (Remember that since 85 percent of today's churches are not growing, "typical" is not necessarily ideal.)

- The typical growing church sees 21 percent (or about two in ten) of first-time visitors become active.
- But when visitors return a second time, the retention rate nearly doubles (from 9 percent to 17 percent in nongrowing churches and 21 percent to 38 percent in growing churches).
- When people visit the same church three times in a six-week period, about one-third of them stay (36 percent), even when the church is declining. And in growing churches more than half of them stay (57 percent).

To put this research, and the apparent facts, into a simple statement: *The more often people visit, the more likely they will stay.*

■ What We Can Do about It

The first thing we recommend you do is to sit down and compose two more follow-up letters, one to second-time guests and one to third-time guests (assuming you already have one for first-timers).

Next, invite a group of four or five people (include some new members) to help design a system to identify, follow up on, and monitor involvement levels of second- and third-time guests.

Your primary goal is to connect second- and third-time guests with regular attendees they have things in common with (such as interests, marital and family status, age, gender, or occupation). There is clear evidence that the more friends a person has (or makes) in a new church, the more likely he or she will become active and involved.

Remember, visitors represent 100 percent of your church's growth potential. It's a wise investment to give them the time, honor, and attention they deserve.

#12 THE VISITOR AGENDA RULE

Know what visitors are looking for and provide it.

■ Introduction

Visitors who are open to becoming part of your church will evaluate their initial visit based on six factors. They are listed below in their probable order of importance. However, all of these factors contribute to the first impressions that visitors have about your church, and all play a role in the visitors' decision to return.

■ Explanation

Are you providing what visitors are looking for in each of these six areas?

1. *The friendliness and warmth of the church.* It is difficult for people who have been regular attendees in a church to accurately judge the kind of impression their church gives to newcomers in the area of friendliness. The best indicator is to check the return rate of your first-time visitors. If less than 25 percent return within six weeks of their first visit, it may indicate a problem in this area.

2. *The character of the worship service.* People are looking for integrity and meaning in worship. They want the service to enable them to experience the presence of God. They hope to hear a word from God. They are looking for clarity and guidance, joy and hope, God's love and grace.

3. *A place for children.* For some visitors, this is the most important issue. Parents may be willing to be ignored and uncomfortable on their visit if it turns out their kids had a great experience. And if moral and spiritual values are creatively taught to their children, some parents will be willing to overlook everything else.

4. *The adult program.* A better scenario, of course, is a church that brings benefit to kids and their parents. Bible studies for adults provide some of the greatest evangelistic opportunities today. As a recent cover story in *Newsweek*[1] magazine indicated, the American public is fascinated with the person of Jesus. Other adults are looking for answers in areas such as marriage enrichment, financial management, coping with loss, even understanding Islam. The more options, the more outreach.

5. *The church building.* For both the exterior and interior, cleanliness is crucial. Outdoor landscaping and paint make important first impressions. Interior decoration, paint, and smell are important. The nursery and women's restroom can be a deal breaker if not well kept.

6. *The church's image.* By far the best way to create or improve a positive community image is through need-meeting ministry. Allowing community groups to use the building will also enhance the image of a church and generate goodwill. A third way to improve image is pastoral visibility in civic groups, community, and local school activities. Your image can also be enhanced through periodic high-visibility events and related publicity.

■ What You Can Do about It

Conduct an informal survey among your church leaders and ask them how they think visitors would rate your church in each of the six categories. For the purpose of comparison, ask them to respond to each item on a scale of 1 to 7 (1 low, 7 high). Then average and summarize the results and use them as a discussion topic for an upcoming leadership event.

Based on these six characteristics, develop a visitor response card. Include this postage-paid reply card in your visitor gift bag and ask visitors to take a moment to respond to the survey on a similar 1 to 7 scale. Also include the survey on your website. (Both should be anonymous.)

Using these six categories, evaluate your church's present ministry and ways to improve the first impression you make on visitors.

#13 THE INFORMATION CENTER RULE

Have an easily accessible location where church and visitor information can be obtained.

■ Introduction

Both the authors have had the same independent experience when landing at Incheon Airport serving Seoul, South Korea. The shock comes after clearing customs when entering the terminal area through the sliding glass doors and being confronted by a sea of Korean faces, Korean signs, and Korean language. As you walk alone in the terminal, somewhat aimlessly and anxiously, your eye catches a sign, like this $\boxed{i}$. You walk up to the young Korean woman behind the counter and ask somewhat tentatively, "Do you speak English?" "Yes, of course," comes the reply. Ahhh. Your anxiety drops immediately. Probably most of you have had a similar experience when entering a foreign country.

Such an experience has many similarities to that of the newcomer attending your church for the first time. He or she is confronted with a sea of unfamiliar faces, unfamiliar signs, unfamiliar language. Why not help lower their anxiety with a $\boxed{i}$ in your church? Or, more specifically, an information center.

■ Explanation

If visitors' first impressions are important to you (and they should be), an attractive and inviting information center is a great way to say: "Welcome! We were expecting you. How can we be helpful?" And if you're a newcomer, that's a particularly nice thing to hear.

We like the name and idea of an information center, visitor center, or welcome center, since it will encourage *all* attenders to make use of it. Tickets for the upcoming church play are on sale here. Flyers describing the adult class topics and locations may be picked up here. This is where families register their kids for summer camp. And this is also where information on the church is available to newcomers. It's easier for a guest to approach a center where other people are gathered in a hubbub of activity.

People may visit the information center before or after the service, so it should be "open for business" twenty minutes before the first service (or class hour) through twenty minutes after the last service ends.

Ask different people to staff the center, rather than the same ones each week. This gives a variety of members the opportunity to interact with newcomers, which is always an enjoyable experience. Recruit people who are friendly and outgoing and who know how to listen, maintain eye contact, and carry on a comfortable conversation. (See #44, The Learning to Listen Rule.)

Your goal is to make it easy and desirable for newcomers to stop by the information center. One of the best ways to connect is to offer a nice gift to your guests. A gift says you appreciate them and the valuable gift they have already given to you—their time. We've seen a variety of creative gifts for kids and adults: candy-filled mugs, small potted plants, imprinted pens and flashlights, highlighters, umbrellas, memo books, crayons and coloring books, stress balls, jigsaw puzzles, music CDs, gift certificates, even polo shirts with a stylized church logo on the front (with a choice of size, gender, and color). Some churches even have gift *bags* filled with lots of fun things. If this all sounds a bit "cheesy" to you, think of it from a different perspective. When you receive a genuinely well-intended gift (which hopefully your gifts are), don't you feel a sense of gratitude, importance, and appreciation? And don't you want to give something in return? For your guests, their return gift may well be a return visit.

Here's an idea that takes gift giving even further. Give *three different* gifts—one to first-time guests, another to second-time guests, and still a different one to third-time guests. A growing church in Baltimore uses three different colored gift bags: red, white, and blue, depending on whether you're a first-, second-, or third-time guest. (They didn't tell us what people get for their fourth visit—maybe offering envelopes.) The information center host said they put items worth fifteen to twenty dollars in each bag, such as a CD, a copy of *The Message*, Starbucks gift certificate, a nice pen. "And," she said, "the value in the bags increases with each visit."

Meaningful Dialogue

Good questions are a great way to nurture a conversation with guests. Questions show interest, affirm value, and create history. Plus, the answers to those questions will give you information for later follow-up. There are actually two different kinds of questions: "open" and "closed." Open questions (preferable) require an answer of more than one or two words and generally begin with *what, how, who,* or *when.* Be careful asking *why* questions since they can begin to sound like an interrogation. Closed questions (less desirable) inhibit discussion since they can be answered in a few words, and generally begin with *are, can, did,* or *do.*

Good conversationalists will also be aware of the four different levels of a conversation: exchange of clichés, exchange of facts, exchange of opinions, and exchange of feelings. While not every conversation needs to delve into the inner-most emotions behind our masks, guests who leave your church should feel that they have had a meaningful connection with one or more people. They have had a chance to tell a part of their story to someone who was genuinely interested, perhaps as Jesus would be.

Relevant Information

The reason to gather information about your guests is for effective follow-up. This means connecting newcomers with people in the church who share similar age, interests, concerns, and marital and family status. Such a "matchmaking" process, of course, requires good information. Name and best contact information for the guest is helpful. Sometimes email is the most comfortable first step, since many visitors are hesitant to give out their phone number or address without knowing what you're going to do with it. (Incidentally, if they do trust you enough to share their address, *don't* breech that trust and show up at their door—uninvited or unexpected—the following week!) The more you know about your newcomers, the more likely you can connect them with others of similar interests in your church.

In gathering this information, names and ages of children are helpful. Occupation, special interests, needs, or concerns of the person or family will help you be carriers of God's love to those who took the initiative and risk of coming to your church.

■ What You Can Do about It

If you don't presently have an information center, the first obvious step is to create one. You could have one up and running within a month. It doesn't need to be anything fancier than two nicely covered four-by-eight-foot tables and a sign, for starters. A better design is a kiosk that gives both permanence and dignity to the process.

If you live in a part of the country where the information center can be out-doors, it should be within sight of the parking lot or campus entrance. (A growing Lutheran church in Southern California has a campus with parking on both sides of the building. Undeterred, they set up *two* information centers, one on each side of the campus.) If your information center must be inside, it should be visible the moment people enter the front doors. If that's not possible, an obvious sign with an arrow pointing to the information center is a must.

Regardless of the size and shape of your information center, location is important. A position where all four sides are accessible is better than something backed up against a wall. It should be well identified and, as we said, easily visible.

Invite one or several people in the church with a good taste for design to lay out the center in a way that is visually appealing and well organized (versus loose papers, books, and brochures laid out all over). For a functional *information* center, additional signs identifying available materials will be helpful, such as "Education/Classes," "Music Ministry," "Camping," "Information for Newcomers." It's also nice to have a good supply of kids' activities (coloring books, small stuffed animals, M&Ms, puzzles, and the like) for kids who will be sitting in the service.

Coffee, doughnuts, and other refreshments shouldn't be far from the information center. A good host should be ready to step away with a guest to share some coffee and a more extended conversation (a good reason to have multiple hosts at the information center). Another reason for a center staff to move out from behind the table or kiosk is to introduce the newcomers to the pastor, a staff person, or another member. A quick tour of the facilities could be an option if time and interest allow. After the service the information center is a perfect place to begin a short tour of the church building for anyone interested.

Several information center teams can be helpful. First, decide on the appropriate number of people to staff the center, depending on your church size. You should have no fewer than two people, though three are preferable. Then identify three different teams, so they can rotate from one week to the next. With three teams, the schedule could be two weeks on, then four weeks off, then two on, four off, and so on. Or it could be one month on, then two months off. This allows more people to have a part in the process (a good thing), and does not require someone to be on duty every Sunday for the next year or two (a bad thing).

If you decide to give a gift of some sort, put the gifts out in clear view even before the service begins. There's nothing like some pretty colored bags at the information center to whet people's curiosity as they go into the service. Then announce the gifts and where to get them at the end of the service.

As mentioned above, an important responsibility of the center staff is to note any information that may be helpful in following up with guests. For example, if the family has a second-grade daughter, the host might ask the mom if she would be interested in a phone conversation with the second-grade Sunday school teacher later in the week. Perhaps the mom would be interested in connecting with another mom in the church who also has a daughter in second grade, to learn more about the kids ministry. The host might make a note about the dad who has just been laid off and send the information to the church office for connections regarding job opportunities in the area. A good conversation will lead to all kinds of possible "connection points" to bring old-timers in the church together with newcomers who share common interests. Of course it is important that someone in the church follow up on this information.

If you expect to see visitors return, it's important to treat them like honored guests. Treat them the way you would want to be treated if you were feeling alone in the world, looking for some hope, some community, some love. The benefit is far greater than the time and effort you will expend.

3

Ministry Rules for Worship

Churches conduct a wide variety of activities, events, and ministries that affect many people in a typical month. But it is the one-hour weekly gathering, called the worship service, that seems to (rightly or wrongly) define a church. Pastors spend hours preparing their message. Choirs practice. Music groups rehearse. Programs are printed. It's a big deal in the life of nearly every congregation.

Some have suggested that if the same amount of time that is now put into planning and participating in the worship service were dedicated to other functions of the local church—such as prayer or service or evangelism or Bible study—the church would be a different place. Quite likely this is true. But unless you are a revolutionary, or plan to start your own church around a different paradigm, most pastors see the weekly worship service as one of their prime responsibilities. Assuming you are one of those, this chapter is intended to provide some helpful guidelines on how to see your worship service be a stimulating, equipping, and enabling experience that encourages participants in their Christian walk.

#14 THE GROWTH RATE RULE

A healthy growth rate in worship attendance
is 7 percent or more each year.

■ Introduction

A church is a living organism. It's natural for an organism to grow and it's natural for a church to grow. When a church is not growing, it is quite likely that something is wrong. In the United States a healthy church will see between 7 and 12 percent growth in worship attendance each year.

■ Explanation

There are a number of indicators that could be used to evaluate whether a church is healthy. One could analyze the budget. The number of visitors, and visitors who stay, in a church might be a good indicator. The percentage of members who read the Bible and have regular devotions could qualify. Perhaps the dollars and hours spent in local community service projects should be considered, or the number of corporate hours in prayer. The number of small groups in a church, or the percentage of members involved is often important. Does the church have adequate and qualified staff? The number of conversions per year could (and should) be measured. And there are other measures. So what is the key indicator of a healthy church?

After years of study, it is our contention that the *primary* indicator of a church's health is its worship attendance growth rate. A negative rate normally means the church has one or more significant problems. A positive growth rate indicates that, for the moment, ministry and mission are likely going well. Of course there will be exceptions in either case. But rules are generalizations of what is the case far more often than not. We suggest the following guidelines for growth rates as an indicator of health in a local church, a regional cluster, and a national denomination:

Poor growth: less than 2% per year

Fair growth: 3–5% per year

Good growth: 6–8% per year

Excellent growth: 9–11% per year

Outstanding growth: 12–15% per year

Incredible growth: 16–20+% per year

It is not uncommon for pastors to be distressed over a discussion that suggests worship attendance is the key reflector of church health. They may respond with something like: "We are not an old-fashioned 'attractional' church and don't define success by how many people come to us. We are a 'missional' church and define our success by how many people we go to." While there is certainly nothing wrong with going *to* people in the community, the idea of creating a dichotomy between "attractional" and "missional" is often a smoke screen typically raised by those in churches that are not growing. Pastors of growing churches know quite well that a church can be both missional, as defined by their focus, and attractional, as shown by their growth.

Worship attendance is the heartbeat of a healthy church. Like a human body, there are indicators of health other than a heartbeat, but in the absence of this critical measure, the other indicators are rather meaningless.

■ What You Can Do about It

We believe that 70 percent of churches in America have the potential to grow by at least 4 percent per year with very little effort. We know this may sound naïve, simplistic, or presumptuous, but sometimes people tend to make things seem much more difficult than they are. A church of one hundred would need a net of only five new worshipers each year for five years to average a 4 percent annual growth rate! If a church of one hundred worshipers added just ten new people per year for ten years, it would average 7 percent growth per year.

Congregations that wish to be healthy should "check their pulse" at least once a year. Here is how to get started. First, look through your church's records and calculate the average weekly worship attendance for each of the last ten years. If you do not have records for some years, talk to people who attended the church at the time and inquire as to their best recollection of attendance.

Once you have the yearly totals, calculate the average percentage of growth or decline from the first year to the second year, the second year to the third year, and so on. For example, suppose the first year's attendance was 73 and the second year's was 78; subtract the first year from the second (78 − 73 = 5), then divide that number by the first year's attendance (5 ÷ 78 = .064 or 6 percent). In this example the church grew at a 6 percent rate over one year. Do the same calculation from year two to year three, year three to year four, and so on.

Note that your calculation may result in a negative number. For example, if the first year's average attendance was 295 and the second year's was 245, the calculation would be 245 − 295= −50; divided by 295 = −16.9 percent decline. Calculate the average growth or decline rate for every year over the last ten years.

Next, plot your ten yearly averages, as in the illustration on page 55.

Add the growth rates for the ten-year period and then divide by ten to get an average growth rate over the ten years. In the example notice that only three down years severely limited this church's growth rate. The church grew 29 percent but lost 23 percent for a gain of 6 percent in ten years, or an average gain of just over ½ percent per year.

Once you have determined your average annual growth rate for the last ten years, think deeply about what the information is telling you concerning the health of your church. Based on the scale we suggested, is your growth rate poor, fair, good,

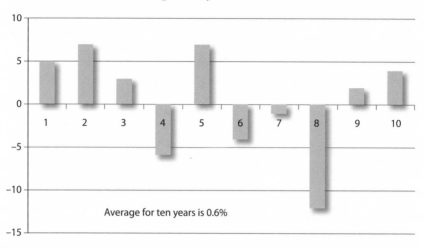

Average Yearly Growth Rates

Average for ten years is 0.6%

excellent, outstanding, or incredible? What are your thoughts on this situation? What do you think God's thoughts are?

Developing such a ten-year chart for your church gives a helpful perspective. It will stimulate a productive conversation among your church leaders about where you are, where you have come from, and where you are going. Keep this chart current from one year to the next. In so doing you will be better able to track your pulse rate and monitor the results of any changes you introduce.

#15 THE SERMON PREPARATION RULE

Effective preachers spend at least fifteen hours
in sermon preparation each week.

■ Introduction

"For I have not hesitated to proclaim to you the whole will of God" (Acts 20:27). Pastors and preaching go together like soup and a sandwich. When a prospective pastor is evaluated, church members wouldn't think about extending a call without first hearing the candidate preach. When church members discuss the strengths and weaknesses of pastors, the typical first criterion is their preaching skill. Obviously preaching is an important part of any pastor's ministry. So can a pastor become a better preacher? Is there a correlation between time in preparation and quality of presentation? Good preaching, of course, depends on a number of factors, but we have found that the best preachers spend a *minimum* of fifteen hours each week in sermon preparation.

■ Explanation

There are three broad ingredients in a successful sermon:

1. *Identifying* the topic and the issues that connect with the people in the congregation
2. *Organizing* the content in a logical way that hearers will understand and remember
3. *Presenting* the message in an engaging and persuasive manner

Taking these things into consideration, as a rule, a pastor should spend at least fifteen hours each week in sermon preparation, divided over at least two weeks. In the first week the pastor spends about seven to eight hours exegeting the passage(s) of Scripture to understand it. The big idea or eternal principle is defined, and a tentative outline is laid out. Then many pastors will let the message percolate during a week of prayerful reflection. The following week, an additional seven to eight hours are given to filling out the outline with illustrations, stories, testimonies, and other didactic techniques. Most good preachers recommend practicing the delivery as well.

Here's a brief glimpse at how two noted orators prepare their messages. John Stott, in his book *Between Two Worlds*,[1] shared the preparation steps he used.

- Choose the text.
- Meditate on the text.
- Isolate the dominant thought.
- Arrange the material to serve the dominant thought.
- Add the introduction and conclusion.
- Write down and pray over your message.

John Piper, popular orator and expositor, shares his approach.[2]

- Read the text in English and Greek (or Hebrew), writing down important points.
- While writing, ask God to make clear what is in the passage for the congregation—what's really there, not just something in the preacher's head that he forces into the text.
- Pray for wisdom to turn the paper into a sermon.

- Look for the two, three, or four points that will be the outline of the sermon.
- On another sheet of paper, order the points, asking the question: "How will these points fit together?"
- Take a break and come back to write out the sermon manuscript (normally ten double-spaced pages).
- Go to bed.
- In subsequent days, internalize the sermon by marking it up and working through the manuscript. This marked-up manuscript is an outline that Piper takes to the pulpit.

Other factors, of course, affect how a pastor prepares his or her sermon. Experience has a major impact on the time necessary to prepare a sermon, with younger pastors typically taking longer, and more experienced pastors needing less time. The genre being preached affects preparation time. Is the message from a psalm or a passage in Revelation? Some parts of the Bible are just easier to get a handle on and thus take less time to develop.

But regardless of the topic, time, or context, Paul's words to Timothy should resound in the ears of every preacher: "Avoid irreverent babble, for it will lead people into more and more ungodliness" (2 Tim. 2:16 ESV). What should be the focus? To the church at Corinth, Paul said that while the Jews demanded signs and the Greeks wanted wisdom, "we preach Christ crucified" (1 Cor. 1:23 ESV).

■ What You Can Do about It

The steps to put this rule into practice are fairly obvious. First, look back over the last three months and determine how much time you typically put into sermon preparation. If it is more than fifteen hours, you are doing well. However, if it is substantially less than fifteen hours, you may not be doing the best job of which you are capable.

Try splitting your sermon preparation time in two halves. In the first week, spend time just understanding the passage. Do quality exegesis of the passage. Think and pray about how the eternal principles could impact the lives of your people. In the second week, refine your outline and add illustrations that connect to your people. Write out the sermon. Practice preaching it at least three times out loud. Pray that God uses you to speak to the hearts and minds of your people.

#16 THE VISITOR HOSTILITY RULE

Visitor-sensitive churches avoid visitor-hostile services.

■ Introduction

Worship services can be very attractive and inviting to newcomers, or they can be very hostile. Services that are visitor friendly are always intentionally designed as such; they don't just happen. Services that are visitor hostile are not intentionally so, but they occur when church leaders design the services only for the interests, preferences, and concerns of their own members. It's not hard to guess which churches are growing.

■ Explanation

A visitor-hostile church service occurs when the activities, worship style, and jargon are so foreign to newcomers that they have no desire to return. The apostle Paul, in speaking to the Corinthian church about the use of tongues, talked about a seeker-hostile service and presented a broader principle that applies to every church: "If then I do not grasp the meaning of what someone is saying, I am a foreigner to the speaker, and the speaker is a foreigner to me" (1 Cor. 14:11). Paul went on: "But in a church meeting I would rather speak five understandable words to help others than ten thousand words in an unknown language" (v. 19 NLT).

Why would Paul be so concerned with communication that was understandable? Because he assumed there would be unbelievers in the midst of their Christian worship. It was important to Paul that the services not be an obstacle to understanding the gospel. He wrote, "If you come together as a congregation and some unbelieving outsiders walk in on you as you're all praying in tongues, unintelligible to each other and to them, won't they assume you've taken leave of your senses and get out of there as fast as they can?" (v. 23 Message).

All services, whether believer-focused or seeker-focused, should be visitor-friendly. Unfortunately not all services are. The Service Evaluation Scale on the next page can be helpful in evaluating and planning the service(s) in your church. If your church service (or a new service you are planning) is seeker-focused, with the planning and attention on outreach to non-Christians, you will want to design your service to be far right on the X-axis and far up on the Y-axis. If your service will be believer-focused, and the primary purpose is the spiritual growth of believers, you will want to design your service to be far left on the X-axis but still far up on the Y-axis.

We have encountered more than a few services that fall in the bottom left portion of this scale. And surprisingly, some misdirected services fall into the bottom right.

The X-axis on this scale measures the *content* of the service. The Y-axis measures the *comfort* of the visitor. For example, an emphasis on redemption is seeker-focused. An emphasis on sanctification is believer-focused. If the language is clear and understandable to an outsider and the welcome is warm and hospitable, you are visitor-friendly, regardless of the content of the message. If the service is filled with religious jargon and the newcomer is ignored or uncomfortable, you are visitor-hostile.

Service Evaluation Scale

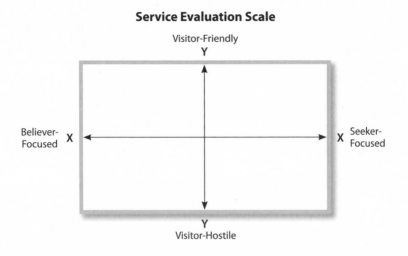

Visitor-Friendly
Y

Believer-Focused   X ←————————————→ X   Seeker-Focused

Y
Visitor-Hostile

An important part of your service evaluation is the music. The *words* of the song identify the music's location on the X-axis (seeker-focused or believer-focused). The *attractiveness* of the music (rhythm, melody, tempo, and so on) to an unchurched visitor defines its place on the Y-axis.

In general the Y-axis evaluates the *medium,* while the X-axis evaluates the *message.*

■ What You Can Do about It

Ask some of your church leaders and worship planners to identify where they feel your services are on the X-axis and the Y-axis. Then compare each other's notes and use the results as a discussion starter as to whether this is where you *want* your services to be. And if they aren't where you want, what can be done to move the services in the right direction? The goal, as Paul reminds us, is, "If some unbelieving outsiders walk in on a service where people are speaking out God's truth, the plain words will bring them up against the truth and probe their hearts. Before you know it, they're going to be on their faces before God, recognizing that God is among you" (1 Cor. 14:25 Message).

#**17** THE NEW SERVICE RULE

An additional worship service for a new target group will help you reach more people.

■ Introduction

"Half of all the churches in North America need to expand their weekend worship services," says Lyle Schaller.[3] And since you're reading this book, you are probably in that 50 percent category. If you would like to see an increase in your total worship attendance, in your total giving, and in your total number of visitors, an additional worship service may be for you. Whether you have one service and add a second, two services and go to three, or three and are contemplating four, the principle holds: *new service = new growth*.

■ Explanation

Here are seven reasons we believe most churches should add a new-style worship service in the next twelve to twenty-four months. One reason may resonate with you more than another. In reality it is not necessary that everyone in the congregation share one *motive* for beginning a new service. What is important is a shared *goal*—namely, to begin a new-style service within the next two years.

1. *A new service will reach the unchurched.* When you begin talking about the idea of a new service, many people will ask, "Why can't they come to the service we already have?" The essential answer is that if they haven't already come, they probably won't. The motivation for starting a new-style service is to connect with people who are *not* presently attending your church.

2. *A new service will minister to more Christians.* Approximately 80 percent of the congregations that move from one worship experience to two find their overall attendance jumps by at least 10 percent. Whether the new service is on Saturday for the people who work on Sunday, or Thursday evening for young families taking weekend minivacations; whether the new service is for those who prefer contemporary music, or for parents who want to worship with their children in a family service, the more options you have, the more people you will reach.

3. *A new service will reach new kinds of people.* Your present service style is attractive to some people and not attractive to others. "The simple truth is that worship cannot be culturally neutral," says James White.[4] If you desire to reach *new* kinds of people in your community, you will need a new service with a style that will speak to them.

4. *A new service will help you break out of your normal life cycle.* The life cycle of a church has three parts: infancy, maturity, and death. The sobering fact is that at least 80 percent of churches today are on the flat or backside of their life cycle. Beginning a new-style service will often start a new life cycle in a church as it regenerates a sense of mission and outward focus and breathes new life into an old, perhaps tired, congregation.

5. *A new service allows for change while retaining the familiar.* If you wish to attract new kinds of people to your church, you have three options: (1) completely redesign your present service, (2) incorporate more variety into your existing service, (3) add an additional service that offers a clear choice of style. We know from experience that the first two options will cause considerable disruption in your church. The third option is based on the important principle of innovation: change through *addition* is more successful than change through *substitution*.

6. *A new service will activate inactive members.* In many congregations only 40 percent of the members who could be in church on any given Sunday actually are. Churches that have added a new-style service often experience a serendipitous benefit—the percentage of inactive members decreases. It is not uncommon to see a new-style service boost the member attendance from the 40 percent range to 60+ percent.

7. *A new service will help your denomination survive.* Denominational church families that desire to be effective and vital well into the twenty-first century must see a large percentage of their churches practicing either one of two growth strategies: actively starting new churches or intentionally starting new services.

We won't presume to suggest that a new service in your church is the simple solution to all your problems. But we can tell you, with utmost certainty, that as long as there are unreached people groups in your community, there is an opportunity for God's love to be shared with them. For many of these people, that love may well be experienced through a new service.

■ What You Can Do about It

A five-year research study examined churches that added a new service. The results were summarized in a 268-page report.[5] Here is a brief summary from this resource of the recommended steps for successfully beginning a new-style worship service:

Step 1. *Identify your target group.* Churches that effectively add a new-style service have a clear understanding of the people group they want to reach. The difference between the current congregation and this new group may be age, spiritual maturity, music preference, language, ethnic identity, or some other significant definer. Such churches realize that one service cannot be all things to all people.

Step 2. *Define the goal of the service.* A goal statement for your new service should include who the service is for, why the service is needed, and what change the service will create in the lives of participants. This goal statement will help your congregation understand the reason such a high-visibility (and possibly high-risk) endeavor is being undertaken. If your church has a mission state-ment, explain how the new service contributes to the pursuit of that mission.

Step 3. *Identify appropriate themes.* Learn as much as you can about the "typical" person in your target group. Here are three questions you should ask about them: What do they worry about? What do they wonder about? What do they wish for? Identify these issues and the gospel's good news answers. Then plan your service around them.

Step 4. *Design the service.* When you begin planning, keep this principle in mind: the sermon is not the message; the *service* is the message. Form a worship planning team (see #18, The Planning Team Rule) and encourage creative preparation that communicates your message through a variety of media and learning experiences.

Step 5. *Determine a place and time to meet.* Many churches begin in schools, hotels, or restaurants. All of those are less threatening to people who haven't been in church lately. (And hopefully they are your target audience.) Just because you have a sanctuary/worship center is not a sufficient reason to use it for your new service. Multiple sites and simultaneous services are growing in popularity.

Step 6. *Invite your target audience.* The best way to get a "critical mass" in your first few services is through the networks of your existing people. Nearly one in three unchurched people say they would attend a church event if asked by a friend, whereas just one in one hundred will respond to the invitation of a stranger (or institution) by phone or mail. Print an attractive flyer about the new service and distribute copies for members to give to friends and relatives. Public advertising can complement these efforts but should not replace them.

Step 7. *Follow up with visitors.* A successful new service requires effective visitor flow. Research shows that the visitor return rate is highest when the follow-up contact (ideally a phone call) is made within the first forty-eight hours. After that, return rates drop off progressively.

As you and your church leaders look to the future, you should find inspiration in the words of the apostle Paul: "I have become all things to all people so that by all possible means I might save some" (1 Cor. 9:22). We believe Paul's words apply to churches that step out in faith to begin a new worship service to reach new people.

#18 THE PLANNING TEAM RULE

A worship planning team will enhance the quality, relevance, and message of your service.

■ Introduction

Have you ever attended a worship service where those on the platform seemed as unsure of the next event as those in the pews? A poorly planned service is an insult to church members, guests, and most importantly, to God. It says, *What we're doing here really doesn't deserve that much preparation.* In contrast, a well-conceived and well-prepared service increases the likelihood that participants will have a chance to genuinely worship an impressive God, to confront his penetrating Word, and to consider its application for their life. Every pastor who prepares a sermon assumes the value of some preparation. Why not put as much time and preparation into planning the entire service to glorify God and edify those in attendance? The best way to do so is through a worship planning team.

■ Explanation

A worship planning team (WPT) is a group of four to seven creative people responsible for designing, planning, and presenting your worship service(s).

Here are four important benefits of an effective WPT:

1. It will add creativity, variety, and interest to your service(s).
2. It will utilize the strengths, insights, and gifts of others.
3. It will require you to plan the services and themes further in advance.
4. It will result in a more polished and well-conceived presentation.

Howard Griffith, pastor of a church in Kentucky, used his three-month sabbatical to visit the worship services of growing churches. He observed, "At first glance, the worship style of rapidly growing congregations seems informal. Looking closer, it becomes apparent that the worship service is tightly structured and well-scripted."[6] A well-polished service is never by accident. The worship services in most growing churches have a team behind the scenes that is responsible for the quality experience.

Makeup of the Worship Planning Team

The WPT should be chaired by a worship director. This person (lay or professional) has responsibility over the entire worship experience. His or her task is to be sure that all aspects of the service are well-planned, well-rehearsed, and well-presented. The role of the worship director is similar to that of the film director for a motion picture. Film directors do not decide what the movie will be about; that's the producer's (pastor's) job. Film directors do not appear on the screen; that's the actor's (platform personnel's) job. Film directors coordinate the production, coach the actors, blend the ingredients, and orchestrate the entire potpourri into a smooth, coherent, moving message to the viewers (congregation). While the worship director may never appear on the platform, the ultimate responsibility for a well-presented service is largely dependent on this individual. Our recommendation is that someone other than the pastor serve in this role, even in smaller churches.

In addition, the following individuals should be on the WPT:

- pastor
- a worship leader (the platform "emcee")
- music coordinator
- drama/arts coordinator
- engineer (sound/lights/props)
- two or three people who are creative and who understand the dynamics of effective communication, rotating on and off the WPT every six months to keep creativity fresh and involvement high

Responsibilities of the Worship Planning Team

For each service the WPT should

1. identify the *theme* of the service
2. identify the *attitudes* that worshipers have about the topic
3. identify the *message* that the overall service should communicate
4. identify the best way to *communicate* the message

■ What You Can Do about It

Your WPT should have two weekend planning retreats per year and then meet every week to prepare for the upcoming services. The goal of the retreats is to work with the pastor on the service themes for the coming six months. The purpose of the weekly meetings is to put together the various ingredients of the services.

The Theme Planning Sheet (on the next page) will help your WPT organize each service. The first three items (theme, attitudes, message) should be completed for each service for the next six months by the time you finish the retreat. If ideas grow out of your retreat for communicating the message in music, drama, sermon points, testimonies, and so on, they can be noted on the sheet.

At the end of the retreat, give one set of theme planning sheets to each member of the WPT. A loose-leaf notebook is helpful to organize the material. Ask members to keep their notebooks handy and jot down ideas that come to mind in subsequent days for effectively communicating the message on that Sunday. Encourage team members to be on the lookout for illustrations or ideas related

Theme Planning Sheet

Service Date(s):

Theme of the Service:

Common *Attitudes:*

Message:

Ideas for *Communicating* the Message through

    Music

    Drama

    Sermon

    Testimonies/interviews

    Other

to these themes. Real life stories, cartoons, anecdotes, television shows, news stories, and articles related to each week's theme can be added to the notebook.

Then the WPT should meet weekly to decide the best ways to communicate each theme. The planning process for each service should take between five and six weeks.

#19 THE MESSAGE RULE

The sermon is not the message; the service is the message.

■ Introduction

An assumption in many churches is that the sermon is the most important part of the worship service. So common is this assumption that the sermon is often referred to as "the message" by members and preacher alike. Paul Anderson has observed that, because of this perception: "Pastors may spend fifteen hours on sermon preparation and fifteen minutes throwing the service together."[7] A better paradigm, as you design your service, begins with a very different assumption: the message is conveyed via the *entire* service.

■ Explanation

An important goal of most worship services is to communicate God's timeless truths so that participants incorporate them into their lives. This goal may—or may not—be best accomplished through a twenty-five-minute sermon. That's a hard one to swallow for many preachers. But if a pastor can reframe his or her thinking in this way, it will be a wonderful, freeing breakthrough in the worship service planning.

My (Charles) postgraduate degree is in instructional technology, which is the study of how to facilitate the greatest learning, given: (1) the unique *characteristics* of the learner, (2) the specific *objectives* of the lesson, and (3) the instructional *media* available to the teacher. The task of an instructional technologist is to create a learning experience that will most likely result in the student's desired behavior change.

The goal of a worship planning team (see #18, The Planning Team Rule) is similar to that of an instructional technologist, namely to consider the unique *characteristics* of those attending the service, identify the specific *objectives* of that particular service, and use the communication *media* that will create the best learning experience and behavior change. (Incidentally, instructional technology studies reveal that the unsupported spoken word—which describes the communication style of most sermons—is one of the weakest mediums for changing behavior.)

This instructional technology approach to worship service planning may mean in some weeks there is no sermon delivered at all, and the message is delivered through different media. Other services may have no music. Some "sermons" may be entirely a dramatic presentation. Avoid filling slots in a canned liturgy. Rather, focus on communicating a clear message through the entire worship service.

■ What You Can Do about It

Given that the *service* is the message (rather than the sermon alone), work with the worship planning team to utilize many different tools to best communicate your message.

- *Music* is the most important ingredient in a successful service. Good music = good service. Poor music = poor service. Of course good music + good preaching + good drama + good pace + good transitions = a great service. Whereas the sermon speaks to the mind, music speaks to the soul.
- *Drama* is a powerful tool to communicate a message. Good drama can highlight the theme of the service, heighten the attention of the congregation, and enhance retention of the viewers. It can range from a three-to-five-minute sketch that illustrates a problem to be addressed in the sermon to a twenty-minute "sermon" given by a person in biblical character.
- *Storytelling* takes listeners into the realm of their imagination. Whereas a good sermon illustration *clarifies* a point in the sermon, a good story *makes* a point, which the sermon clarifies. Think about Jesus's parables. Were they sermons or stories? Jesus knew the indelible image that is created in one's memory by a stimulating, well-told story.
- *Puppets* capture the imagination and a sense of childlike innocence in people. Whereas people may be judged by their appearance, their manner of presentation, or their body language, puppets are immediately accepted. Puppets can teach many moral and spiritual lessons that might be lost if told by an adult.
- *Multimedia* means using a variety of media to make the point. Media can include video, posters, audio, objects, art, slides, noises, smells, tastes. The more senses involved in processing a message, the more likely that message will be remembered.
- *Preaching*, according to the New Testament, is essential to faith, conversion, and Christian growth: "So faith comes from what is heard, and what is heard comes by the preaching of Christ" (Rom. 10:17 RSV). The preached word is a channel through which God, by his Holy Spirit, invites, instructs, challenges, comforts, and energizes people.

- *Testimonies* are true-life stories—told by firsthand witnesses. Though a dramatic impact can be made by telling a good story, an even more powerful impact can be made when people tell their own stories. It's hard to argue with someone whose life has been changed.

When a worship planning team grasps the idea that the entire service is the message, and makes a commitment to use all creative means possible to communicate that message, there will be a discernible increase in the impact of the message and the number of people who are affected by it.

#20 THE SERMON SELECTION RULE

When church members help select sermon topics, they are more likely to come hear you preach on them.

■ Introduction

If you are like most pastors, you often ask the question, What should I preach on? Sometimes it may be the topic of a churchwide study. Other times it's related to a book just read. Perhaps it's an issue you are wrestling with in your own life. Whatever the topic, your prayer is that the message will be relevant and used by God to speak to people's lives.

Wouldn't it be nice to know that when you sit down to research and prepare your sermons you can be *guaranteed* people will be interested and looking forward to hearing God's words with eager anticipation?

■ Explanation

Some years ago we conducted research for the U.S. Navy Chaplain Corps. The chaplains wanted to know the attitudes of incoming eighteen-, nineteen-, and twenty-year-old recruits toward religion and church. We interviewed young men and women in mainstream America and asked, "What is your opinion of church?" Two words came back over and over: *boring* and *irrelevant*.

Relevance is one of the secrets of an effective, contagious church. When attendees find their church speaking clearly and directly to their life issues, not only do they return, but they invite their friends. Relevance applies to the words and rhythm of songs and to the style and appearance of the facilities. Relevance applies to children's Sunday school and to topics in the adult classes. But perhaps the key area where relevance is essential is the sermon.

In his book *Relevant Preaching: What They Didn't Teach You in Seminary,* James Emery White talks about how to make preaching relevant: "The most important issue has to do with your sermon topics. They should address people's life issues and questions about the faith. . . . That means you try to bring as much of the counsel of God as you can to them through the door of their interests."[8]

How do you find out the interests, concerns, and needs of your congregation so you can connect God's Word with their world? Rather than guess, why not ask them?

■ What You Can Do about It

Insert a 3x5" card in each church bulletin or program for the next several weeks and point it out during the service. Explain that two of your goals, as pastor, are to be sure the Word of God is understood and applied to daily life, and that it is relevant to both those in the church and those in the community. Ask people to take a moment to think about their answers to three questions and write them on the card.

1. *What do you wonder about?* What do you just not understand—or wish you did understand—about how life works? Is it why bad things happen to good people, or does prayer really work? Perhaps you wonder about what happens when people die, or why innocent children suffer. If there is more than one thing that comes to mind, write them all down.
2. *What do you worry about?* What keeps you up at night, causes your heart to beat faster, your anxiety level to rise? Perhaps it's a financial issue, maybe a relationship gone bad. And in your worst case scenario, is there realistic hope?
3. *What do you wish for?* If money were no obstacle, if time and other commitments could not stop you, what is your dream? What would you love to see or do? Maybe travel somewhere? Perhaps you would like to have lots of money, or a particular job, or a special relationship. Dreams are powerful things. What are yours?

At the end of the service congregants should drop their completed cards into one of several marked boxes by the exits. The cards should, of course, be anonymous.

Repeat the process for the next two weeks. Many will have thought about your questions and have additional ideas to add. People who did not attend the previous week can also contribute.

Then transcribe the responses to each question into a separate document on your computer. (Having a secretary can come in handy at this point.)

Spend time reviewing the responses to each question and look for common issues. Try to make general categories and then place tic marks under the category when you encounter a similar response. Repeat the process for the other two questions and identify the most frequent responses to each question.

Your congregation will be interested in the results of the "survey." On the Sunday after your last survey, share the list and frequency of the responses. A visual illustration, graph, or printed document will add interest.

Explain that you will be taking these issues seriously, doing research, and sharing messages in the coming months that speak to them. If you are organized enough, you might print a list of upcoming dates of which services will be addressing these issues. Encourage members to invite friends or relatives on the day(s) when the topic may be of interest to them.

Such a list of topics is certain to tweak the interest of your members as they know the service will be speaking to issues they (or others) care deeply about. Advertise upcoming dates and topics so that previous visitors, parents of VBS kids, inactive members, and other groups who have a loose connection with your church will be aware of them.

Don't forget #19, The Message Rule: *The sermon is not the message; the service is the message.* Use the entire service to examine the issue: drama, panel discussions, music, personal testimonies, video clips. And then remember #18, The Planning Team Rule: *a worship planning team will enhance the quality, relevance, and message of your service.* This series on life's issues is a great time to invite a group of creative people to help plan the services (and the series), making them ring with reality and relevance!

#21 | THE ATTENDANCE TRACKING RULE

Monitor attendance to close your "back door."

■ Introduction

The most accurate indicator of people beginning to drop out of church is a fluctuation in their worship attendance. They miss a Sunday for no particular reason. Then they are back for the next several months. (They probably wonder if anyone missed them.) Then a few months later they miss another Sunday, maybe two. They return (still wondering). Then there are three or four absences in a row. They come back once more. The next time they attend is Christmas. Then Easter. In addition to their spotty attendance, their giving drops off. For all practical purposes they have left the church. While the length of time it takes people to physically drop out of church is often six to eight months or more, the time it takes people to psychologically drop out of church and sever their emotional ties is only six to eight weeks. Sadly, in most cases, this pattern could have been prevented.

■ Explanation

If you take seriously your responsibility for the spiritual life, health, and growth of your congregation, we suggest you increase the quality of information gathered from your weekend worship service(s). With better information you will be a better leader, a better steward, and a better shepherd of your people. Every church should do the following:

1. *Obtain* attendance information.
2. *Monitor* attendance patterns.
3. *Respond* to attendance indicators.

Obtain Attendance Information

This does not mean just counting heads. While graphing attendance for the past several years is interesting, it is a *reactive* process able only to stimulate the casual observer to a thoughtful "hmmm." The *proactive* approach gathers more "intelligent" information and then acts on it. Such information goes beyond knowing how many were present and allows you to know who was in church and who was not. This is important because a fluctuation in worship attendance is the first sign of a person beginning to drop out.

So, how do you find out? Here are some ideas used by various churches:

- A "pew pad," located at the end of each row, is signed and passed down the row. Most people will sign a sheet when it is handed to them, so it is usually an accurate indicator of who is in the service and who is not. The downside is that it's not very private and thus people may not feel free to share additional information, such as prayer requests, name and address, or notes to staff.
- Registration cards in a rack on the seat back are completed by each attendee (not just the visitors). Newcomers don't like to be publicly identified, so asking them to reach forward and fill out a visitor card lowers the percentage of people who will do so. A large Lutheran church in Houston uses one card with two sides—the blue side for all members and regular attenders, and the green side for those who still consider themselves visitors. Good idea.
- A perforated flap in the printed program is completed by each attendee, torn off, and dropped into the offering plate. This approach allows for more confidential information to be shared and gives all members and visitors an opportunity to put at least something in the offering plate as it goes by. (Of course, some pastors prefer a different approach for that very reason.)
- A church in Southern California preprints the names of each member and regular attender on 4-across computer labels (each label is approximately 1" by 2½"). The continuous form paper is torn into 5-foot lengths and the

strips of labels are taped to the wall in the church lobby. Worshipers enter the building, find their nametag (listed in alphabetical order), peel it off, and stick it on their shirt for the morning. It's a handy way to help people remember names. In addition, the nametags that remain on the 5-foot sheets after the last service show who was *not* there that Sunday. (Visitors or guests can get a similar nametag printed at the information center, which also gives the church a record of visitor information.)

- A country church in Kansas has appointed a woman in the choir to check the membership list against people in the pews as the choir sits on the platform facing the congregation. Having identified the visitors, she takes the initiative to introduce herself to them after the service.
- Small groups and adult Bible classes can be asked to check worship attendance of the people in their group.
- A few examples on the high-tech side include: One large church in Atlanta has two video cameras mounted in the worship center that scan and record those in attendance using facial recognition software. Another church scans the congregation with a video camera and the following week has a staff member name the faces on the screen while another checks off the names on a membership list. They report that it takes only five minutes to check their three hundred attendees.
- A church in Las Vegas issues magnetically striped wallet-sized cards to each member and regular attender. The cards are used for childcare check-in, financial contributions, member voting, and other church activities. And located at all doors are wireless readers that automatically register the names of cardholders who pass through on Sunday morning—they don't even have to swipe their cards. (Members are aware of this process and love it!)

Monitor Attendance Patterns

For monitoring attendance patterns, your computer is your best friend. Whether it's a bells-and-whistles commercial church software, or a homemade spreadsheet with a few formulas, you'll need a way to enter *and* evaluate the data. At the beginning of each week print a report that provides you with the following:

- First-time visitors (names and addresses, if available)
- Second-time visitors and the date of their first visit
- Third-time visitors and the dates of their first and second visits
- Percent of visitors to total attendance (numerical and graphical format for the previous six months)
- Members and regular attenders who were absent (totals and percentages for the previous six months)

- Members and regular attenders who have missed three services in a row
- Any additional information you may find helpful

Respond to Attendance Indicators

Some churches have a system to send out a card, email, or letter to any regular attender who was not present on Sunday. The communication is not a "Where were you?!" interrogation. It is simply a note that says, "We missed you. You're an important part of our church family. Things just aren't the same here without you."

Some churches wait for two misses in a row before the "take action switch" is flipped. Still others wait for three consecutive absences.

You might develop a system in which the names of those who missed the service are forwarded to their small group leader or Sunday school class teacher or deacon. It is important for pastors or staff people to contact any member or regular attender who is gone three Sundays in a row, since research indicates half of such people will be gone within a year.

■ What You Can Do about It

Discuss with your church leaders the idea of tracking attendance. Some pastors don't feel comfortable with the idea and prefer to remain in the dark about who is attending and who is absent. And some church members feel like "big brother" is watching over their shoulders. So it will be helpful to discuss the benefits and risks.

If you are curious about the value of tracking attendance, talk with several pastors who do so. Find out how they do it and the results they are experiencing. Ask them if, in their opinion, it's worth their trouble. Then make up your own mind. (If the idea is adopted, or tentatively adopted, be sure to read chapter 13, "Ministry Rules for Change." There are some important guidelines for successfully introducing and adopting new ideas.)

Organize a task force to develop a plan for each of the three processes: obtaining attendance information, monitoring attendance patterns, and responding to attendance indicators. The task force should research methods and models that are currently in practice. Realize that you probably won't get it exactly right the first time, so continue to evaluate whether you are reaching your goals in the first few months. You may want to introduce the process to the congregation as an "experiment" and then ask for feedback after three or four months.

4

Ministry Rules for Connecting with and Assimilating Newcomers

A recent survey found that only 3 percent of churches in the United States have a specific group, committee, or task force charged with welcoming visitors and integrating newcomers. This is in contrast with 21 percent of churches that have an outreach and/or evangelism committee, 68 percent with a team that oversees the worship ministry, and 84 percent of churches with persons responsible for the Christian education program. Perhaps it is not a surprise, given these figures, that only 15 percent of the churches in America today are growing.

The typical American church sees only one of every ten first-time visitors come back to become an active participant. And the reason has little to do with the preaching, facilities, theology, or location of that church. In this chapter we think you will find some helpful·rules of thumb that will focus on the issues that cause more visitors to return and become assimilated into the life and fellowship of your church.

#22 THE FRIENDSHIP FACTOR RULE

Newcomers must have seven-plus friends in the church
within the first six months to become fully assimilated.

■ Introduction

Why do some new members become actively involved in their new church, participate in groups and activities, serve on planning committees, sit with friends in church, go out afterward for a meal, while others disappear into the woodwork, never connect, never volunteer or join a small group, or serve in ministry? Is it all just luck? Do extroverted newcomers get assimilated but introverts don't? Do some churches simply have more to do, so more volunteers get involved? There are many reasons, of course, but from our research and experience, there is one *most important reason* that some newcomers stay in church, while others drop out. It is the number of new friends that new people make in their new church. Friends are the "bridge" for outsiders to become insiders in a church family. And the first six months are critical.

■ Explanation

The number of friends that newcomers make is crucial to whether they "stick." A researcher interviewed one hundred different people a year after they had joined a church—fifty who had become active and fifty who had dropped out. The question posed to each person was, "How many friends did you make in your new church?" The chart below shows his findings.[1]

Number of new friends	0	1	2	3	4	5	6	7	8	9+	Avg.
Actives	0	0	0	1	2	2	8	13	12	12	7
Dropouts	8	13	14	8	4	2	1	0	0	0	2

Newcomers who developed a significantly larger number of friends remained active in their church, while those who had fewer friends left the church. The average active member had made seven friends, the average dropout, two. This leads to an inverse rule of thumb: *Newcomers who make fewer than two friends in the first six months are more likely to drop out.*

Here's the bottom line: If you can help newcomers develop seven or more friends in your church within the first six months of their initial visit, there is a strong likelihood they will become integrated into the life and fellowship of your church. If they make three to five friends, their participation is tenuous. If they make two or fewer friends in those first six months, it is likely they will be gone by their first anniversary.

■ What You Can Do about It

The best way to create a "friendship greenhouse" in your church is to regularly *begin new groups for newcomers*. Becoming involved in a small group is the best way to make friends. Groups provide a time and place to know and be known, to share, question, laugh, cry, encourage, and grow together. The more things that newcomers in a group have in common, the more likely they will become and remain friends for a long time. (See #32, The New Groups Rule for more on why and how to start new groups.) As you start new groups for newcomers, plan on growing together. Here are a few ideas:

- *Eat together.* John Chandler, a longtime student of effective churches, observes, "Not all groups that grow eat together. But all groups that eat together seem to grow. It is my overwhelming experience that eating together is one of the best ways to build community."[2]
- *Celebrate special days.* Members of the group should be encouraged to share special events and problems in each other's lives: graduations, new babies, illness and other health concerns, job promotion or loss, engagements, grandchildren.
- *Care for needs.* If special needs arise in the life of a group member (and they will), make an effort to respond in love and care to the person. Bring meals to their home, pick up their kids from school, do their grocery shopping or whatever else is needed. Loving acts in times of need will build relationships like nothing else.
- *Go to special events together.* If there are activities (church-related or otherwise) that sound like fun, go together. This might include seeing an appropriate movie, hearing a special speaker of interest to the group, attending a conference or seminar, going for pizza after church, attending a church- or community-sponsored event together, working on a church- or community-sponsored service project.

Your church should be, in the best sense of the phrase, a "relational cupid," working to bring newcomers together with other newcomers and longtime members, in meaningful relationships that will last a lifetime.

#23 THE VISITOR RETENTION RULE

Twenty percent of your visitors should become involved
in your church within a year of their first visit.

■ Introduction

A few years ago I (Gary) consulted with a church that, during the previous year, had seen 197 visitors come through its doors on Sunday mornings. Unfortunately only three had stayed to make the church their home.

Many pastors make the mistake of assuming that the secret to church growth is simply more visitors. This assumption overlooks a key part of the growth equation—visitor retention.

■ Explanation

Visitor retention is defined as the percentage of your visitors who become involved in your church within a year after their first visit. They may not have yet joined as members but they are regular attenders at one or more church activities.

Whether you know your church's visitor retention rate or not, you do have one. Discovering your visitor retention rate will help you know if you have enough visitors to grow. And this information will go a long way toward explaining your church's recent growth or decline.

In our research we have found that the typical nongrowing church has a retention rate of 9 percent. That is, only about one in ten first-time visitors to the church who could come back actually do. This is in contrast to *growing* churches that average approximately 21 percent visitor retention (or about two in ten).

The best way to calculate your visitor retention is to list each new person who has visited a church event (worship service or otherwise) in the past two to eighteen months. Then determine whether that person is now a regular attender. An example of a chart for determining your visitor retention is given below. (An actual chart would be much larger, allowing for each visitor's name to be listed.)

Once you have completed this chart, simply add the number of times you put "yes" in the right column and divide that number into the total number of visitors on the chart. The result will be your visitor retention.

Name of visitor	Date of first visit (in past 2–18 months)	Now regularly attending? (Yes/No)

As the rule indicates, a healthy visitor retention rate is 20 percent or better. If you are keeping one out of five visitors, you are doing very well. (We have actually seen some churches that place a high priority on visitor follow-up averaging 30+ percent.) If your visitor retention is less than 20 percent, you should consider focusing on how to better identify, connect with, and assimilate newcomers.

■ What You Can Do about It

The first step is obvious—calculate your visitor retention rate and complete the above table. Take this information to your next leadership meeting and talk about the implications.

Research shows that when newcomers visit a church twice within a six-week period, their eventual affiliation rate doubles. And when they visit three times within six weeks, affiliation rate triples! So, the more you can do to see them back the following Sunday, the more likely you will see them back for years to come. Here are some suggestions to see visitors return:

1. *Obtain visitors' names and contact information.* Newcomers will only give you their name and address if they are comfortable with what you're going to do with it. Practice the *principle of disclosure*. That is, be up front and honest with people about what you will do with their information (such as sending alerts of special church events), and what you won't do (such as showing up on their doorstep unannounced). Make the benefit worth the risk. By the way, visitors are more likely to give you their email address than their physical address. So, give them the chance.

2. *Make a follow-up contact within 48 hours of their visit.* A phone call or email is best. A personal visit is usually too presumptuous. Research shows that the highest visitor return rate the following Sunday occurs when the church's follow-up contact is made the Monday or Tuesday after the first visit. The later into the week the contact is made, the fewer visitors return the next Sunday.

3. *Laypersons should make the email or phone contact, not clergy.* Visitor return rates nearly double when a church member makes the connection. It's just a more believable conversation. And the best members to make the contact are ones who have something in common with the guest. Common age, family status, interest, or occupation increases the likelihood of a relational connection and a return visit.

4. *Invite guests back and offer to meet them.* "Can I meet you in the lobby next Sunday?" is much more effective than, "I hope you come back next Sunday."

5. *Involve them in a small group.* The most important ingredient in connecting newcomers to your church will be relationships. The more friends in the church, the more likely the newcomer will stay. And, the best way to make friends is through a small group. If the newcomer already has one or more friends in a church group, that is the best option. If the newcomer does not have any friends in church, the best approach is to involve them in a *new* group that has been meeting less than a year, with people of similar characteristics. Ideally, they can be part of a group that is just beginning.

#24 THE NEW MEMBER MINISTRY RULE

Nine of every ten new members should be involved in a ministry role or task.

■ Introduction

Eleven years ago I (Charles) joined a new church with my wife and son. I remember how alone I felt on Sunday mornings during the first three months. My wife was a better "joiner" than I. She had made some new friends and seemed to be increasingly at home in the new church. But not me. One Sunday morning the announcement appeared in the bulletin of an all-church workday in two weeks. *Why not?* I thought. That Saturday I arrived at 8:30 a.m. and was assigned to paint the walls of room 14. When I walked in, I saw two other people I didn't know who were already working away. We introduced ourselves and spent the next three hours painting the doors, closets, walls, and floorboards. Of course you can't be in a room with two other people for three hours without conversing, and it was a nice time. But the next Sunday I discovered I had made some new friends. It was easy to strike up a conversation with them in the lobby after church. And as we chatted, I introduced my new friends to my wife. Ten years later I still call these people friends.

What happened? The same thing that will happen when your new members work together with other church members on a common task—they will get to know each other. While my experience was just for one day, sharing in ministry over a period of weeks or months will result in new members building important new friendships with others in the church during that first crucial year.

■ Explanation

The initial months of a newcomer's connection with your church are both important and perilous. As we have already noted, the "friendship factor" is the key ingredient in whether a newcomer becomes a long-term attender or simply slips away.

The two best ways for newcomers to develop friendships are to be involved in a small group and to have a role or task in the church. Actually it should be both-and rather than either-or. We address small groups in chapter 5, so we'll look here at ministry roles or tasks. While it's especially helpful for *newcomers* to have such involvement, it's just as important for *everyone* in your church to have something meaningful to do.

The chart below will give you a quick reference guide to determine how well you are (or are not) involving your members in ministry. (Note that diagnostic items 7–12 are specifically for newcomers.) To assess your church, first fill in the blank at the top left on line 1 with your total church constituency. This number reflects your overall church family—that is, a combination of church members and regular attenders. Next, determine in which column your church falls on lines 2–18. (All the numbers are percentages.) Calculate your percentages based on your total church constituency (line 1), unless noted otherwise.

If you find your scores fall primarily in the left columns, the focus of your lay ministry is likely to be inward and your people might be better characterized as "workers." The farther your scores are to the right, the more likely you have an outward focus and your people are more likely "ministers." Note in particular where your newcomers are located. It is on the right side, obviously, where effective ministry most often occurs. Such ministry is about growing people in Christ, not filling slots to accomplish our institutional needs.

"Workers" ◄————————► "Ministers"

		Problem area	Needs attention	Average	Good	Ideal
People Involved	**1. Total Church Constituency:**_____					
	2. Constituents with a specific role/task	0–20	21–29	30–49	50–69	70+
	3. Constituents with a "church-focused" role (% of #2)	96+	95–86	85–75	74–61	60>
	4. Constituents with an "outward-focused" role (% of #2)	0–4	5–9	10–14	15–19	20+
	5. Constituents who attended worship 1+ in past 4 weeks	0–34	35–44	45–59	60–69	70+
	6. Total # of constituents involved in a small group	0–10	11–29	30–45	46–64	65+
New Attenders	7. Constituents who began attending in last 12 months	0–2	3–4	5–6	7–10	11+
	8. New constituents (from #7) with a role/task	0–29	30–44	45–59	60–69	70+
	9. New constituents (from #7) involved in a small group	0–29	30–49	50–69	70–79	80+
	10. Constituents who began attending 12–24 months ago	0–2	3–4	5–6	7–10	11+
	11. Constituents (from #10) with a role/task	0–29	30–44	45–59	60–69	70+
	12. Constituents (from #10) involved in a small group	0–29	30–49	50–69	70–79	80+
Ministry Positions	13. Total role/task positions available in the church	0–20	20–29	30–49	50–69	70+
	14. Role/task positions with written job descriptions	0–10	11–29	30–50	51–74	75+
	15. Positions with specific pre-service training	0–10	11–29	30–50	51–69	70+
	16. "Maintenance" oriented role/task positions (% of #13)	90+	89–80	79–70	69–60	59>
	17. "Outreach" oriented role/task positions (% of #13)	0–8	9–15	16–20	21–34	35+
	18. New roles/tasks created in the last 12 mo. (% of #13)	0–2	3–4	5–6	7–10	11+

Source: *The Growth Report* Vol. 2 No. 6, Institute for American Church Growth (Pasadena, CA)

■ What You Can Do about It

For the most part, assume that newcomers will act like "relational introverts." That is because they are not generally comfortable around people they don't know and situations with which they are not familiar. Thus the discomfort of volunteering for anything the first time will keep many newcomers on the passive sidelines. Go out of your way to be sure newcomers are *personally invited* to do the following:

- *Help in church-related projects.* Special activities that are already on the church calendar (for example, decorating for Christmas, painting the church, repaving the parking lot, recarpeting the nursery) are great opportunities for newcomers to help out and make new friends in the process.
- *Go on special church outings and events.* If you have any family camps, mission trips, or summer picnics planned, personally invite newcomers to be a part. In fact, ask them to help in the planning process as well.
- *Assume a responsibility in a class or group.* If the newcomer is already part of a small group (hopefully so), ask if he or she would be willing to help bring refreshments, photocopy handouts, or occasionally host the meeting at his or her house.
- *Serve as greeter or usher in the worship service.* We recommend multiple usher and greeter teams that rotate throughout the year so more people, especially newcomers, can be involved. (Greeters and ushers don't need to be members!)

Help newcomers find a place of service in your church that matches their particular interests; then the new role will be a ministry rather than a job. When you do this, many more of your newcomers will begin to feel that "your" church is becoming "our" church.

#25 THE NEW MEMBER ORIENTATION RULE

One hundred percent of your new members should participate in your new member orientation class.

■ Introduction

Years ago, as an entering freshman at Seattle Pacific University, I (Charles) recall our entire freshman class being taken to Camp Casey for a three-day orientation. We met the president of the school and heard his vision and passion for higher education. We met the senior class president, our faculty advisors, and fellow freshmen students. We learned (and sang numerous times) the school song. (I can still sing it to this day!) We learned about the history of SPU. We received a map of the campus and an explanation of each building's use. And there were numerous planned events to help us get to know our fellow classmates.

I haven't been on a college campus during freshman week since then, so I don't know if such goings-on continue. I suspect they have faded like many traditions of my youth. But as I look back on that assimilation process, I see many things that helped me develop an identity as an SPU Falcon. And these were principles that can still be applied to the process of assimilating newcomers in a church so that they feel a part of the family.

■ Explanation

In churches, as well as many other gatherings of people, the move from being an "outsider" to an "insider" is not always easy. In some churches, unfortunately, it seems nearly impossible. But as members of the body of Christ, we must open our arms and welcome new family members who have been adopted into the faith community. One of the best ways to facilitate this welcome is through a well-conceived new member orientation process. Every church should have one.

The reason it's important to spend time, effort, and money on new member orientation is that assimilation of newcomers *does not happen automatically*. It's surprising how many churches think it does. A survey we conducted a few years ago asked pastors if they had an evangelism/outreach committee in their church. Twenty-one of every hundred said yes. The next question was whether they had an assimilation committee in their church. Only three in a hundred said they did. Many pastors and churches seem to think that assimilating new people happens by itself, without any need to oversee the process.

The truth is, however, that if anything happens automatically, it is that the newcomers will *not* be assimilated. There are many reasons for this:

- Newcomers don't know any (or many) people in the church and they feel uncomfortable, thinking they are the only ones who don't know anyone.
- Most newcomers are not extroverted enough to push themselves into existing conversations or groups.
- Newcomers are hesitant to volunteer their ideas for fear of looking silly because of not understanding the history of the church.
- Church groups and classes that have been meeting for more than two years are socially difficult to break into.

It's common to hear people in a church say with conviction, "We are a warm and loving church." The implication behind their belief is that any newcomer who joins will automatically feel the same sense of warmth and love that they do. It's likely, however, that the members who are so convinced that these qualities characterize their church have been in the church for at least five years and more likely twenty-five years! It is common for visitors and new members to feel quite a different (lesser) degree of warmth and love than the longtime members. Thus the more intentional and proactive a church is in welcoming newcomers into the flock, the more newcomers will remain and become longtime members.

■ What You Can Do about It

Here are some ideas for your new member orientation process that we suggest you consider:

- *Overnight retreat.* There is a long-term bond that develops when people "camp out" together. Find a nice getaway place and treat your new members to a weekend together. Ideally make it a two-night event (Friday and Saturday). Include get-acquainted events, small group activities, devotionals, social time, quiet time. Make it fun and be creative. Then plan a retreat to celebrate their first anniversary as new members.

- *New members class.* Your newcomers will feel closer to other new members than they will to "old-timers" in your church. So build on this natural bond to develop a sense of camaraderie and community among them. Usually the class works best on Sunday morning. We recommend that a new members class last long enough to develop a relational bond and to cover the key things every new member should have a chance to learn in depth. Here are a few possible topics:

    Discovering and using your spiritual gifts

    Learning the vision and goals of the church

    Taking a tour of the church facility

    Who we are, as a church family, and what we believe

    The Christian disciplines and their application in your life

    Nurturing deeper relationships with others in the body of Christ

    Finding (or starting) a small group in our church

    The importance of Christian worship

    How to be an effective witness with friends and family

    The power of prayer and how to tap into it

- *Monthly social events.* There are all kinds of fun things to do together as new members—bowling, concerts, movies, picnics, game nights, street fairs, ball games. These events are especially important during the first year, which is the most critical time for newcomers in the assimilation process. But chances are good that these new members will find the monthly gatherings so enjoyable, they'll want to keep meeting beyond the first year. So, do it! Actually you should start a group for newcomers at least every year (ideally every six months) rather than trying to add new members to what will become an increasingly older (and more closed) group as relationships mature.

- *Monitor attendance at church events.* Studies have shown that it takes only three absences in a row for a person to have a fifty-fifty chance of dropping out of church. With each additional absence, the likelihood of the person leaving out the back door increases. When people (new or older members) have been sick or out of town for a few weeks, they wonder, *Did anyone miss me?* Just a casual, "Hey, it's good to have you back," or a card in the mail that says, "We missed you," can go a long way toward closing the back door of a church. As we have seen, some congregations monitor the attendance of everyone (not just new members), knowing that their duty of "minding the flock" is a trust God has given them as spiritual leaders.

#26 THE NEW MEMBER SPONSOR RULE

One hundred percent of new members should have a sponsor.

■ Introduction

There I (Charles) was thirty-five years ago, standing with eight others at the front of the church looking at 700+ people, while they looked back at us. The eight of us were about to become new members of the church, and the pastor had asked us to come forward during the service. Like most new members, I knew only a few people in the pews, and most of the members did not know me. I wondered whether I could make any friends in that church. Could I become part of the activities and enjoy the fellowship as it seemed most other members did? Then, as we stood there, the pastor told us that we each had been given a sponsor. He read the names of the sponsors who stepped out of their seats and came to stand behind us that day. As I saw my sponsor come forward, I felt as if I had been thrown a life preserver. I had someone who would help teach me how to swim in this new pool called First Church.

■ Explanation

A new member sponsor program is a great idea. A sponsor helps newcomers get acquainted with longtime members and find their niche in the church. A sponsor provides information and assistance to new members about activities, special events, committee opportunities, and questions on the workings of the congregation. A sponsor is a sort of midwife who helps the newcomer become an old-timer in the life of the church.

Actually a new member sponsor is not an idea unique to the church. Assimilating newcomers happens all the time in all different places, because assimilation is primarily a sociological matter. For example, here is the job description for mentors of new members in the Lions Club. As you can see, it's not all that different from what a similar role might be in the church.

> As a Lions mentor you should:
> Continue to introduce the new member to Lions they have not met, helping them feel part of the group.
> Offer to accompany them to meetings. Stay in touch.
> Make sure they are allowed to express their thoughts and ideas.
> Serve as a source of inspiration and advice.
> Consider entering into the Lions Mentoring Program, where you and the new member can continue to grow as Lions.
> Encourage the Lion that you sponsored to be active and to live up to the Lions' motto: "We Serve."[3]

■ What You Can Do about It

The best first step for beginning a new member sponsor program is to introduce the idea at a church leadership meeting for discussion. Here's a general template for introducing any new idea in the church. In this case, use it for introducing a new member sponsor program.

1. Explain the situation as it exists today.
2. Describe where the church will be if the present situation continues.
3. Present the possible options, one of which is to do nothing.
4. Propose what you feel is the best option and why.

To create ownership of the new member sponsor program among church leaders, ask for ideas on what the responsibilities of the sponsor would be. As a group, brainstorm a job description (or a ministry description) for a new member sponsor. The group is likely to come up with a good list.

A good sponsor is someone in your church who has a genuine care for people, who knows about the church programs and people associated with the programs, and who is respected in your congregation. Perhaps most important, a good sponsor *wants* to be a sponsor.

Sponsors must be trained. A good ninety-minute session should be adequate to accomplish this. You may want to use the following agenda:

1. Why new member sponsors are important
   a. to the new member
   b. to the sponsor
   c. to the church
2. Specific responsibilities of the sponsor
3. A typical month in the life of a sponsor
4. Testimony from recent new members
5. Role-playing
6. Questions and answers
7. Closing prayer

The pastor (or appropriate staff) should be in touch with the sponsors at least monthly. If there is a concern regarding the new member, the sponsor should be in touch with the pastor as soon as possible. A monthly report would include such things as recent contacts with the new member (what and when) and any noteworthy information and recommendations for follow-up.

#27 THE ASSIMILATED MEMBER RULE

Your church should have a list of characteristics that describe a fully assimilated member.

■ Introduction

Jesus said, "Go and make disciples" (Matt. 28:19). Have you ever wondered exactly what *is* a "disciple"? We're called to make them, but how do we know when we've succeeded? Would you know one if you saw one? And here's another question: Is a *disciple* synonymous with an *assimilated member* in your church?

■ Explanation

We recommend that you and your leaders take some time and list the measurable characteristics of an ideal assimilated member in your church. One reason is that it will help you plan your assimilation strategies so as to instill these qualities into the lives of your new members. Another reason is that it will help you evaluate whether your present ministry activities are actually contributing to the goal of making disciples.

We've been thinking about this for a while and would like to propose a starting list. You may want to add or subtract from it for your church. But you will find the process of developing a list to be a thought-provoking and clarifying activity.

1. *An assimilated member attends the worship service regularly.* For most Christians the Sunday morning service is the focal point of the church calendar. It's hard to imagine a disciple not regularly participating in the sacrament of worship and celebration of God. "Worship the Lord your God" (Luke 4:8 ESV).

2. *An assimilated member is growing spiritually.* Every believer needs to feel a sense of spiritual movement and growth. The Spirit despises "lukewarm" Christians (see Rev. 3:16).

3. *An assimilated member has friends in the church.* Research indicates that assimilated members have an average of seven friends in their new church; dropouts had made only two. "I no longer call you servants. . . . Instead, I have called you friends" (John 15:15).

4. *An assimilated member has affiliated with the church body.* The value of a public commitment, through baptism and church membership, solidifies the identity of the believer with the body of Christ. "There are many parts, but one body" (1 Cor. 12:20).

5. *An assimilated member is praying.* Growing in one's understanding of how, when, why, and where to pray is important for a follower of Christ. "Lord, teach us to pray" (Luke 11:1).

6. *An assimilated member identifies with the goals of the church.* Clear and specific goals in a church allow members (new and old) to rally around a common focus. "I press on toward the goal for the prize of the upward call of God in Christ Jesus" (Phil. 3:14 ESV).

7. *An assimilated member has a ministry role or task.* Service is a key part of the identity of a Christ-follower. Jesus said, "The Son of Man did not come to be served but to serve" (Matt. 20:28 ESV). So should his followers.

8. *An assimilated member is involved in a fellowship group.* The best place to grow spiritually and relationally is in a small group. Jesus led a small group for three years, and they changed the world. "They devoted themselves to the apostles' teaching and to fellowship, to the breaking of bread and to prayer" (Acts 2:42).

9. *An assimilated member tithes regularly.* Assimilated members give back to God what is his to begin with. "The place where your treasure is, is the place you will most want to be, and end up being" (Matt. 6:21 Message).

10. *An assimilated member participates in the Great Commission.* A disciple is spreading the Good News in his or her social network and beyond. "You will be my witnesses" (Acts 1:8).

■ What You Can Do about It

Make your own list of characteristics of an assimilated member. Try it out with your church leaders the next time you're together. Give each one an opportunity to develop his or her own list; then compare notes and review the list above.

Such a list can provide a helpful way to evaluate your church constituency in how well you are doing at making disciples. Create a spreadsheet that lists each of your assimilated member characteristics along the top, one characteristic per column. Next, list all your members and regular church attendees down the left side, one per row. Finally, consider each member or attendee in light of each characteristic. Place an X in the corresponding cell if, to the best of your knowledge, the person exhibits that particular quality or characteristic. An example might look like this:

Member Assessment Chart

Church Member/Attendee	Attends worship	Is growing	Has 7+ friends	Has joined	Is praying	Has same goals	Has role or task
Alexander, Chris	X		X	X			X
Bell, Kevin	X	X					
Herman, James			X			X	X
Herman, Sue	X					X	X

Filling out such a spreadsheet will give your church leadership a snapshot of the people God has put under your spiritual guidance. You can quickly see the status of each person and the overall assimilation level of the body.

If "grading" the assimilation level of people sounds a little presumptuous, you can involve each member in their own self-assessment. These characteristics could also be used as a personal goal-setting matrix to help people consider where they would like to be in the coming year. Perhaps you are uncomfortable giving people an arbitrary list of characteristics. If so, have them develop their specific criteria for a disciple.

Then look at your present church programming. Are you strong at equipping the saints in certain areas but weak in others? Is there a relationship between the predominantly empty columns in the above chart and a lack of training provided in those areas? Identify where programs and training are needed, based on obvious weaknesses in the member assessment chart. Set about addressing these weaknesses in the future.

#28 THE FIRST YEAR RULE

Pay particularly close attention to first-year members.

■ Introduction

Of all the people who drop out of church, *82 percent leave in the first year!* The first twelve months are critical in the life of new members if you hope to see them around beyond that first year.

■ Explanation

It is true that most people who drop out of church do so in the first year. On further study, however, we learned that they do not leave in random fashion. There are two definite "spikes" when an inordinate number of new members stop attending. The simplified pattern looks like this:

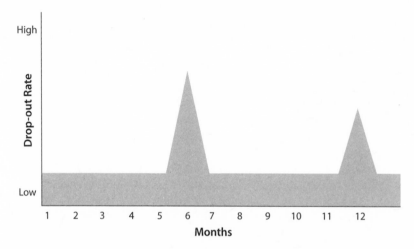

Our curiosity, of course, was aroused. We interviewed thirty-six people who had stopped attending their church after six months, then another thirty-six who had stopped attending after a year. What happened? We asked them to tell us their story.

After conducting the interviews, we replayed the recordings and listened for common themes. We found some! New members, it turns out, are asking questions. Often they are not even consciously aware of their concerns. But in these "postmortems," the issues became readily apparent. During the *first six months* new members are asking:

1. *Can I make friends in this church?* As we already noted, new members who remained active in their church made an average of seven friends in their first year; those who dropped out made less than two.
2. *Is there a place I can fit in?* When newcomers feel that there are a lot of people "like me" and groups where they might fit, they are likely to stay in the

church. Common age, marital status, family status, special needs, interests, concerns all help newcomers feel comfortable in their new surroundings.

3. *Does this church really want me?* After the warm words of welcome, new members need to be regularly invited to participate in the ministries and activities of the church.

If new members conclude that the answer to these questions is no, many of them will leave after five or six months. If the answer is yes, they stay around, at least for a *second six months*. But they're still asking questions:

1. *Are my new friends as good as my old ones?* The issue is now not so much quantity of friends as *quality* of friends. New believers, in particular, feel increasingly uncomfortable with their old behavior, old habits, and old friends. That's good. But they're also unconsciously assessing the value and depth of their new friends in the church.

2. *Does the group meet my needs?* They may have found a young singles' group, a senior adult group, or a Sunday school class of people like them (see question 2 in the first six-months). But seven to twelve months later, they're asking whether the benefit of their involvement is worth their cost in time, inconvenience, and social discomfort in the new setting.

3. *Is my contribution important?* The question is now not so much one of involvement but of *significance*. Am I doing busywork or kingdom work? "I wanted to have an impact on people's lives," one dropout told us, "but all they asked me to do was set up chairs for the church dinner."

Do everything you can to be sure your new members give a resounding yes to these six questions. If they do, you will see them actively involved in your church for years to come.

■ What You Can Do about It

What can you do to help new members make it through the first year? Here are a few suggestions related to these questions; you can no doubt come up with more.

1. Make a list of each new member who has joined your church in the past nine months. Next to each name (list couples individually), note as many things as you know about this person (for example: age, gender, marital status, number and age of children, special interests, particular concerns, hobbies, careers, and other defining characteristics). Then under each new member, list the church members and regular attenders who have several characteristics in common with the person. Keep in mind that the more things people have in common, the more likely they are to become good

friends. Then over the next few months, make a point to introduce your new members to those in the church with whom they have things in common.

2. Identify all the groups and classes in your church in which the new member might feel socially comfortable. Contact the group leader or teacher and provide him or her with the name, contact, and other related information on the newcomer. Ask the leader to initiate a contact and invitation to the new member during the next few weeks. Encourage the leaders you contact to go out of their way to introduce themselves to the new person or family, befriend them, and introduce them to the others in the church.

3. Contact church leaders who oversee the selection, nomination, and appointment of people for ministry positions in the church. Provide them with information on the new members and encourage them to consider these people as they replace those whose terms are coming to an end.

4. Encourage group and class leaders to nurture relationships among participants to a deeper level throughout the year. Discussion of curriculum is important but does not always connect people at a deeper level. Rick Warren gives his list of deeper needs that people desire:[4]

    Support—Everyone wants to know they're not alone.

    Stability—People are looking for a foundation to build their life on.

    Self-Expression—People want an opportunity to express their uniqueness.

    Significance—We all want to know that our life matters.

5. Regularly start new groups and classes so that new members can participate. As we discussed, many groups stop growing after several years since the relationships become so strong that it's hard for a newcomer to break in. (See #29, The Group Diversity Rule, and #32, The New Groups Rule for guidelines on starting new groups and classes.)

6. A pastor, staff person, or lay leader should meet with each new member (or couple) every three months for the first year. The leader's role is more of a listener than a talker. Look for clues related to the six questions new members are asking in their first year. Perhaps start with a few questions like: How are things going? How do you feel about the church? Is the benefit worth the cost? Have you found a class or group you feel comfortable with? Do you have any suggestions for how the church could better serve new members? Do you have anything you'd like help with?

As you monitor the involvement of your new members, stay in touch with them on a regular basis, initiate relationships, and ask important questions, you will see fewer people dropping out in that critical first year. And if they make it past the first twelve months, you will probably see them for the next twelve years.

5

Ministry Rules for Small Groups

In our opinion, small groups provide the best possible means for the church to actually *be* the church. These groups provide opportunity for people to worship God, support others in need, pray and care for others, grow in spiritual depth and character, develop close relationships, and participate in ministry and service.

But small groups can also be one of the most devastating of church activities. They can nurture destructive gossip, create exclusive cliques, breed antagonism toward other members, and cause people to leave the church in large numbers.

Is the benefit worth the risk? We think so. We also think the rules of thumb in this chapter will increase the possibility that your small group ministry will be a *healthy* small group ministry.

#29 — THE GROUP DIVERSITY RULE

The more kinds of groups in the church, the more people will get involved.

■ Introduction

Small groups are something like airplanes—there are many different kinds with many different purposes. Some planes (airliners) are designed to carry hundreds of people thousands of miles. Others (jet fighters) carry just one or two pilots. Some (transports) carry thousands of gallons of fuel, while others (gliders) have none. Some (supersonic) fly thousands of miles per hour, while others (trainers) seldom top one hundred. In the same way, there are different groups for different purposes. Some church groups meet weekly, others monthly. Some meet to discuss the pastor's sermon, while others meet to talk about dog training. One small group may be led by a skilled therapist, while another has no formal leader at all.

Just as one airplane cannot do everything, one small group cannot be everything to everyone. Thus the rule: *The more kinds of groups in the church, the more people will get involved in a group.* And the more people involved in a group, the more people in your church will experience the joy and growth that such involvement can provide.

■ Explanation

People's experience with small groups spans a wide spectrum. Some church members report that they love being in a small group, that they have been in their small group for years and couldn't conceive of a balanced life without their group. Others have no experience in a small group and no inclination to join one. What's a pastor to do?

First, realize that not all small groups are—or should be—the same. Groups must be different, because people are different. Here is a list of five different kinds of groups and some of the characteristics of each:

1. *Covenant Groups*
   - Long-term commitment. Groups meet from six months to two-plus years.
   - Group consent. Members decide on the topic of discussion and the day and time they will meet.
   - Between four and twelve people. This size is best to facilitate sharing and building friendships.
   - Similar ages, marital status, interests, occupations, or other characteristics. The more characteristics members share, the more likely relationships will flourish.

2. *Study Groups*
   - Predetermined topic of study. The common interest in study is what draws the group together, rather than age, gender, or marital status.
   - Short-term commitment. Groups last from six to twelve weeks and may be led by a subject matter expert.
   - Avoids long-term commitment. These groups are easier to join for people who have not been part of a group before. It's emotionally safer to focus on a topic than on relationships.

- Flexible schedule. This appeals to people who can't commit to a long-term group.
- Appeals to those with past negative experiences in a group. It's less threatening to join a group that is short-term.

3. *Evangelistic Groups*
- Builds relationships with unchurched people. This kind of group may be the first time many Christian participants have really connected with non-Christians.
- Topical or investigative study. Subjects cover a range of interests of both Christians and non-Christians (for example, Who Is Jesus? Healing Our Image of God, Successful Parenting, Social Justice, Healthy Family Relationships).
- No time commitment. Each session is independent; people may come and go from week to week. The duration is similar to study groups (six to twelve weeks).
- Neutral location. Meetings work better in homes (neutral territory) than in the church building.

4. *Action Groups*
- Focuses on a benevolent task. Participants share a passion for resolving a community or human need.
- Involves members and nonmembers. A shared cause transcends religious affiliation and builds new relationships.

5. *Support Groups*
- Focuses on a life challenge. Participants confront life's tough challenges, such as divorce, alcoholism, overeating, or substance abuse.
- Provides emotional and spiritual support. Although not intentionally evangelistic, the spiritual dynamic often plants seeds that bear fruit later.
- Leadership varies. A professional counselor may lead the group. Other times a book or study curriculum may be used with various members of the group leading.
- Flexible size. If the gathering is larger than twelve people, smaller discussion groups are helpful following a general session.

Churches may decide to focus on one or several kinds of groups. Some will specialize in support groups, others in small face-to-face covenant groups. Sermon-discussion groups are popular in some congregations. You don't need to provide every kind of group, but the more options you provide, the more bridges you are building into the community where people can plug in and feel comfortable.

■ What You Can Do about It

Leadership training is one of the biggest concerns for a small group ministry. One of the best ways to find leaders is to find the "passionaries" in your church— those people who already have a strong interest in something particular. For example, there are some in your church who have long been involved in small groups and credit much of their spiritual growth to this experience. These are people who will be most interested in helping you start longer-term *covenant* groups. Others in your church will be knowledgeable in a particular topic. It may be related to Scripture, such as prophecy, creation, Pauline Epistles, or faith. Others will be more knowledgeable in a topic that could be addressed from a Christian perspective, such as stress, marriage, child rearing, C. S. Lewis, or Hollywood movies. Usually such people are open to teaching a *study* group related to their particular interest. Still others in your church have a spiritual gift of evangelism or hospitality and would be interested in helping with an *evangelistic* group. And there may be people in your church who are activists for a certain cause. Perhaps it is green living or social justice or children with special needs. Such passion can easily be channeled into an *action* group that brings people together around a shared cause. And those who have overcome an addiction or a relationship or an obsession could be the nucleus of a great *support* group.

But not everyone has the leadership ability, administrative wherewithal, or even the social skills to be a successful small group leader. So if you have an enthusiastic content expert but your intuition tells you a group is not likely to come together under his or her leadership, try the tag-team approach. Look for someone with the spiritual gifts required for a good small group leader (leadership, teaching, shepherding, encouragement, discernment), and introduce him or her to the subject expert. The result can be the best of both worlds—a well-facilitated group with a knowledgeable teacher.

This rule book is not the place to explore a detailed approach to small group leader training. There are dozens of excellent texts, curricula, websites, and conferences to get your leaders (and potential leaders) well trained before the group begins. If you cannot identify a leader for your small group, put the idea on hold until one is forthcoming. Leaders are critical to the success of a group.

#30 THE NUMBER OF GROUPS RULE

Your church should have seven small groups for
every one hundred church constituents.

■ Introduction

A few years ago we were consulting with a growing church in El Paso and conversing with a husband and wife who were members of that church. Jeff was telling us how he had turned down a job promotion that would have required them to move to Nashville. The reason, he said, was that a move would mean they would have to leave their small group. Jeff and his wife had discussed the pros and cons of moving and decided that the relationships they had developed and growth they were experiencing in the group were higher on their list of life values than the money and security of the promotion. Now that's a small group that means something!

Do you have enough small groups in your church to allow for such life-influencing relationships to be experienced by everyone?

■ Explanation

How many small groups is enough? One variable, of course, is the number of people you want to be involved. Larry Osborne, pastor of North Coast Church who puts a high priority on small groups, noted in a recent email to us: "For the 26th year in a row, we far surpassed our goal of 80 percent of our weekend adult attendance in a weekly small group. . . . That means this idea has now scaled successfully from 180 to now over 8,000 in weekend attendance." The best way to know how many groups you should have is to use a ratio that will give you a target number, regardless of how many people are in your church. As we noted above, the ratio for a healthy church is 7:100. That is, for every 100 constituents, a church should have 7 small groups.

You're probably asking, "What do we count as a group?"

Good question. Here are four criteria that we use to define a group. To call a gathering of people a *group*, they should have all four of these criteria. In other words, it's not 1 or 2 or 3 or 4. All four criteria are necessary.

1. *Size of fewer than twenty-five people.* Of course for some readers this will be the approximate size of their church! And most small churches are, in reality, a small group. The purpose of a group will affect the ideal size of the group. Here are three different purposes for groups and the ideal size to accomplish each purpose:

Purpose	Ideal Size
Intimacy/sharing	3–8 people
Study/task achievement	9–15 people
Fellowship/socializing	16–25 people

2. *Strong and close sense of belonging.* In a healthy group people are missed when they're gone and welcomed back when they return. There is genuine

interest among members about the well-being of each person in the group, and time is gladly given when a member is in need.

3. *Minimum of one meeting per month for at least six months.* Effective groups build trusting relationships among members. And trust takes time. A minimum of six meetings is required before members in a group start remembering names, building history, and creating a sense of identity. Of course groups that meet more than once a month develop that community even faster.

4. *Contributes to the emotional, spiritual, and relational needs of participants.* The bottom line for group members is: Do I get more out of this group than I put into it? That may sound selfish, but ultimately it is how everyone makes decisions about their time. Does the benefit outweigh the cost?

Calculating your small group ratio is easy. First, determine the number of groups you have in your church, based on the above four criteria. Realize that they may be formal groups with a name or just regular gatherings of friends. With the above definition, some Sunday school classes are groups; others are not. A choir can be a group if it meets all the criteria, but not all choirs do. The same with a church board. In general, most task-oriented gatherings do not meet all the criteria.

Next, count your total constituency (that is, members, plus attenders who are not members). Pick a cutoff age with which you are comfortable. Some churches use thirteen years old, others fifteen, some eighteen. When calculating your members, include even those who are not regular attenders. While you may not see them often, they are still on your roll and are persons for whom you have some spiritual responsibility.

Finally, divide the number of small groups in your church by the number of your church constituents. For example, if you counted 5 groups in your church and you have 75 constituents, divide 5 by 75, which gives .067 as the result. Then multiply .067 times 100 for your ratio. So .067 x 100 = 6.7:100. This means your ratio is 6.7 groups per 100 people.

■ What You Can Do about It

If you have a ratio of significantly less than 7:100, you may want to begin thinking, talking, praying, and planning for some new groups. In #32, The New Groups Rule, we provide ten helpful questions that will be a guide to starting one or more healthy and growing groups.

Here are some reasons starting new small groups can be a health tonic for your church. With more new groups:

- more people in your church will be involved, because you have more places for them to be involved.

- more entry paths will be available for non-Christians to come to faith, because people are at different places on their spiritual pilgrimage.
- the church will be more in touch with people's needs, because new groups tend to focus on needs (while older groups focus on relationships).
- fewer people will have a *job* (that drains energy) and more will have a *ministry* (that generates energy).
- the pastor will have less need to shepherd people, because more pastoral care will occur in the small groups.
- the spiritual growth and enthusiasm of members will be greater, because spiritual growth fosters enthusiasm.
- the congregation will be better able to endure church transitions or crises, because members of small groups tend to ride out the storms.
- more inactive members will begin to get re-involved in the church, because members of small groups attend worship more often, volunteer more often, and give financially more often.

#31 THE NEWCOMER BONDING RULE

New members will always feel closer to other new members.

■ Introduction

You've probably seen in your present or previous churches the bond that develops between new members who join at the same time, particularly if they have gone through the new members orientation together. It's a bond that transcends age, marital and family status, ethnicity, and gender. Newcomers share a common anxiety about what's ahead, and the security of knowing that someone else shares those same feelings transforms former strangers into friends for life. This natural magnetism can be a great asset in connecting your new people to each other and to the church.

■ Explanation

If you moved to Lynchburg, Virginia, in the last five years, you were invited to join the Lynchburg Area Newcomers Club. "The object of our club is to bring newcomers together into an organized group to promote friendship and aid them in learning about the Lynchburg area."[1] Or you can join the Charlottesville [Virginia] Newcomers Club if "you have been a resident of the greater Charlottesville area for less than 3 years, or experienced a change in life circumstances (e.g.

retirement)."[2] The purpose of this club is to "meet people and make new friends, attend social and recreational activities together, learn about the area, and get involved in the community."

Virginians are not the only hospitable people. In fact, there are newcomers clubs in all major (and hundreds of minor) cities in all fifty states, as well as dozens of countries around the world.[3] The attraction of these clubs is that they draw people who are new to the area and have no connections. The need they fill is for community, camaraderie, and companionship. And many of the newcomers club websites tell about members who have been active in their club since the day they joined—thirty or forty years ago!

We hope you're seeing some implications for the church. New members in your church are new to the area and have no connections. They also have a need for community, camaraderie, and companionship.

It would be nice to think that your church is full of members who will take the initiative to pursue and nurture friendships with newcomers. The reason this is unlikely, however, is that most people in your church:

- already have friends, and don't feel a great desire for more.
- consider themselves quite busy, with little or no time for additional activities.
- believe their church is already friendly and it will be easy for newcomers to get connected.
- are not aware of the important need for new members to make friends quickly in their new church.

As we have seen in #22, The Friendship Factor Rule, the new member who *stays* beyond the first year has made an average of seven new friends in the church. It is our conviction that the responsibility for initiating and nurturing these new friendships among new members rests primarily with the church. In other words, it is *not* the responsibility of the newcomer to take the initiative to make friends.

■ What You Can Do about It

What can you do to create a "relational greenhouse" where strong friendships grow that will keep your new members active and involved for years to come?

- Plan your new members class to build relationships among participants. Don't focus just on content, theology, and curriculum. Spend time deepening relationships and nurturing love (see chapter 7). This means your new members class should last longer than a few weeks. Lyle Schaller suggests: "A good model is provided by some churches that expect each adult new member to be in a new member's class for 30 to 45 weeks."[4]

- Keep the class together after you have completed the new members orientation. If the class meets for three to four months, it is likely that the class has actually transformed into a group, and the new members have developed a genuine sense of belonging. Everyone (with the exception of one or two longtime members who shepherd the class) becomes a "pioneer" in the creation of the new group. Subsequently the new class becomes a part of the ongoing program structure of that congregation.
- Plan special outings that the group can share beyond the one-hour class on Sunday mornings. Go to a ball game, movie, seminar, picnic, parade, or any other activity that the group agrees on.
- The group can go to each other's homes for dinner, to play table games, or to watch the World Series.
- They will want to celebrate special events together (birthdays, anniversaries, weddings).
- The group will also share common sorrows together (loss, grief, transitions).

#32 THE NEW GROUPS RULE

One of every five groups in your church should be less than two years old.

■ Introduction

Imagine a sponge that has been sitting on your kitchen windowsill for weeks and is bone-dry. Turn on the faucet to a slow drip and hold the sponge under the faucet. The sponge begins to absorb the water. Eventually the sponge reaches a point where it can no longer hold any more water. One drop in the top means one drop out the bottom. The sponge is saturated. Here's the insight: Just as sponges have saturation points, every group in your church has a saturation point. It is that point at which the group can no longer hold any more new members. Growth through addition will cease, and only growth through substitution will occur.

Knowing when groups reach their saturation point is important if you expect to see new people become involved in your church groups. You may have enough groups based on the previous 7:100 rule of thumb. But if you don't have enough *new* groups, you won't see many (if any) new people become part of your groups. The secret? *Start new groups!*

■ Explanation

There are many reasons a small group can become saturated. Here are some of the most common. The first two reasons, by the way, are the reasons the great majority of groups stop growing.

1. Length of Time the Group Has Been Together

Our experience is that fully half of all groups stop growing after being together for just one year. And 90 percent of all groups stop growing after two years together, which means most groups in your church that have been together for more than two years will not grow beyond their present size. This is because the people in those groups have been together for so long they have developed real community, traditions, and a genuine Christian love for each other. The group doesn't intentionally exclude newcomers. It's just that the shared history has created a natural bond that is quite strong. If you've ever been part of a group that shares this intimate sense of community, you know it's a rare and wonderful human experience. That's the good news. The bad news is that when newcomers try to get involved, it's *very* difficult. The social barriers are unseen but very real. Unless a newcomer already knows or is related to someone in the group, becoming part of the group is a real challenge.

2. The Purpose of the Group

Different groups have different reasons for existence (see #29, The Group Diversity Rule). Some groups are task-oriented. Their purpose may be to study a book together, view a video series, or learn more about a particular topic. Some adult Sunday school classes fit into this category and become saturated when their size reaches twenty-five to thirty people. (Often larger churches have adult classes that reach one hundred or more, but these gatherings do not meet the criteria for being a group.)

While some groups are task-oriented, others are more relationship-oriented. These groups nurture a sense of community among members who share life's joys, challenges, and sorrows together. Such groups become saturated at eight to twelve people. If new people continue to join these groups beyond their twelve-member saturation point, the group loses its ability to provide intimacy, and the result is either a high dropout rate until the group stabilizes at eight to twelve people, or an evolution of the group into a larger study group without the interpersonal dynamics that were initially intended.

3. The Ability of the Leader

Some group leaders can perceive and guide the dynamics of a group better than others. It's almost a sixth sense. More people will be comfortable in a group with an exceptional leader, and thus the saturation point of some groups will be larger.

4. The Size of the Meeting Room

It is a curious phenomenon, and no one is entirely certain why it's true, but it is. A group becomes saturated when the facility they are meeting in (classroom, sanctuary, living room) starts to reach its physical capacity. At somewhere around 80 to 85 percent of the room capacity, people start feeling increasingly uncomfortable and eventually give up trying to fit in the space. There are exceptions for special events, when room capacity can get to 100 percent or more. But for regular group meetings over a six-month period, the number of participants will level off when the capacity approaches 85 percent.

■ What You Can Do about It

The answer to the saturation condition is easy. As we said above, start more groups; and not just more of one kind but more *different* kinds of groups.

Here are ten questions that will guide you in successfully starting a new group, regardless of what kind it is. If you ask—and answer—these questions, you will be well on your way to starting successful new groups in your church.

1. Who is our target audience?
2. What kind of group would best meet their need(s)?
3. Where will the prospective group members come from?
4. How will this group contribute to the purpose of the church?
5. Who will lead the group?
6. Will training be necessary for the leader?
7. What support will the leader and group need to assure success?
8. How will we publicize the group and invite prospective members?
9. When and where will the group meet?
10. What are the specific goals of the group? How will we know when they are accomplished?

#33 THE PARTICIPATION LEVELS RULE

Churches that emphasize small groups can see 70 to 80 percent of their total constituency involved.

■ Introduction

Most church leaders would agree that the purpose of bringing believers together on a regular basis is to nurture their spiritual maturity. The higher the percentage of church constituents who participate in such activities, the deeper will be the spiritual maturity of the congregation. Churches that emphasize small groups as their primary means of spiritual formation can realistically expect 70 to 80 percent of their total constituency to be involved. There are few, if any, other programs in which such a high percentage of a congregation will be involved.

■ Explanation

It is quite possible for one congregation to be more spiritually mature than another. The church in Berea, for example, was characterized as being "of more noble character than those in Thessalonica, for they received the message with great eagerness and examined the Scriptures every day to see if what Paul said was true" (Acts 17:11).

The purpose of every letter the apostle Paul wrote to the early churches was to encourage spiritual maturity. His letter to the Christians at Colossae typified this priority: "We continually ask God to fill you with the knowledge of his will through all the wisdom and understanding that the Spirit gives, so that you may live a life worthy of the Lord and please him in every way: bearing fruit in every good work, growing in the knowledge of God" (Col. 1:9–10). This same desire and challenge remains for pastors today. How is it best accomplished?

Average attendance in church-sponsored small groups throughout the United States is around ten people. Thus a church of one hundred people with seven small groups (see #30, The Number of Groups Rule) will have approximately 70 percent of its people involved in this process of spiritual development. This is a good number and percentage of people in a church who are striving to be "bearing fruit in every good work, growing in the knowledge of God."

There are reasons why, in some churches, fewer than 70 percent of the constituents will be involved in a small group. Some can't participate because of work or family commitments. Others cannot drive at night. Some don't feel attracted to small groups, preferring larger fellowship gatherings. In churches that stress adult Sunday school classes, attendance in small groups that meet during the week will be less. And churches that don't have enough groups or enough *new* groups (see #32, The New Groups Rule) will see fewer involved.

In most situations, however, a strong small group ministry, which church leaders prioritize in the overall ministry of the church, will see more than 70 percent of the adult congregation participating.

■ What You Can Do about It

Educate your church leaders and members about the benefits of involvement in small groups. Some of the benefits are:

- You can talk more in small groups than in larger gatherings.
- You can discover that others have similar life challenges.
- You can use your spiritual gifts.
- You can be encouraged and grow in your faith.
- You can have help through life transitions.
- You can get positive accountability.
- You can be prayed for.
- You can put into practice what you are learning.
- You can make and grow good friendships.
- And, of course, you can give, as well as receive!

Educating your congregation about the value of small group involvement takes more than just one exposure. Here are some suggestions for building a small group consciousness in your church:

1. *Sermons.* What is endorsed from the pulpit obviously carries more weight than what is not. Give the biblical rationale for small groups, including Proverbs 27:17; Matthew 18:20; Acts 2:42, 46; 5:42; 20:20; Ephesians 4:15–16; 1 Thessalonians 5:11; Hebrews 10:24–25. Encourage everyone to at least try a short-term group to see how it feels.
2. *Information meetings.* Meetings can be scheduled to inform people about the nature and variety of the small groups available.
3. *Personal letters.* Write a personal letter to every person or family in the church informing them of the small group ministry, its purpose, and your passion for their spiritual development.
4. *General communication.* Promote new small groups in church publications, such as your website, newsletter, and bulletin.

Compile a list of people (including nonmembers) who could be personally invited to attend a small group, and identify the group(s) in which they would most likely be comfortable. Such a list will also help you determine how many small groups will be needed and how many will need to be started. As noted earlier, seven small groups for every one hundred people (one small group for every eight to ten people) is a good rule of thumb.

Some churches hold "Sign-up Sundays" to bring attention to their small group opportunities. On these Sundays the worship service and sermon focus on the small group ministry. Testimonies are given. Small group leaders share their expectations. A brochure is distributed with a description of each small group, including purpose, content, meeting length, time, location, and any age, gender, or other characteristics of the group. Sign-up sheets should be available, with a limit of ten people per group.

#34 THE GROUP LIFE CYCLE RULE

Every church group has a life cycle.

■ Introduction

Living things are born, they grow, and they die. Small groups could be considered living, since they are parts of the body of Christ, which is certainly a living organism. But while the life of the greater church is eternal, local congregations—and the small groups within those churches—have life cycles. Groups are born, they grow, and they die.

■ Explanation

Social scientists have conducted a good deal of research on the life cycle of small groups. The consensus is that all groups (religious or otherwise) go through three life stages in their development, analogous to the human being: infancy, adolescence, and adulthood. And, like people, groups eventually die.

- *Infancy.* Individuals are eager and somewhat anxious when a collection of people first comes together. The attitude of participants is positive and expectant. In this first stage dependency on the convener is common. Members begin to take baby steps as they get closer to each other. Growth spurts toward community happen quickly. As the group defines itself through spoken and unspoken rules, expectations, and other behavioral traits, a self-identity begins to form. The group leader, like a good parent, should encourage this growth of relationships by providing facilitative exercises, outings, and other experiences.
- *Adolescence.* This can be a challenging time in the life of a group. Members are moving beyond superficial relationships and becoming more vulnerable. Feelings can get hurt, tears can be shed, and arguments may disrupt the equilibrium of the group. But during this stage, conflict is easily forgotten and reconciliation strengthens relationships. Participants may blame the leader

for lack of progress in the group. Power plays, when a member tries to use his or her influence in the group, are not uncommon. The struggles of the group in this adolescent stage, however, are necessary for the group to move on. In fact, avoidance of the unpleasant aspects of this second stage can lead the group back to the infancy stage rather than on to the adult stage.

- *Adulthood.* With the frustrations of adolescence behind them, the group begins to get their act together and show signs of maturity. Words and actions that would have been inflammatory in the adolescent stage are now absorbed with grace and compassion. Group members are not as concerned with the activities as with the progress of the group. Members become less self-conscious and more others-conscious, and the well-being of fellow members takes on significant importance.

- *Death.* The natural tendency for people who have grown up together is to want to stay together as long as possible. But just as an individual must face the inevitability of life's end, eventually a group must die. It may be because the group has accomplished its purpose or that the time designated for its termination has arrived. It may be simply that the group can no longer contribute constructively to the health of its members or the church. At some point, the group must decide whether it will redefine itself and continue, or simply dissolve. As with any loss, the death of a group is often accompanied by pain and grief. But in death can come the rebirth of new life through a new group and the beginning of a new life cycle.

■ What You Can Do about It

One of the most helpful benefits of this rule is simply awareness—the realization that groups have life cycles with recognizable characteristics and behavior. It is also important to realize that not all groups "grow up." Some never leave the infancy stage, while others get stuck in adolescence. If group leaders are made aware of these stages, they will be better able to recognize the characteristics and guide the group to a productive adulthood.

Examine the groups you presently have from the perspective of the life cycle stages. Which groups seem to be making progress in their growth? Which are stuck in infancy or adolescence? Remember that not all groups move through these stages with equal speed. Sometimes groups move naturally from one stage to the next. Other groups may need help in being made aware of their stage of growth and encouraged to think about what might be involved in facilitating their own maturity.

Another implication of the life cycle of a group is the final stage of death. Are there groups in your church that need to die, that have reached a point where they have completed their useful purpose? There may be some groups that have become detrimental to the health and purpose of the church and whose members need to be released for other ministry. At the same time, don't be too quick to pull the plug on a group that may actually be providing a real sense of meaning, value, love, and caring for participants who might otherwise not experience these important feelings. An axiom about small groups is that it's better to add new groups by addition than by replacement.

6

Ministry Rules
for Christian Education

When Jesus was asked about the greatest commandment, he referenced the passage in Deuteronomy: "Love the LORD your God with all your heart and with all your soul and with all your strength" (6:5). Thousands of years before Jesus was asked the question, God had given the Israelites this command and then added, "These commandments that I give you today are to be on your hearts. Impress them on your children. Talk about them when you sit at home and when you walk along the road, when you lie down and when you get up" (vv. 6–7).

It has been this process by which people through history have preserved God's Word. They have talked about it, taught it to their children, applied it in their own lives and the life of their family. God has given us the same command he did to the ancient children of Israel. And it is such a process that is the heart and soul of Christian education.

This chapter provides rules of thumb that will enhance the life and health of your Christian education ministry among adults and children.

#35 THE CLASS AGE RULE

One of every five adult education classes should
have been started within the last two years.

■ Introduction

A curious thing happens when a new class is begun. It grows! If you want to see your Sunday school enrollment and attendance increase, the most predictable way to do so is to begin new classes. The proven formula behind this rule of thumb is this: new classes = new growth.

■ Explanation

There are two related rules of thumb concerning the number of education classes in your church: (1) merging classes inhibits growth, and (2) creating classes encourages growth. Actually these principles have been shown to be true from children's elementary classes to senior adult classes. As one example, Richard Myers described his research in the article "Sunday School and Church Growth."[1] Using two equally divided groups of pastors, each representing one church, the first group was told, "If a teacher in your children's Sunday school resigns this year, do not replace him or her. Instead, combine that class with another of about the same age to make one larger class. Keep a close watch on the attendance in the new class and record what happens."

The second set of pastors was given different instructions: "In every children's department with two or more classes, add another teacher and another class. Reassign the existing pupils to give all classes an equal enrollment. Monitor the growth patterns of these classes for the coming year."

In a year's time, dramatic changes took place in both groups. In the first group, attendance in every combined class had declined to the size of the original groups, resulting in decreased Sunday school attendance. In the second group, just the opposite happened. By the end of the first year, all the classes that had been divided had grown back to the size of the original class, resulting in increased Sunday school attendance.

Myers notes:

> The experiment provides a certain degree of evidence that the addition of classes may be an important variable to Sunday school growth. Attendance in two classes will likely be larger than the attendance would have been with only one class. Eventual attendance in three classes should be larger than in just two. As the Sunday school provides the opportunity for more persons to be involved in meaningful programs, attendance grows.[2]

In our book *Growth: A New Vision for the Sunday School,* Win Arn and I (Charles) provide eight reasons for establishing new classes:[3]

1. New classes provide a positive answer and response to human need.
2. New classes are often more effective at incorporating people into caring, belonging fellowship.

3. New classes enlarge the appeal to new "kinds" of people.

4. New classes are needed to replace those classes that have stagnated or have reached their saturation level.

5. New classes provide more people with meaningful involvement and service opportunities.

6. New classes discourage clustered, self-serving attitudes and programs.

7. New classes are usually more effective in winning new people to Christ and the church.

8. New classes help the "single cell" church begin the process of cell multiplication and growth.

■ What You Can Do about It

The best intervention to stimulate a healthy increase in attendance, membership, and enrollment in your education classes is to start new classes. Here are some steps for doing so:

1. Identify a "people group" for your next class. This group may be based on age, marital status, family status, special interests, problems, concerns, or any other combination of factors in a person's life.

2. Learn more about the people in this group and the kind of class that would meet their particular need.

3. Find two church members or regular attenders who are willing to help start such a class. The leaders should be similar to the target group or at least able to identify with the group.

4. Select a topic for an initial eight-to-twelve-week class. The topic should be based on research of topics of interest to the people in this group.

5. Search for a curriculum, book, or video series that will guide the study and discussion.

6. Determine the best time and place to meet. It is best to ask people in the target group what they think would be the best time and place to meet.

7. List (by name) prospective attendees of the class. Build this list from friends, neighbors, relatives, and other contacts of people who would have an interest in the topic. Include people both inside and outside the church.

8. Develop a flyer or brochure explaining the class content, purpose, curriculum, when and where the class will be meeting, and any related costs.

9. Extend personal invitations to the first class session. Invite members, attendees, previous visitors, inactive members, and any other contacts that come to your mind.

10. In class focus on studying the topic as well as developing relationships among members.

11. At the conclusion of the eight-to-twelve-week class, present the option of either concluding the class or continuing to meet. If the leader has focused on nurturing relationships in the class, normally the class will want to continue. If so, continue meeting on a longer-term basis.

Who are your prospects for starting a new class? You have three choices:

1. Church members or attenders who are currently enrolled in a class
2. Church members or attenders who are not involved in a class
3. Those who are not active in church or any education classes

Many churches make the mistake of starting a new class by simply taking members from existing classes. While research and experience indicate that this will likely work, it is probably the least desirable way to begin a new class. The best strategy is to identify and invite people from inside and outside your church who are not presently involved in a class. Starting new classes through *addition* is a better strategy than starting them through *division*.

#36 THE ROOM CAPACITY RULE

On average a classroom needs a minimum of twenty-five square feet of space for each student.

■ Introduction

Many church leaders inadvertently apply the "bonsai principle of growth"[4] to their Sunday school and education classes. It says, "To keep the bonsai small, you must keep the pot small." In a similar way, many churches keep their Sunday school enrollment, attendance, and classes small because they keep their facilities small.

■ Explanation

While church leaders are usually aware of the need for adequate seating in the worship services of their church, often less attention is paid to the proper amount of space for educational classes. Yet inadequate space for children, youth, and adult education can be a very significant growth-restricting obstacle. The room capacity rule of thumb will vary with the age of the student. For example, classrooms for smaller children should provide twenty-five square feet per child, while adult meeting places need only about ten square feet per person. However, if you intend to grow in attendance and have enough space for additional people to join, then it is best to plan for more space per class member.

As churches grow, it is important to anticipate the need for extra seating and parking. Appropriate space for children and youth classrooms should also be anticipated. For example, suppose a church averages 200 people on a Sunday morning, with 75 (37.5 percent) being children and youth. If this church grows to 400, with the same adult-child balance, there will be 250 adults and 150 children. It is possible that this church might have enough parking and seating but be stunted by the bonsai phenomenon because it has not provided adequate space for the children and youth. Growth must be kept in balance—as adult attendance increases, additional space must be provided for the children and youth.

■ What You Can Do about It

For a church to experience balanced growth for both adults and children, the following guidelines should be followed to allow for adequate space:

- 80 square feet per child on the playground
- 35 square feet per person in early childhood rooms (babies to five-year-olds)
- 25 square feet per pupil in classrooms for children (grades one through six)
- 20 square feet per student in classrooms for adolescents
- 10–15 square feet per person in classrooms for adults (eighteen years and above)

These numbers seem more realistic when you realize that they include space for chairs, tables, cabinets, pianos, and other furniture in a classroom. To visualize 10 square feet of space (the minimum adult requirement), cut and paste sheets of newspaper together into a 2.5-feet wide by 4-feet long rectangle. Lay it on the floor. Then put a typical classroom chair on one end of the paper and sit in it. Notice how little space is left. Now lay out additional 10-foot-square sheets. It's easy to see why this is the minimum suggested space requirement.

If you find that space is at a premium in your church, but you want to allow room for growth, the best option is to add another Sunday school/education hour. It's common practice for churches to add a second (or third or fourth) worship service when space becomes saturated. The same principle applies for providing adequate space to the Sunday school and education process.

#37 THE TEACHER-STUDENT RULE

The younger the student, the more teachers are needed. A general rule of thumb is one teacher for every ten students.

■ Introduction

Most of us can remember a favorite teacher who made an impact in our lives. It may have been a teacher who helped us understand math, or the one who taught us a foreign language. Maybe it was a Sunday school teacher who helped us take a giant step forward in our relationship with Christ. Teachers are important in our lives and in the lives of our children. From an administrative planning viewpoint, how many teachers do you need for the most effective teaching-learning experience?

■ Explanation

The number of teachers per class is affected by the maturity level of the students. The chart below provides a simple diagram of the relationship. The more mature the students, able to think and act on their own, the fewer teachers are necessary. Conversely, the less mature the student, the more teachers or attendant adults are needed.

The following are good rules of thumb for the number of teachers (adults) needed for each age group:

- One teacher for every two to three babies
- One teacher for every four toddlers
- One teacher for every five pre-K and kindergarten children
- One teacher for every eight elementary school children
- One teacher for every ten junior or senior high youth
- One teacher for every thirty adults

■ What You Can Do about It

The obvious issue this rule of thumb raises is teacher recruitment. Here are a few tips we've picked up in conversing with Christian education leaders on this topic:

- *Recruit one teacher for the regular school year and another teacher for summer.* This provides the school-year teacher with a much needed, and appreciated, break in the summer. Usually it is easier to recruit summer teachers, because it's only a two- or three-month commitment. And the summer teachers become a resource pool from which to recruit school-year teachers. (This is a better approach than what many churches do, which is to simply cancel Sunday school for the summer.)

- *Recruiting two school-year teachers can be easier than recruiting one.* A team-teaching approach halves the responsibility for preparation and presentation and doubles the support and encouragement each teacher receives. In addition, a team-teaching approach makes it much easier to cover a teacher's unexpected illness or need to be out of town.

- *Ask prospective teachers to consider being an assistant for a semester.* This will help eliminate some of the fears of teaching a Sunday school class that might keep potentially good teachers who have never led a class from accepting a position. It also gives the apprentice teacher a chance to learn at a slower pace from an experienced teacher.

- *Ask current teachers whom they might recommend as a future teacher.* Sometimes another teacher can see potential in someone you might never otherwise have considered.

- *Ask someone to lead a six-to-ten-week class on a topic in their particular expertise.* People are much more comfortable teaching about something they already know.

- *Invite prospective teachers to consider being an emergency teacher.* These are people who have a lesson prepared, but no class to teach. With an emergency teacher pool, if you get a call on Saturday night from a teacher who is suddenly ill, you just smile and say, "No problem. Hope you're feeling better by next week," and dip into your pool.

- *Don't ask a potential teacher to make a decision about your invitation on the spot.* Give him or her a chance to think about it, talk about it, pray about it, and then respond. Under pressure the instinctive response is no. When time, and God, have had a chance to work, the answer may be yes.

- *Invite prospective teachers to sit in on your teacher training sessions.* (You do have teacher training sessions, don't you?) This will give them a chance to meet some of the other teachers and get more of a feel for training that is available to them. Often training will reduce fears of the unknown.

- *Express regular appreciation (public and private) to your teachers.* Have an annual teacher appreciation banquet. Honor them in the worship service. Give them free tickets to a special event in town. Let them know, on a regular basis, how valuable they really are to your church and to the kingdom!

#38 THE SUNDAY SCHOOL FOCUS RULE

Effective Sunday schools are outward-focused, not inward-focused.

■ Introduction

What is the goal of your Christian education ministry? If it is similar to the goal of most churches' educational ministry, it may explain why your Sunday school and adult classes are not growing. Purpose is everything. More than fifty years ago, D. Campbell Wykoff emphasized the role that *purpose* has in the church's educational ministry: "All education clearly implies a process toward an end. The end—the goal—gives it direction. Purpose, to a large degree, determines what shall be included in the educational process, what shall be stressed and what shall be played down or omitted."[5] It is important for church leaders to confront the question: What is the purpose of our Christian education ministry? Your answer will, to a great extent, determine the health, growth, and vitality of your Sunday school.

■ Explanation

The exclusive purpose of most declining Sunday schools is ministry to existing Christians and nurture to members of existing churches. While a concern for the spiritual health, the personal growth, and the social fellowship of Christians within existing Sunday schools is necessary, in declining Sunday schools these concerns become the *entire* preoccupation of the classes and curriculum.

What happens when the priority of Christian education focuses exclusively on the nurture of existing Christians? People are urged to participate in the Sunday school because it will help *them.* The church is thought of as a place for fellowship with other believers, a personal and spiritual center where *believers* are nurtured to spiritual maturity.

An example of the curriculum emphasis of an inward-focused Sunday school can be seen in the following actual statement of purpose we found in one (declining) denomination's curriculum: "The _____ Church Curriculum centers in these Christian tasks, which are all part of one's pilgrimage of faith: (1) to grow in relation to God; (2) to develop trustful and responsible relationships with others;

and (3) to become a whole person." There is nothing wrong with these important tasks. They are *parts* of the total emphasis, but for inward-focused Sunday schools, they become the *entire* emphasis.

Unfortunately the belief that Sunday school growth will naturally result from the personal growth and spiritual development of existing members is one of the primary reasons many Sunday schools today are declining. Such self-centered education *does not* motivate people toward involvement in the church's mission of outreach and growth. Education that concerns itself only with the spiritual nourishment of its own members contributes significantly to a "self-service mentality" that effectively seals off the Sunday school from the outside world.

The purpose of most growing Sunday schools, on the other hand, is quite different. Outward-focused Sunday schools exist to obey Christ's Great Commission and to equip people for ministry to the world, not to each other. While concern for spiritual growth and nurture of existing Christians is a part of all curricula and activities, it is seen as a means to an end, not an end in itself.

Christian education is missionary education by definition. It is participation in Christ's invitation to join in God's mission to the world. God's mission—his purpose and plan for the world—is that he desires all people to be saved and come to the knowledge of the truth (1 Tim. 2:4). Outward-focused Sunday schools see evangelism and education as two sides to the same coin, two tasks to achieve one aim.

Noted Christian educator H. W. Byrne observed: "Evangelism is the chief work of the Sunday school. In fact, Christian education cannot be Christian unless it is evangelistic. To fail here is to fail in our primary reason for existence."[6]

In outward-focused Sunday schools, each class and each department gives high priority to seeking, reaching, teaching, and discipling men and women, boys and girls. The focus of the entire organization, events, classes, curriculum, and activities of outward-focused Sunday schools is toward one purpose: *making disciples!* And the result is growth—God gives the increase.

■ What You Can Do about It

There are several ways to determine if your Sunday school program is outward-focused or inward-focused.

- Over the next few weeks, do a casual survey of people in your church. Ask them, "In one or two sentences, what would you say is the purpose of our Christian education ministry?" Mentally classify the responses you hear into inward-focused or outward-focused purposes.
- Review the agenda of several recent Christian education leadership meetings. Put an *I* (for inward-focused) or an *O* (for outward-focused) next to each item. Then evaluate the percentage of time spent on both.

- Review the budget for your Sunday school and/or Christian education ministry. Put the same *I* or *O* next to each line item. Then evaluate the total dollars spent and overall percentage of money spent in both categories.
- Make a list of everyone who spends time during the week related in some way to the Christian education ministry of the church. Include paid and volunteer staff. Next to each person's name, estimate the number of hours he or she contributes each week to each activity and break down the total time into the two categories (inward-focused and outward-focused). Beside each name you will have: I: ___ hours and O: ___ hours. Evaluate the total number of hours spent in both categories.

Once you have finished this internal audit, share the results with your Christian education leaders. Ask whether this distribution of time, talent, and treasure is appropriate for your church and situation. If it is (like most churches) overly weighted toward the inward-focused side, discuss how the priorities could become better balanced in your church.

#39 THE TWO STEP RULE

Your adult education options should include both short-term and long-term classes.

■ Introduction

Here's the good news about adult Sunday school classes—they are a great place to make friends. Here's the bad news—the longer a class has been together, the harder it is for newcomers to make friends. As we discussed in the last chapter, adult groups and classes have a saturation point—after two years they are relationally full. After that it becomes very hard for a newcomer to break into that class. There is a solution, but not many churches know it or use it.

■ Explanation

The solution for dealing with a saturated adult class or a saturated Sunday school is simple—*start new classes*. But how, exactly, does that work? There is a rule of thumb called the two-step approach to starting a new class. But first, the background.

Some churches organize their adult classes on an elective basis. New classes on new topics are begun each quarter, and people select from this list of classes based on their particular interest. This approach has some benefits:

- It provides a variety of interesting topics about which people can learn.
- It is easy for visitors and new members to join because basically everyone is new.
- Different church members teach a short class in their particular area of interest and knowledge.
- It provides a flexible schedule for summer.

Other churches organize their adult classes on a longer-term format, meeting for an indefinite period of time. This approach also has some benefits:

- Class members grow to know and love each other as they share life's ups and downs.
- Members rally around and support fellow class members in times of need.
- Those involved in these classes tend to be regular attenders in worship and bigger financial givers to the church.
- Usually these classes have the same teacher year after year, which provides consistent leadership.

The two-step approach to starting new adult classes integrates the strengths of both the short-term and long-term groups.

■ What You Can Do about It

The two steps of the process are start short, then go long. It refers to the length of time the class meets. Here's how it works.

Start Short

Initially a new class should plan to gather for six to ten weeks. Six weeks is the minimum number of meetings people need just to get to know each other, remember names, develop a sense of community, and begin creating a history together. A *collection* of people starts to become a *group* of people after five or six times together. On the other hand, if you ask people who have not recently been involved in a class to commit to more than ten meetings, they will be less inclined to do so. So don't ask them—yet.

In your first meeting, inform the class that you will be meeting for a certain number of weeks (somewhere between six and ten). Explain that, at the end of that time, the class will discuss whether they want to continue meeting.

In each of the six to ten meetings, spend time nurturing relationships among members and developing a sense of camaraderie. Ice-breaker activities are fun and productive. Sharing prayer requests builds strong bonds together. You will probably not see intimate friendships develop among group members during the first six to ten weeks, but it is likely that people will get to know each other, remember names (use nametags in each class), and develop a sense of comfort and enjoyment in being together. Encourage and facilitate a growing sense of community among members. Perhaps go out to dinner after church or bring in a pizza for the class and family members.

By their third week participants will have begun to develop a sense of familiarity with the people, the place, and the experience. With each subsequent meeting (assuming you continue to nurture and encourage relationships), the sense of community in the class will strengthen. Eventually, after about six weeks, an interesting thing happens. The satisfaction that members gain from the class experience comes more from the new friendships with fellow class members than from the knowledge gained in the actual study. And an amazing thing has occurred—the class has become a group!

Go Long

Now, for the second step. At the next-to-last scheduled meeting, the teacher should ask the class to think about what they would like to do in terms of the future. Tell them that this issue will be discussed at the following (and final) class session. Essentially the options are to keep meeting or stop meeting.

The following week, the teacher should ask class members for feedback on how they liked (or didn't like) the class. Ask for suggestions on how the class could be improved if it is offered again. Finally, ask the class what they would like to do—continue meeting or stop meeting. Encourage discussion on the options. Leave the discussion—and decision—up to the class. Explain that if they were to continue meeting, it would not mean everyone needed to participate. Some might drop out. A few others might join.

If the class decides to keep meeting, here are some ideas that we've included in previous chapters on how to build and nurture a sense of community in the class:

- Go out to eat after church.
- See a movie together.
- Travel to hear a special speaker.
- Attend a church- or community-sponsored event.
- Work on a church- or community-sponsored service project.
- Have parties to celebrate birthdays, new babies, engagements, a returning military loved one, a job promotion, or for most any reason!
- Help someone in need.

As the new class moves beyond a short-term topical focus to a longer-term relational focus, an important benefit will appear. Participants will develop what may be, for many, a new sense of belonging, of caring, and of community in their new group.

Be sure that once you've succeeded in starting a long-term class (the second step), you repeat the two-step process by starting a new class so that new people can also find a place in a group.

#40 THE PARTY RULE

Each class or educational department should hold a social event at least once every twelve weeks.

■ Introduction

We have mentioned that friendship is the most important ingredient in assimilating newcomers into the church. The stronger and more meaningful those relationships become, the more likely it is that newcomers will be active and involved in your church. A great way to encourage and nurture these new relationships is through regular social time outside of the normal Sunday classroom.

■ Explanation

The Party Rule applies to every class in your church, from primary to senior adult. It is at social events that new friendships will be established and casual friendships deepened. These social activities are also a great opportunity to begin friendships with *prospective* class members who may not yet have attended a class or even a church service. Often Sunday school leaders and teachers assume that the primary function of their class is to teach the Bible. While this is certainly a major goal of a Sunday school, our experience is that the primary reason people continue to participate in adult classes is relationships with others.

One study found that the number of friends a person develops in church has a direct relationship to that person's involvement in the church. If a person has few or no close friends in class, the chances are lower that he or she will be active. If the person has more friends in class, the chances are good that he or she will be more involved. A simple rule, but true.

In the overall context of a local church, the children and adult classes are ideal for building new friendships and providing a sense of belonging. Classes that are successful in assimilating newcomers have found ways to actively encourage the development of close friendships among new and older members alike.

■ What You Can Do about It

Each class at the high school level and above should have a social committee of three people. Their task is to schedule a year's worth of just plain fun things to do together. Put creative and fun-loving people on the committee and you'll have everyone looking forward to each month's event. Some of the activities we've heard that classes have organized include:

- broomball
- frisbee golf
- scavenger hunt
- bowling
- board game night
- picnics
- ice cream socials

In addition to just having fun, a great way to build friendships and have an influence in people's lives is through class service activities. There are many people in your community with needs or hurts to which your class can respond. Here are just a few service activities we've seen classes conduct:

- mowing the lawns of widows
- hospital Christmas caroling
- helping at a Special Olympics event
- planning a Memorial Day or Veterans Day program
- decorating for Christmas at a local nursing home
- organizing an Easter egg hunt for needy children
- raking leaves at elderly people's homes

#41 THE TOP FORTY RULE

Adult classes and groups will not exceed forty active participants, and, depending on the purpose, may peak much earlier.

■ Introduction

When people gather in groups, the natural limit of active participation is no more than forty people.[7] In fact, almost all adult groups and classes tend to stabilize at one of three different sizes: five to eight, nine to sixteen, and seventeen to forty. Of course adults do gather in larger public events, such as worship services, concerts, and rallies, yet in most situations that involve personal interaction, people prefer smaller settings where they can maintain relationships.

■ Explanation

Different factors impact the size of a class. Seating arrangements, room size, and teacher skills all affect the total number of participants. Even the use and shape of tables, placement and style of chairs, and home or church facilities affect the maximum class size.

Bible study and prayer groups desiring an intimate atmosphere that encourages discussion usually peak at eight people. This ceiling applies when group members desire heart-to-heart relationships that go deeper than surface discussion. Also work groups, task forces, and committees in Sunday school seem to function best with eight or fewer members.

Classes with nine to sixteen people are classified as a fellowship group. People in this size class remember each other's names and keep mental track of each person's attendance. They develop casual relationships. This size class is excellent for group discussions and individual processing, since everyone can participate.

When a class reaches eighteen to forty in size, it takes on more of a teacher-student environment. While class members can still relate to each other on an individual basis, deeper intimacy and community are difficult to establish and maintain. The class is so large that not everyone can participate and the best style of teaching is usually lecture.

■ What You Can Do about It

Churches will have many different size classes. In fact, it's good to have such a variety. Review the number, kinds, and purposes of your classes. How many adults could you theoretically accommodate, based on the above categories? How many people are actually in those classes? How many more could be accomodated before you reach the size ceiling?

Set a goal for the number of people you would like to see involved in your adult classes. (We recommend 80 percent of your average worship service attendance.) Examine the number of classes you presently have, their purpose, and how many are in each class. Then calculate the number of new classes you will need to start to reach that goal. Keep in mind that the kind of class you desire will dictate the maximum number of students you can accommodate. Also realize that some people will be more comfortable in a lecture-style class, while others will prefer the closer and deeper sharing that comes in a smaller group.

Slightly larger groups (fifteen to twenty-five) tend to assimilate new people more easily, since the strong emotional bonds of the small group are less developed. Newcomers may feel threatened in small, intimate settings but find it more comfortable to engage new friends in a larger group. However, the best kind of group to assimilate visitors and newcomers is a *new* group, where members make history together.

7

Ministry Rules for Love and Caring

Today there is a veritable famine that has left our country starving for love. Mother Teresa once told an American couple, "I have seen the starving. But in your country I have seen an even greater hunger. That is the hunger to be loved. No place in all of my travels have I seen such loneliness as I have seen in the poverty of affluence in America."[1]

Love should be an integral part of every local church. Love is certainly the message of our Christian faith: "God is love," "The greatest of these is love," "Love your neighbor," and "Love your enemy." It is one of eight common denominators of healthy churches.[2] Love is more frequently experienced in growing churches than in plateaued or declining ones.[3]

But can a church become more loving? Can people learn to love better than they are loving now? We believe so. We have seen churches become more loving when they set out to do so. We have seen pastors prioritize this ingredient in the mix of their church and have seen people respond.

Thus we have included in this rule book a chapter on love, though our intent is not to demote the nature or character of love to a set of rules. Here are a few guidelines we would like to suggest to help you create a "love greenhouse" where "the greatest of these" can flourish.

#42 THE LOVE DEFINITION RULE

Love must be defined before it can be taught.

124

▪ Introduction

The command to love is the most frequently given command in Scripture. It defines the essence of Christianity—God's love for us and our love for God as expressed through our love for others. The apostle Paul's great treatise on love in 1 Corinthians 13 describes the characteristics of love (patient, kind, consistent, etc.), but a specific definition of agape love is needed before you can build and lead a loving church.

▪ Explanation

Many people associate the word *love* with feelings and emotions. However, when the word is used in the Bible, the vast majority of verses are in the context of action. For example:

> For God so loved the world, that he *gave* his only Son (John 3:16 ESV).

> But God *demonstrates* his own love for us in this: While we were still sinners, Christ died for us (Rom. 5:8).

> No one has greater love than the one who *gives* his life for his friends (John 15:13 NIrV).

We would like to propose a specific definition of love that may be helpful as you teach and nurture this most important quality among your people: Love is intentionally doing something caring or helpful for another person, in Jesus's name, regardless of the cost or consequence to oneself.

Consider the key words and phrases of this definition:

- *Intentionally*. Love does not happen by accident. Love happens because it is planned and premeditated. "Let love be your greatest aim" (1 Cor. 14:1 TLB).
- *Doing something*. Love is action. If it is not seen or observed or experienced on a regular basis, there is cause to doubt whether it is really love. "Don't just talk about love. Put your love into action. Then it will truly be love" (1 John 3:18 NIrV).
- *Caring*. The word means "a feeling of concern and protection." The ultimate caring for a person is giving one's own life to protect the object of one's love. "This is how we know what love is: Jesus Christ laid down his life for us. And we ought to lay down our lives for our brothers and sisters" (1 John 3:16).
- *Helpful*. The Greek word means "lend strength to." Where a need exists, love responds. Ecclesiastes says that, whereas one person is weak, two are strong (see 4:9–12). Love builds up the other person.

- *For another person.* Love is always focused on a person. Love does not exist in a vacuum. We cannot sit alone in a corner and love. The well-being of the person who is loved motivates action. "Love your neighbor as you love yourself" (Matt. 22:39 NIrV).

- *In Jesus's name.* We are doing an act of love in the spirit of Jesus, with the same motivation that Christ would have had when he did something caring. "As I have loved you, so you must love one another" (John 13:34).

- *Regardless of the cost or consequence to oneself.* True love does not say, "I love you if it doesn't cost anything . . . or if it's convenient . . . or if I don't hurt myself in the process." Can you imagine God putting those conditions on his love for us? "Follow God's example, therefore, as dearly loved children, and walk in the way of love, just as Christ loved us and gave himself up for us as a fragrant offering and sacrifice to God" (Eph. 5:1–2).

■ What You Can Do about It

One of the best ways to get people talking about any topic is to ask questions. Here is a list of ten questions you can ask—a "love quiz." You will see some of the characteristics of love Paul speaks about in 1 Corinthians 13 hidden in these questions. Use them in your next sermon as you begin teaching your congregation about love. (See #43, The Teaching Love Rule.)

1. Do you find it difficult to become interested in the people from your daily life beyond a superficial level?
2. In a disagreement, is it hard for you to understand why other people feel the way they do?
3. Do you get nervous when your reputation is in the hands of someone else?
4. Are you often bothered by fears of being stupid or inadequate?
5. In conversation, do you usually do more talking than the other person?
6. Is it difficult for you to accept criticism from others?
7. Do you ever apologize to someone whose feelings you think you may have hurt?
8. When people do things you consider stupid, do you secretly enjoy seeing them pay for their mistakes?
9. Do you find that you often forget about commitments you make to other people?
10. Do you find yourself feeling supportive or envious when someone in church receives public recognition?

If the answer is yes to many of these questions, it may be an indication that the responder would benefit from a commitment to learn more about love.

 **THE TEACHING LOVE RULE**

A church becomes a more loving church when its members learn how to love.

■ Introduction

Is love taught . . . or is it caught? Can a person become more loving? Can a church become more loving? The answer to both of these questions is yes! We *can* become more loving. In fact, Paul assumes this when, after finishing his great treatise on love in 1 Corinthians 13, he says: "Let love be your highest goal" (1 Cor. 14:1 NLT)! If we can learn to love, then why is it so many people aren't better lovers? Some may have had poor examples. Others have inaccurate assumptions about what love is. Quite a few simply haven't had a teacher or mentor from whom to learn. One of the most important contributions your church can make to members—and nonmembers—is to teach them how to love.

■ Explanation

Jesus taught about love more than any other topic. In his Great Commission, Christ told his followers to make disciples, and then teach these new disciples "to obey everything I have commanded you" (Matt. 28:19–20). That is, teach them to love.

Helping people learn to love—to love with Christ's *agape* love—is quite possible. As you equip your saints for a life of loving, here are eight practical steps they can follow:

Step 1. *Make a love covenant with God.* A love covenant is a statement to God that you want to make loving the priority in your life. A love covenant should have the same faithful intent that God has in his covenant with us: "Though the mountains be shaken, and the hills be removed, yet my unfailing love for you will not be shaken, nor my covenant of peace be removed" (Isa. 54:10).

Step 2. *Identify those who need your love.* There are people in your life whom God wants to love—through you. It's helpful to make a list of these people who are your "love connections." They include: *family* (Exod. 20:12; Eph. 5:28; 1 Tim. 5:8), *friends* (Prov. 18:24; Eccles. 4:9–12; John 15:13–15), *acquaintances* (Mark 12:31; Rom. 13:10), *enemies* (Matt. 5:44; Luke 6:27), and *needy people* (see Deut. 15:7; Pss. 41:1; 82:3; Matt. 19:21; Gal. 2:10).

Step 3. *Act first.* Often we wait for the other person to make the first move. Will he speak first? Will she call first? Will they invite us over? Don't wait for the other person. Always act as if the responsibility for the initiation and growth of a loving relationship depends on you. This is true for strengthening old loving relationships and initiating new ones.

Step 4. *Communicate.* As communication grows, love grows. And the level at which we communicate affects the degree to which we can love: level 1—the exchange of clichés; level 2—the exchange of information; level 3—the exchange of opinions; level 4—the exchange of emotions.

Step 5. *Empathize.* The word means "identification with or vicariously experiencing the thoughts, feelings, or attitudes of another person." In a sense, you become that person. You see through the person's eyes. You experience what he or she is experiencing. You feel the way the person feels. As the old Native American saying goes: "Don't judge a man until you've walked two moons in his moccasins."

Step 6. *Identify a love opportunity.* Everyone has needs. It may be a physical, emotional, relational, or spiritual need. As you spend time with a person, through good communication (step 4) and empathy (step 5), you will discover opportunities for loving actions. Then you can take the next step.

Step 7. *Respond with a caring gift.* A good gift is a unique expression of love. Learning how to give gifts is a giant step toward learning how to love. A good gift is *meaningful*, based on the needs of the person receiving it. A good gift is *sacrificial*, or it's just a convenience. A good gift is *unexpected*, rather than expected because of protocol. A good gift is *motivated by love*, unconditionally with no expectation of something in return.

Step 8. *Share yourself.* Sharing yourself is when love actions become a way of life with your love connections. Sharing yourself is loving another person as yourself (see Mark 12:31). Sharing yourself is taking the first seven steps over and over with the people in your love connections so you actually *become* a loving person. You are Ebenezer Scrooge on Christmas morning! You have discovered that love really is the answer when it is shared through sharing yourself.

■ What You Can Do about It

There are several practical ways to help your congregation think about why and how to be more loving. Here are some suggestions:

- A church-wide study on love will bring great results. Learn about the different kinds of love (*agape, phileo, eros*). Study the steps of love, the obstacles to love, models of love. There are excellent books on the topic for small groups and Sunday school classes.

- Preach a series of sermons on love—what it is, and how we can improve in loving others. First Corinthians 13 provides a wealth of issues to dissect and apply to life.
- Ask members to write their own definition of love and compare their definitions.
- Encourage members to make a list of the people in their "love connections" and keep a diary of the love actions they take and the results of each experience.
- Teach about the four characteristics of a good gift, and encourage members to give such a gift once a month.
- Do a word study on how and where the word *love* is used in Scripture. Discuss whether it is used to describe a feeling or an action.
- Brainstorm with others on how a creative emphasis on love could take place in your church and what steps could be taken to help members learn to love. Go beyond just studying about it.

#44 THE LEARNING TO LISTEN RULE

When people learn how to listen, they are learning how to love.

■ Introduction

Paul Tillich, German philosopher and theologian, once said, "The first duty of love is to listen." No single characteristic of people reveals as much about them as the ability to pay attention to others. Even though we are born with the capacity to hear, the ability to listen must be deliberately cultivated. How odd that this skill so central to loving, to community, and to healthy relationships is so seldom taught in our churches.

■ Explanation

People pay hundreds of dollars an hour to have someone listen to them. Therapists would likely be out of a job if more people knew how to listen and put this skill to use. How do you feel when someone really listens to you? Most likely you feel validated, rather important, perhaps wise, maybe even loved.

There is a particular kind of listening that can be taught to the people in your church that will greatly enhance the communication between them and bless your members' personal lives. It is called "active listening." It is a conscious effort not only to hear the words of the other person but also to understand the complete message being conveyed. Here are a few tips you can share with others on how to be an active listener:

Pay Attention

- Look at the speaker directly but don't stare.
- Avoid thinking of a response before the speaker has finished.
- Mentally block out things that are going on around you, such as distracting noises and people.
- Pay attention to the speaker's body language.
- Avoid side conversations in a group setting.

Show That You Are Listening

- Nod occasionally.
- Smile and use other facial expressions.
- Don't sit or stand with your arms crossed or be physically turned away from the speaker.
- Encourage the speaker to continue with small verbal comments like "yes," and "uh huh."

Provide Feedback

- Paraphrase: "So, you're saying that . . ." is a great way to show that you're listening and to clarify the meaning.
- Question: "What do you mean when you say . . .?" or "Is this what you mean?"
- Summarize: "It was good talking with you about . . ."

Dietrich Bonhoeffer underscores the importance of love in the church:

> The first service one owes to others in the fellowship consists of listening to them. Just as love of God begins in listening to His Word, so the beginning of love for the brethren is learning to listen to them. It is God's love for us that He not only gives us His Word, but lends us His ear. So it is His work that we do for our brother when we learn to listen to him.[4]

■ What You Can Do about It

In this book on congregational health and growth, it may seem unusual to find techniques for listening. But if you believe one of the church's important roles is to teach members how to love, then it's not far-fetched to be teaching them about a key part of loving—listening.

Why not offer a class on active listening? Obviously you will want to approach the topic from a Christian perspective and help class members apply the concepts to their own life. Google "active listening" and you'll get nearly two million hits. Add "Christian" to the search and it's still nearly two hundred thousand. There are many excellent books and resources on the topic. Many people will sign up for an eight-week adult class on how to be a good listener.

A sermon series called "How to Be a Better Lover" would certainly get people's attention. One of the sermons could be on the subject of being an attentive listener. James 1:19 is a good Scripture reference: "Be quick to listen, slow to speak and slow to become angry." The topic easily lends itself to a creative drama presentation. The service could include audience participation in listening. Prepare a quiz. Have a panel discussion. Use the entire service as a creative opportunity to learn together.

You may want to suggest that your small group leaders study a book by a Christian author on listening or communication with their groups. Talk with your youth leader about doing a study on listening with the youth group. What parent wouldn't support that? Why, they'd probably buy the materials for you! Eugene Peterson's *The Message* records the verse in James this way: "Lead with your ears, follow up with your tongue, and let anger straggle along in the rear."

#45   THE BIRTHDAY CELEBRATION RULE

Each member and regular attender should receive a personal birthday card from the pastor and staff.

■ Introduction

There's something about getting a birthday card in the mail that just makes us feel special. Maybe it goes back to our childhood and the cards from Grandma each year with a dollar bill inside. Or probably it's just that warm feeling when we realize that someone thought enough about us to buy and send a card on our special day. (And if they planned ahead so the card actually arrives in the mail on our birthday, that's *really* special!) Are you telling the members in your church that *they* are really special?

■ Explanation

What an opportunity most churches miss by not having a system to send birthday cards from the pastor to each person in the church family (especially the kids)!

Dennis Wiggs, who retired after many years in the ministry, says, "I discovered that a birthday card goes far beyond recognizing a church member's birthday. It expresses a deep appreciation for that person."[5] Sure, in a larger church that's a lot of people. But guess what? For each person in your church, that one day is one of the most important days of the year. Why not affirm your people on their big day?

■ What You Can Do about It

Here are a few tips on how to take this simple idea and make it your great idea:

- For several weeks, include a bulletin insert to collect the name, mailing address, and birthday of every church attender and child. (Don't forget members who may not have been present on those weeks.) The information need not include the year of birth, since some people are sensitive about their age, and it's really not important, anyway. Do this annually to update the list of people who are coming and going, and add newcomers as they become regulars. Then enter each person's name and data in a spreadsheet that can be sorted by day of the month.

- In addition to your members and regular attenders, try to gather information on your "regular visitors" and others who have a casual relationship with the church (VBS kids and parents, newlyweds whom you married, nonmembers in church groups or clubs who don't yet attend the service, and the like).

- Have an assistant or volunteer handwrite the person's name and address and use a first-class stamp (rather than a computer-generated label with machine-generated postage). Resist the temptation to use email.

- Buy eight or ten different kinds of cards so that family members don't all receive the same one. You may want to note which card was sent to which family member.

- Don't discuss the practice from the pulpit once you have the addresses and birth dates. Make it a silent ministry.

When you get a birthday card in the mail, you know it's from someone who cares about you. (Unless it's from your insurance agent.) So why not celebrate the special day of all the special people in your church? A personally signed card will do wonders for their commitment to the church. And it's a great way to say, "We love you."

#46   THE SHORT-TERM MISSION RULE

Approximately 75 percent of your congregation should participate in a short-term mission trip in the next five years.

■ Introduction

This Short-Term Mission Rule could easily be in the evangelism chapter, since it will have a big influence on those who share the gospel and hopefully on those who hear it. Or it could be in the assimilation chapter, since going on a short-term mission trip is a great way to bond newcomers and longtime church members together. It could be in the chapters on education or lay ministry or revitalization or small groups. Short-term mission trips have many positive benefits in many areas of a church. But we put it in the love chapter because that should be our primary motivation for going on a mission trip—to let people know we are Christians by our love.

■ Explanation

A megachurch in Pasadena is so dedicated to missions that their goal is for 75 percent of their members to go on a short-term mission trip in the next five years. Some of these opportunities will be close to Pasadena; some will be on the other side of the world. Whether a person is eleven or ninety-one, the church has provided a way for them to be missionaries. We like that idea. And if three thousand people in one church can do it, your church (which may be somewhat smaller) could do it too.

Approximately 1.6 million North Americans participate each year in various types of short-term missions. Of that number, about one-third go on domestic trips, one-third go to Mexico, and one-third go overseas.[6]

Short-term volunteer missions can range from a weekend jaunt across a nearby border to an extended three-week trip; from college students going on spring break to couples spending two years or more as "tent makers." Short-term missionaries cross cultural and geographic boundaries to use their skills in constructing buildings, teaching English, installing computers, helping in orphanages, fitting eyeglasses, tutoring missionary children, helping with disaster relief, training leaders, and responding to medical needs. In the vast majority of these endeavors, the motivation of participants is love for God and love for God's people.

There are excellent books, websites, organizations, and experts available to help in organizing short-term missions. Missiologists highlight the benefits of such short-term missions in three areas: the effect on the field, the effect on participants, and the effect on the sending church.[7] Here is a brief summary of these three effects from the perspective of helping people to love:

1. *Effect on the field.* Some of the most significant benefits to short-term missionaries going to a different culture are the relationships generated during the experience. Pastors in the receiving countries, whose churches have hosted short-term volunteers, frequently talk about how the presence

of a volunteer or a group from abroad gave them concrete evidence that they belonged to a global community of faith.

2. *Effect on the participants.* The effect that short-term mission trips commonly have on participants confirms what the Bible says about the value of giving of oneself in service to others. During short-term mission trips, people experience firsthand the scriptural principle that it is more blessed to give than to receive. Frequently on such trips, those who go to minister find that they are equally ministered to by local believers.

3. *Effect on the sending church.* A fair amount of money goes out of the sending church to transport, feed, and house short-term mission participants. The home church begins receiving dividends from that investment when the spiritual fervor of returning participants often ignites new passion in the sending church. Excitement is generated as volunteers come home with stories to tell and retell. Such an experience can shift a congregation's focus away from a maintenance mind-set toward an understanding of their global covenant to share the message of God's love to "the uttermost part of the earth" (Acts 1:8 KJV).

■ What You Can Do about It

There are many resources you can use to get your short-term mission program underway. Google "short-term missions" for a wealth of information and make a list of books, information packets, websites, and sending organizations for further investigation. Contact your denominational foreign mission office to learn more about available short-term trips. For those who cannot be away for a couple of weeks, identify mission opportunities within driving distance of your church.

You will want to discuss with your leadership whether a goal of 75 percent of your congregation participating in a short-term mission trip in the next five years is a desirable goal. If so, appoint a task force to begin organizing the trips and encouraging participation.

One of the goals of this mission task force should be to build a "mission consciousness" within the congregation by encouraging them to read books, study a course, watch videos, and hear from people who have been on short-term trips. Such a missions emphasis can easily move your members' attention away from themselves and onto others less fortunate than they. And that's what love is really all about.

8

Ministry Rules
for Volunteer Involvement

Several years ago we surveyed pastors and asked them to identify the most frustrating part of their job. Can you guess the most frequent response? *Getting laypeople to help with the work and ministry of the church.*

You've heard it before—the hems and haws from church members when asked to volunteer for this task or that job. *REV!* magazine found that our old assumption about 20 percent of the members doing 80 percent of the work is optimistic.[1] It's even fewer!

Here are a few rules of thumb that may be helpful if you share this same frustration with many other pastors in the church today.

#47 THE ONE YEAR RULE

No one should be asked to take a church
responsibility for longer than one year.

■ Introduction

Why is it that so many laypeople dread church work? One reason is that little effort is given to finding the right place for the right person. The qualification to hold many volunteer positions in the church today seems to be the invitee's ability to say, "Well, I guess so." Once the "volunteers" have agreed to take on the responsibility, there is little training, accountability, or evaluation for how they are doing. And many members know that accepting a responsibility in church can easily become a life sentence! It doesn't take too many such experiences for members to become gun-shy.

■ Explanation

What is your approach to inviting people to serve in a ministry role or task in your church? One insight is that the length of time people are asked to serve affects the response they give. The general rule is, the longer the commitment, the fewer people will say yes. In fact, if there is no end date to the duty and the church member is smart enough to know that, it can be next to impossible to find anyone willing to say yes.

So this rule of thumb says, don't ask prospective volunteers to commit to any more than one year for any one position. Applying this rule will:

- increase the number of those who say yes
- decrease the dropout rate of volunteers throughout the year
- increase the percentage of your members and attendees who have a meaningful role or task
- improve the morale of those involved

Each ministry position, from the lowest level of influence to the highest, should be a one-year term. In the minds of your members, one year goes by a lot faster than ten! If they can try a new activity and have the freedom to leave without guilt at the end of the year, many more will be willing to try it.

This doesn't mean that all volunteers must give up their position after one year. In fact if they enjoy the task, if others affirm their skills and gifts in this area, and if they want to continue for another year, by all means let them! Those who are filling ministry positions and who enjoy them should get "first dibs" on that position the following year. But if there are some who find they just don't have the time, desire, skills, or gifts for the task, this policy gives them an easy way out.

■ What You Can Do about It

Review all the roles and tasks in your church—volunteer, elected, appointed. If you have any position (for example, board or committee member, deacon or elder, Sunday school teacher, choir member) that does not have a specific duration, make it one year. If you have any position that presently lasts longer than one year, change it to one year.

We like the idea of some churches that create a written job description (or, better, a ministry description). The document begins with the importance of the position to the overall purpose of the church. It includes an organizational chart showing how the position relates to those above and below on the chain of supervision. A specific description of activities and time requirements is given. The name and contact information of their supervisor is included. Questions and answers that might be pertinent are provided. Finally, a letter from the pastor affirming the important role of each member as a contributing part of a healthy body of Christ concludes the document.

This ministry description booklet can also be given to prospective volunteers as a way to provide expectations and responsibilities of the position. When people can take a copy of this document home to read, think about, and pray over, you will greatly reduce the number of surprises once they take on the task.

#48 THE CLASSES OF LEADERS RULE

At least 20 percent, and ideally 30 percent, of all those who have ministry responsibilities in the church should be serving as Class II leaders.

■ Introduction

Class II leaders? I don't even know what Class I leaders are! you may be thinking. Behind these terms are important insights that can turn a declining and lethargic church around into an outward-focused, growing church.

> *Class I leaders:* Members whose time and energy focus primarily inward on ministry to existing church members, activities, and structures. Choir members, ushers, Sunday school teachers, and board members are generally Class I leaders.

> *Class II leaders:* Members whose time and energy focus primarily on ministry to non-Christians in the church's community. People who follow up with church visitors, lead vacation Bible school, or do community service are examples of Class II leaders.

Here's the key insight: Significant outreach and church growth occurs as a church recruits, trains, and utilizes Class II leaders who are serving in Class II ministries.

■ Explanation

But here's the catch. Most churches have a severe shortage of Class II opportunities available. Our experience is that the ratio of Class I positions to Class II positions in most churches is around 15:1. That is, at least fifteen roles exist for maintenance to the existing church for every one activity that focuses on nonmembers. Another way of saying it is that approximately 95 percent of ministry positions in churches are Class I—inward-focused.

So what is a healthy balance between Class I and Class II positions? After all, there are many activities required to maintain the existing church. We have found that a ratio of around 3:1 provides a reasonable balance. A church should have three "institutional maintenance" positions for every one "community mission" position. Or, approximately a third of all volunteer positions are Class II—outward-focused—activities.

Obviously this points to the need to create new Class II ministry positions. Later in this chapter we share the rule of thumb that a church should have sixty ministry positions for every one hundred church constituents (members and attendees). Based on this rule, you may need to create more roles and tasks for your people, and many of them should be Class II positions.

Developing Class II leaders can begin in your new members class. As you help new members, new believers, and new attendees identify their spiritual gifts, guide them in exploring how those gifts can be used in Class II activities. New people should learn that all Christians are witnesses (1 Pet. 3:15), and our gifts are given for the building up of the body (Eph. 4:12).

In a healthy, growing church, Class II leaders are the hands and feet of Jesus in their community. Recruiting, training, and deploying Class II leaders should be an ongoing priority for a church, and these leaders should be recognized and affirmed for their ministries. Multiplication of Class II positions and personnel is the secret to more effective outreach and growth of the local church.

■ What You Can Do about It

Make a list of all the ministry roles and tasks that presently exist in your church—elected, appointed, or volunteer. A "role" is a responsibility that lasts for at least a year (such as Sunday school teacher, choir member, usher, committee member). A "task" is a shorter-term function that may take a few weeks or months (such as VBS teacher, summer mission trip, fund-raising task force). Once you have listed all the responsibilities, identify which are Class I functions (inward-focused) and which are Class II (outward-focused). Add the number in both categories, then divide the number of Class I functions by the total. This will give you the percentage of Class I positions (and, through subtraction, Class II) in your church. If your church is like most, somewhere around 95 percent of your roles and tasks will be inward-focused. Bring this up at your next leadership meeting and encourage discussion about the implications.

Examine the curriculum for your new members class. In particular, look at how newcomers are introduced to the idea of ministry in your church and how they are expected to find a meaningful place of service. Are most of the positions that are available to new members Class I tasks? If most are inward-focused, realize that you are creating an institutional maintenance mentality among your new members. And that's not good. Do some brainstorming with other leaders about how you could add meaningful Class II opportunities for these newcomers. New members, and particularly new believers, are very eager to help in activities that will extend the message of Christ into the community. Do all you can to give them this opportunity.

As you review the various ministry opportunities in your church, it is a good time to ask whether all the existing positions in your church really need to exist. Honestly evaluate each position in terms of its useful function and contribution to your overall purpose.

To add more Class II activities to your church, ask those in your present Class I activities to brainstorm ways that their Class I role might be broadened to include a Class II function. For example, a church in Knoxville, Tennessee, was determined to become more outward-focused. The ushers (along with other groups) were challenged to think of ways their usher position might become more outward-focused. One of their ideas was to escort visitors at the service to a seat next to a member in the sanctuary and then introduce the member and visitor with the idea of encouraging a conversation between the two. It was a small effort, perhaps, but one that could go a long way toward making a good first impression on church visitors.

Another way to add more Class II activities is to encourage the creation of new "side-door" ministries. As we saw in chapter 1, a side-door ministry is a church-sponsored class, group, club, or activity that is intentionally designed to include nonmembers, with an ideal ratio of 50:50 (members to nonmembers). Successful side-door ministries bring people together who share a common interest or concern, anything from raising a child with special needs to coping with prostate cancer. Some churches have side doors for people who are unemployed or looking to change jobs. The possibilities are endless. But in side-door groups where participants share important things in common, friendships sprout quickly. And often those friendships with non-Christians become the bridges of God over which many walk into new life and fellowship in the church.

#49   THE TWO FOR ONE RULE

When looking for a person to fill a position,
look for two rather than one.

▣ Introduction

As we mentioned earlier, one of the most common frustrations of pastors and church leaders is finding people to fill ministry positions in the church. For many it's like pulling teeth to identify volunteers who are not only willing but capable of serving, and it's not unusual for bulletin notices, pulpit announcements, even personal invitations to come up dry. This rule of thumb, therefore, seems counterintuitive but actually works: ask two people to fill each ministry position in your church when the job calls for only one.

▣ Explanation

Here are some of the reasons people shy away from volunteering for church responsibilities. They feel:

- unqualified for the task
- uncertain about the requirements
- unsure about taking on the responsibility
- isolated and alone with their task
- unwilling to give up their discretionary time
- unable to identify with the mission

Obviously one simple rule of thumb won't solve every problem concerning volunteers, but this rule deals with several of these obstacles. When you are looking for a person to fill a role (Sunday school teacher, choir member, usher, committee chairperson, and so on), recruit *two people* to serve together who can share the responsibilities. For example, two people could teach the same Sunday school class—one could take the class for September, the other for October. Or they could alternate each week. Or they could team-teach each week.

How about ushers? A medium-sized church in California actually recruits thirty-six people as Sunday morning ushers, when most churches would recruit only six. Here's how it works. The sanctuary has three aisles that divide the pews into four sections (far left, left center, right center, far right). There are two ushers per aisle, or six per service. The church has two services. But rather than ask six people to usher both services for all fifty-two weeks of the year, they have six teams of six. Team 1 (of six people) ushers in the first service for the first month. Team 2 ushers in the second service for the first month. Then Team 3 ushers in the first service for the second month, and Team 4 ushers in the second service for the second month. Then team 5 is responsible for the first service in the third month, and Team 6 handles the second service during the third month. After a full three-month cycle, Team 1 is back on duty for the first service. This is a great way to involve more people as ushers, demand less time of each usher, and have a pool of qualified people to substitute if a scheduled usher is out of town or gets sick the night before.

How about the chairperson of your Christian education committee? Some folks are willing to serve on a committee, but being chairperson may be a little too daunting. It's much less intimidating to divide up the responsibilities. The cochairs can share duties or specialize. One can stand in if the other is out of town. As each supports the other, their creative power is doubled.

With the prospect of sharing responsibilities, along with a one-year commitment (see #47, The One Year Rule in this chapter), you'll find it much easier to identify willing and able volunteers in your church . . . especially for those new Class II positions you'll be creating. (See #48, The Classes of Leaders Rule.)

■ What You Can Do about It

Refer to your list of ministry positions from the exercise in the previous Classes of Leaders Rule. Work with several other people and put a checkmark beside each position that could possibly be handled by two (or even three) people. When you have finished, consider your significant accomplishment of dramatically increasing the number of ministry opportunities available in your church!

Before you dive entirely into this new policy change, identify several positions with which you can experiment. Sit down with the person who is now responsible for this task and brainstorm how the position would work with two people sharing the duties. Create or revise the ministry job description with the idea of two people sharing the responsibilities. However, don't assign specific tasks to one or the other person; let them work that out themselves. Then the next time this position becomes vacant, try recruiting two people and see what happens. Even if the person who is now in that position wants to continue, have him or her look for one more person to share the tasks. Then monitor what happens, get feedback from the involved persons, and learn from experience. It could give you all kinds of opportunities for new ministry.

#50 THE MINISTRY MATCHING RULE

Different people do different things well.

■ Introduction

It's quite possible for two identical churches to have identical ministry structures, identical ministry positions, and the identical number of men and women involved, but one church is moving forward, while the other is going in circles. The difference is that one church has the right people in the right positions—or in the case of the second church, the wrong people in the wrong positions. So how do you do it right?

■ Explanation

Different people in your church have different skills and different strengths. One secret for effective ministry is to put people in positions that complement their strengths. Applying this idea is not as complicated as it might seem, since people generally fall into only one of three categories. Some people in your church are inclined and gifted as visionaries, some as administrators, and some as workers.

1. *Visionaries.* These people have bold, creative dreams of new advances for God and his kingdom through your church. Visionary people share God's dreams and challenge God's people to launch out in faith and decisive action. They are stimulated by thinking and talking about big ideas for the church and are usually dissatisfied with the status quo.

2. *Administrators.* These people think organizationally and bring a necessary plan to the vision in order to see it accomplished. Administrators have strengths in identifying alternative solutions, decision making, developing short- and long-range goals, organizing strategy, setting time lines, allocating subtasks, and monitoring and evaluating progress. Administrators provide the critical link between the impossible dream and the step-by-step process of moving the mountain.

3. *Workers.* These people are those in the body who are granted the gifts and skills needed to get the job done. They work best when given training and assignments with sufficient authority to perform the task. Usually workers are eager to invest their talent, time, and treasure sacrificially in a particular ministry, with little expectation, or desire, to move out of this role.

Here's an important insight: Each ministry position in your church requires one of these three kinds of people for the function to contribute effectively to the mission of your church. When a visionary is placed in a position that requires a visionary, it's a match made in heaven. But when a worker is placed in a visionary position, the result is frustration and inefficiency. The same can be said for any of the three categories. A worker in a worker ministry position is great. But a visionary in a worker position is awful. An administrator who is placed in either a visionary or a worker position will probably quit before the end of the year. An administrator in an administrator position will probably volunteer for another year.

People in one category do not tend to be comfortable in the other two categories. It is a mistake to "reward" active, dependable workers by moving them into administrator positions. It is also a mistake to "reward" productive administrators by moving them to visionary positions.

As you reflect on and talk about this rule in your church, be sure you do not attach a hierarchy of value to these categories. Until all of these three groups work together, little progress will be made. All three functions are equally critical to the success of a church's ministry endeavors.

What You Can Do about It

If you would like to apply this rule in your church, share it with the people who are involved in the nominating process. Include it in your leadership training so that all those who will be recruiting volunteers learn about it. Encourage leaders to keep this rule in mind as they go about enlisting workers in the coming year. Then follow these steps for incorporating the rule:

- Take the list of your church's ministry positions from the exercise in #48, The Classes of Leaders Rule, and identify the kind of position each one is. Is it a visionary position, an administrator position, or a worker position?
- Next, review the people who are presently functioning in these positions and mentally categorize them as visionaries, administrators, or workers.
- Evaluate whether you feel there is a match or mismatch in these positions and reflect on whether this match or mismatch has had any bearing on the effectiveness of the ministry over the past year.

#51 THE MINISTRY POSITIONS RULE

For every one hundred constituents (members and regular attendees), you should have sixty ministry positions available.

Introduction

It's an oft-quoted wives' tale (and usually true from our experience): 10 to 20 percent of the people in a church do 80 to 90 percent of the work. But it is not necessary that this be the case for most churches—a much higher percentage of your constituents can be involved in meaningful ministry. The solution to this imbalance, however, is not intuitive. To see greater involvement of more people, *don't* begin with the people. Begin with the positions where people can serve.

■ Explanation

If you have a high "unemployment rate" among your church members and regular attendees, here are some interesting findings of several studies. Almost fifteen hundred churches of different sizes, denominations, and lay involvement levels were compared. A fascinating correlation was observed. In the very small congregations, where few opportunities existed for people to be involved, membership involvement was predictably low. But the percentage of involved members rose rapidly with congregational growth up to around two hundred. At that point, however, the percentage of involved members began to drop, even as church size continued to increase. We might conclude that the ideal size for member involvement is two hundred people. This study, however, did not answer two important questions: Why was there a lower involvement level in larger congregations? What about the exceptions where larger congregations had high percentages of persons involved, while other "ideal size" churches of two hundred had a very low involvement level?[2]

Leaders of growing, plateaued, and declining churches were asked to list all the ministry positions available in their congregation along with the number of members in their church. When the data was correlated, it turned out that the *ratio* of available roles-to-members affected the percentage of members involved. The churches with low involvement levels had not increased their task and role opportunities fast enough to keep pace with their expanding membership. The involvement level was low because there simply were not enough positions to go around. This study identified the following roles-to-member ratios:

- *Growing* churches—55:100 (That is, there were 55 roles or ministry positions available for every 100 constituents in the church.)
- *Plateaued* churches—43:100
- *Declining* churches—27:100

In other words, the fewer places of service there were in relation to the number of members, the less likely the church was to be growing.

The phenomenon plays itself out in many congregations. A church finds a "sweet spot" in the balance between things to do and people to do them. There are plenty of opportunities, and everyone is involved. But then, as the outreach initiatives start to bear fruit, and as members bring friends, the church begins to grow. Unbeknown to church leaders, the number of people with nothing to do also begins to grow. Left unchecked, more and more people become "spectators," while the overall percentage of "players" declines. The result is predictable—attendance plateaus, even while membership continues to grow. The increasing number of "inactives" creates associated problems: decline in giving, drop in morale, inconsistent attendance, difficulty recruiting volunteers. And the institutional phase of the church's life cycle (see #52, The Philosophy of Lay Ministry Rule) has officially begun.

Consider your church. Do you have enough places for people to fit? Are you creating new positions at a rate at least commensurate to the number of people who begin attending?

■ What You Can Do about It

Research your church's role-to-member ratio. Then compare it to the reference numbers of growing, plateaued, and declining churches above. Here's how:

- First, count all the positions in your church (elected, appointed, and volunteer) that require a person to fill them at least four months of the year. In counting ministry positions where multiple people have one title (Sunday school teacher, choir member, small group leader, and so on), count the actual number of positions available.
- Next, determine your church's total constituency. This includes existing members (active as well as inactive) plus regular attenders who are not members.
- Then, calculate your role-to-member ratio by dividing the number of positions by the number of your constituents, and then multiplying by 100. If you need a math refresher course, here's an example:

  Total church membership: 246

  Nonmember attendees: 134

  Total constituents: 380

  Total number of church roles or positions: 147

  Church's role-to-membership ratio: 39:100

  $(147 \div 380) = 0.38684$ (x 100) = 38.684
- Now that you've done the math, discuss what you found with your church leaders. Are there enough places for people to be involved in ministry? Or are you encouraging your new members to find a place of service in the church when there aren't any available positions, at least not enough?

Suppose you find that you need to create new ministry positions in order to create an environment more conducive to ministry and growth. How do you create new ministry opportunities? The answer is easy: *Find the passion.*

What are the "hot buttons" for your members and attendees? What do they care about, worry about, wish for? The best way to begin new ministries is to start with what your people really care about—individual needs rather than institutional needs. (You'll learn more about this in the following rule.) Begin building a new ministry mind-set in your church. Let people know that if they have a desire to focus on certain people with certain needs, or to begin a new ministry around a particular passion or interest, the church will help them do so.

Here are some examples of churches that are nurturing a new ministry mind-set in their people (taken from their websites):

> Ministries begin at Westwood Church through the initiative of Westwood attend-ees and/or staff. If you have the passion to begin a new ministry at Westwood, the process is outlined below . . .

> Do you feel like God has placed a desire in you to start a new ministry at Southwest Community Church? We would love to help you build an action plan for your new ministry by completing the following steps . . .

As you continue to see new people come into your church, be sure to periodi-cally check your role-to-member ratio. Most churches need to increase their total number of ministry positions. If you are one of them, doing so will mean more people becoming involved in ministry and service for Christ and your church. And that's a good step in the right direction!

#52   THE PHILOSOPHY OF LAY MINISTRY RULE

Operate from an individual rather than an institutional philosophy of lay ministry.

■ Introduction

Churches will typically recruit people for service using one of two approaches. While a choice may never have been intentional, every church is clearly in one camp or the other: the institutional approach or the individual approach.

■ Explanation

An *institutional* approach to ministry begins with the needs of the church institu-tion. Every church needs Sunday school teachers, committee members, musicians. There are certain personnel requirements that a church faces if it is to conduct effective ministry. In the institutional approach, when a position opens up in the church, the response is to search for a person who seems most suitable to fill the job and who is likely to accept. Hopefully the person is qualified, gifted, and mo-tivated for that area of ministry, but there are no guarantees. If it turns out that the member is mismatched to the task, the predictable result is that the task is poorly done and the member is frustrated. "Plugging warm bodies into ministry slots in a congregation," says Pam Heaton, "tends to increase volunteer burnout, dissatisfaction, and departure."[3] In the institutional approach to lay ministry, church members exist to serve the needs of the institution.

The *individual* approach is far less widely practiced but tends to be much more effective in member mobilization and higher morale. Here the priority is not so much to fill a vacancy but to identify a place where members (and even nonmembers) can find fulfillment and growth doing what complements their interests and abilities. Rather than beginning with the needs of the institution, the individual approach begins with the strengths of the person. Church members are encouraged to try a position related to their interests and see how it fits. If it does, the member may choose to spend more time in that ministry, and/or receive training to better equip him or her. If the fit is not comfortable, or the person does not feel a sense of calling, he or she is encouraged to explore other ministries that might be more enjoyable. If a natural match cannot be found with any existing roles, the person is encouraged to think about creating a new ministry. In the individual approach to lay ministry, the institution exists to serve the people rather than the people existing to serve the institution.

Consider this matrix that describes the common results of these two approaches:

Ministry Measure	Institutional Approach	Individual Approach
Percent of the church community involved in ministry	Less than 20 percent	More than 20 percent
Individual's satisfaction with ministry task	Often frustrated	Usually fulfilled
Personal energy level as a result of the task	Drained	Rejuvenated
Reason for participating	Doing what I must	Doing what I like
Effect on interpersonal church relationships	Friction	Fusion
Number of people declining to serve	Many	Few
Resignations from the task throughout the year	Frequent	Infrequent
Church leaders' motivation for filling the role	Institutional need	Individual growth
Frequency of new ministries created	Seldom	Often

A church's philosophy of lay ministry, like many things in life, is not always simple to determine. Rather than being an either-or situation, it more likely falls somewhere on the following continuum:

Philosophy of Lay Ministry

Institutional   Individual

To create a culture where the individual approach flourishes, you must keep pushing the church toward the right side of this continuum, because the "gravitational pull" of institutional demands will always work against the individual approach. Rick Warren puts it this way:

> One of the key challenges facing a pastor is to position the church as a creative place that needs the expression of all sorts of talents and abilities, not just singers, ushers, and Sunday school teachers. One of the reasons enthusiasm is so low in many churches is that creativity is discouraged.[4]

Incidentally, this rule differs from #48, The Classes of Leaders Rule, in that it addresses the motive for mobilizing church members. The Classes of Leaders Rule addresses the *focus* of what those members are mobilized to do.

■ What You Can Do about It

How do you move a church toward the right side of the lay ministry continuum if it is currently operating on the left? For starters, realize that such a move won't happen overnight, or even in a year or two. It is a process that may take three to five years before people "get it." Of course, the more people who join your church under the new paradigm of ministry, the more quickly you'll see a critical mass of new thinkers established. Here are a few ideas:

- The first step in moving from an institutional to an individual philosophy is to become familiar with the topic of spiritual gifts. Read several books on the subject and identify a list of gifts that is compatible with your church and theology.
- Next, go back to the list of roles or tasks you developed (see #48, The Classes of Leaders Rule). Identify the spiritual gift(s) that a person in a particular role should have in order to maximize his or her productivity in each ministry. Don't quit until you have every ministry position associated with one or more spiritual gifts.
- Spend four to eight weeks as a church studying spiritual gifts and the role of each person as an integral part of the body of Christ. The study could include preaching a series of sermons on spiritual gifts, exploring and discovering gifts in your church's small groups, studying the topic in adult and young adult classes, and asking members to read one or more selected books or articles on the subject.
- As you work toward developing an individual philosophy of lay ministry, don't forget your new members class. Teach about the call of every believer to be a contributing part of the body of Christ. Study spiritual gifts and help newcomers discover their own gift mix. Review your list of ministry roles and related spiritual gifts with each new member. Don't graduate new members

until you've helped them consider various ministry positions related to their gifts. If there are matches between a person's spiritual gifts and ministry positions, work out a plan with the newcomer to try a ministry for a few months. If there isn't a good fit in the church's present ministry opportunities, discuss the idea of starting a new ministry that would involve the person's interests, skills, and gifts.

- As the terms expire for volunteers, and as the normal attrition of personnel occurs with various church roles and tasks, identify a list of the spiritual gifts the position demands and incorporate them into future ministry job descriptions.
- Use or create a computer program to catalog your church's ministry positions and the associated spiritual gifts. Also list the spiritual gifts of your members and regular attendees. Then when a position becomes vacant, identify the gift mix required and search your constituency for matches. Of course to make this system work, all of your people will need to have gone through a spiritual gifts identification process. So, realistically, this is a process that will take several years before it's fully functional. But take some initial steps toward the goal and add to the list each year.
- Some churches that take lay ministry seriously have one or more ministry counselors who oversee the process of finding the right person for the right ministry. The function is something like the college counselor who guides students in finding the right classes for their chosen career field. In the case of a lay ministry counselor, he or she would meet with those who might be interested in serving somewhere in the church and work with them to find a good match.
- Such a ministry counseling process would obviously benefit from written ministry descriptions for each position. As we have mentioned, there is great value in having these descriptions for each position in the church. Ask each person presently serving in a ministry position to write his or her job description before leaving. (A common template will help to standardize the process.) Then go over the document with the ministry counselor to make any changes before the next person considers the position. A good ministry description will include:

  a list of specific responsibilities
  number of hours required per week
  who the person reports to
  recommended spiritual gifts
  length of position (one year—remember #47, The One Year Rule)
- Such a catalog of ministry positions could be on your website for access by members anytime they have an interest in exploring available ministry opportunities.

Remember, it will take several years to develop an individual ministry mind-set. But the benefit of helping your people find their place in the body of Christ where they can contribute through ministry will be well worth the effort.

9

Ministry Rules for Programs

Quality staff and leadership (see chapter 10) go hand in hand with quality programming. And quality programming goes hand in hand with a quality ministry.

There are many ingredients that go into providing quality programs in your church, but we believe there is one issue that is key, regardless of your church's size, theology, or location. We introduced the issue in #48, The Classes of Leaders Rule, where we discussed Class I and Class II ministry. But not only does this issue relate to deployment of church members, it has much broader implications in the overall programming of the church.

To refresh your memory, Class I describes groups, events, money, and people that focus inward on maintaining the existing church institution. Class I programs are planned exclusively for "our people," they are promoted exclusively among "our people," they are presented exclusively to "our people," and they are deemed successful when a large percentage of "our people" participate. In most churches Class I programming consumes the vast majority of human and financial resources.

Class II programming is designed for churched and unchurched alike. It is planned, promoted, presented, and evaluated to include the unchurched. Class II program planning asks questions such as, Will this address the needs of the unchurched? How will we invite them? Will they be comfortable? And in the evaluation process, how many unchurched people or families participated?

With this overarching principle of programming to include the unchurched in mind, let's look at some rules of thumb for effective programming in your church and community.

#53 THE 80/20 RULE

Eighty percent of the results come from 20 percent of the effort.

■ Introduction

The technical name for this rule is the Pareto Principle, named after Italian econo-mist Vilfredo Pareto who, in 1906, created a mathematical formula to describe the unequal affluence in his country, observing that 20 percent of the people possessed 80 percent of the wealth. The application has since been applied to many other aspects of management and may be stated: 80 percent of the consequences come from 20 percent of the causes. Pareto's observation may also be applied to the distribution of resources (people, time, money) in the church, and further extended as follows:

- 80 percent of the results come from 20 percent of the effort.
- 15 percent of the results come from 30 percent of the effort.
- 5 percent of the results come from 50 percent of the effort.

For example:

Evangelism. 20 percent of your members will be responsible for 80 percent of your new converts; 30 percent of your members will be responsible for 15 percent of your converts; 50 percent of your members will be responsible for 5 percent of your new converts.

Financial giving. 20 percent of your members will provide for 80 percent of the budget; 30 percent of your members will provide for 15 percent of the budget; 50 percent will provide for 5 percent.

Church ministries. 20 percent of your ministries will attract 80 percent of your people; 30 percent of your ministries will attract 15 percent; 50 percent will attract 5 percent.

This rule demands serious consideration when thinking about your church's ministry strategy.

■ Explanation

At first glimpse, the observations behind this rule may not seem all that important, so long as people are reached, the budget is met, and the programs are effective.

Yet the more we think it through, the more we begin to understand its strategic implications. Consider the chart below:

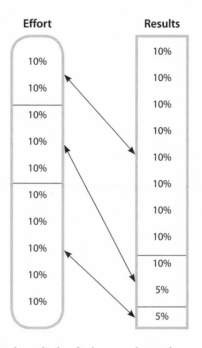

The chart illustrates that a little of what you do produces much of what you get. Time invested in only 20 percent of your activities is usually multiplied fourfold in the final results. Particularly in this day of limited ministry resources, but really anytime as a commitment to good stewardship, you are wise to put your time, energy, money, and people where they will bring the greatest results.

■ What You Can Do about It

Because a limited number of people, programs, and priorities are responsible for advancing most of your ministry forward, it may be the case that a significant number of people, programs, and priorities are actually impeding your church's progress. We suggest the following:

- *Identify your top programs.* List all the programs and ministries your church provides. Then, next to each one, note how many people the ministry touches. Put an asterisk next to the programs and ministries that are in the top 20 percent.
- *Identify your top leaders.* List all the people who have a ministry role or task in your church. Then rank them according to their level of influence in your church, and identify the top 20 percent.

- *Identify your top priorities.* Make a list of all the activities that are a regular part of your personal workweek. Put them in order, starting with the one most crucial for accomplishing significant ministry in your church. Which priorities fall into the top 20 percent?
- *Identify your top goals.* Make a list of all the goals your church has established for the coming year. (Every ministry area of the church, by the way, should have specific annual goals, as we will enlarge upon in #56, The Goal Setting Rule.) Once again, rank them in order, starting with those that are most likely to help your church grow. Consider asking your ministry area leaders to do the same thing with their goals. Which goals fall into the top 20 percent?
- *Identify your top outreach producers.* Make two lists. First, list all the people who are involved in an outreach or evangelism (Class II) ministry. Second, list all the programs that have resulted in individuals coming to Christ and/ or into your church over the last three years. Who are the people in the top 20 percent? Which programs fall into the top 20 percent?

For maximum results and maximum stewardship of your resources, focus 80 percent of time, energy, money, and training on the 20 percent that will bring the greatest return in each particular ministry area.

#**54** THE TWO-HUMPED CAMEL RULE

Focus your efforts to correspond with the two phases of growth in the church year.

■ Introduction

Pastors know it intuitively—the agony and ecstasy of annual attendance patterns. Yearly graphs of churches across the United States show two peaks and two valleys—a pattern commonly called a two-humped camel.

■ Explanation

Most churches find they have two times in the year when attendance peaks: fall and spring. And two times when attendance dips: winter and summer. Church leaders recognize the dip in the summer months and often call it their "summer slump."

Fall's normal attendance pattern finds people returning to church as children start school in September and vacations come to an end. Attendance gradually rises toward a peak at Christmas. Then the following Sunday, and in succeeding months, attendance often drops. Eventually a gradual upturn begins in the spring and peaks on Easter Sunday. Thereafter, attendance again drops to a low in August before the cycle begins anew (see figure below).

The Two-Humped Camel

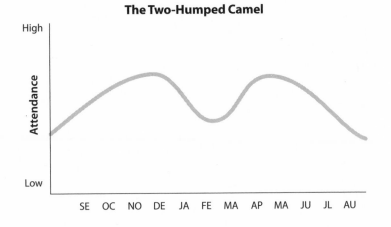

■ What You Can Do about It

Wise leaders use this natural attendance pattern as a "booster rocket" to launch their plans into successful orbit. This means they start new programs in the early fall or late winter to take advantage of the natural upswings. If you are planning to start a second worship service, do so in early September or early March. Follow the same principle with other ministries.

Let us hasten to add, however, that while the camel is alive and well in most churches, the camel can also be harnessed and directed. A church in Carrollton, Texas, makes a point of turning the "summer slump" into their "summer bump." They plan a variety of special events during the summer. They hold one of their worship services on the front lawn in June, July, and August, where members sit on blankets, bring snacks, and have a great time singing and worshiping outdoors. It's a chance to experiment and have some fun in church programming initiatives.

Without thinking about it, many churches apply the summer bump approach to their one or two weeks of Vacation Bible School. Why not get creative and make it a two-month bump instead of a two-week one? Summer activities can be great entry events when churches connect with people in the community who might not darken the doors of a church on Sunday morning.

A summer bump strategy is even more important when you realize that more than 40 percent of all residential moves occur in the three months of summer. And it is during this time of relocation that people are more open to finding a new church home. One pastor we know takes his vacation in the fall, because he knows that people will be visiting the church in the summer, and he wants to be there. So just because it's a natural downtime for church attendance doesn't mean you need to hold your breath for three months and try to survive. Be unnatural—turn the summer slump into your summer bump. We're not aware of any churches that apply this same principle to their winter slump. But why not be creative and try it?

#55 THE RULE OF FIFTEEN

The effective life span of a ministry program is fifteen years.

■ Introduction

All ministry programs have a four-stage life cycle. Peaks in their effectiveness seldom occur beyond the fifteenth year of their existence. Because programs are regularly reaching and passing their point of peak effectiveness, leaders of growing churches understand that launching new ministry programs is essential to the health and relevance of their church.

■ Explanation

The four stages of a program's life cycle include:

1. *Introduction.* This is the most expensive stage of the new program's life cycle. New staff, remodeled facilities, and advertising are involved. And launching a new ministry holds the most risk since it is unclear if the ministry will successfully reach the people for whom it has been designed. During this stage, the emphasis is on communicating and attracting a wide audience. The stage lasts from one to five years. If the new ministry program meets a need and takes hold, it moves into the second stage.

2. *Growth.* This stage is characterized by high interest and an expanding impact on an ever-enlarging number of people. Morale and enthusiasm are high among leaders and participants. Word-of-mouth is the best advertising as people invite friends. The greatest number of persons participate in the program at this stage, which normally lasts from the fifth to the tenth year.

3. *Maturity.* Interest and participation begin to level off. Fewer newcomers visit or attend the events. Other new programs, if they seem similar, attract potential participants. In this stage the leaders who have invested their time and energy into the program become defensive as questions arise about its continuing value and contribution to the church. Those who believe in the

program endeavor to refine or redefine it in order to revitalize it. General appeals for new participants are usually ineffective. People, money, space, and time previously directed to the ministry program are reduced. This stage lasts from the tenth to the fifteenth year.

4. *Decline and death.* The best days of the ministry program are clearly behind it. Significant decreases in participation result in relocating meeting locations and reallocating leaders. Attendance becomes embarrassingly small and visitors, if there are any, don't return. Church leaders must deal with the challenge of closing the program, which can easily lead to damaged egos and hurt feelings. The greatest cost at this stage is emotional stress experienced by those who remain attached to the old programming. This last stage begins around the fifteenth year of a ministry program's existence but may last a long time as some strive to keep it going beyond its useful life span.

While it is easy for longtime leaders to become discouraged and even depressed as the ministry approaches the end of its life, understanding that this is a normal pattern for *all* ministries can relieve some of the personal guilt they may feel at its impending closure. Celebrating the joy of lives that have been influenced by the ministry, and the contribution that leaders have made to those lives, is important. And, of course, a genuine sense of gratitude and appreciation should be conveyed. No doubt God appreciates the efforts that were made. The church should as well.

The silver lining behind closing a ministry is the opportunity it provides to free up people and priorities so there can be a focus on new ministries. The new ministry programs you start will experience the same high energy and positive dynamics as noted in the growth phases.

Here is a summary of some of the benefits a church may experience in starting new ministry programs:

- New people will be reached.
- New kinds of people will be reached.
- More members will be involved.
- More members will be involved in outreach.
- More members will invite friends.
- More new members will be involved in the church.
- Your community visibility will increase.
- You will enlarge your community connections.
- You will be less dependent on walk-in visitors for growth.

■ What You Can Do about It

You have already taken the first step—learning about the natural life cycle of a ministry program. This understanding is important for a church to continue its momentum and growth. Many church leaders think that once a ministry is begun, it can be effective forever. The reality is that all ministries have a fairly short life span during which they impact persons inside and outside the church. Accepting and understanding this fact of ministry life opens the way to strategic thinking about future ministry programs.

Make a list of every ministry program in the church and identify where you think it is in its life cycle. Don't think so much about the number of years it has been in existence as about which of the four stages it seems to be in at this time. The best way to do this is to take a blank sheet of graph paper. Across the top of the page make four columns and label them (from left to right): Introduction, Growth, Maturity, Decline. Down the left side of the page list every program in your church. Then, place an X in one of the four columns for each of the programs in your church. This immediately presents a visual perspective on the life and health of your church's various ministry programs.

It is likely that you will have Xs spread out in all four stages. But an unhealthy picture is when most of the Xs are on the right side of the page in the Maturity or Decline columns. If this is true for your ministries, you should seriously work on starting some new ministry programs in the next year.

Here is a summary of how to start a successful new ministry:

- *Nurture a "greenhouse" mentality for starting new ministries.* Regularly let members know that the church is ready and willing to help them start a new ministry around their particular interest or concern.
- *Find the passion.* Everyone cares about something. Encourage members to start a ministry around their passion, rather than around an institutional need. (See #52, The Philosophy of Lay Ministry Rule.)
- *Form a Ministry Planning Team.* Three to five people who share a passion will accomplish much more through their combined creativity and support than will one or two.
- *Imagine the dream.* What will this ministry look like five years from today as it is coming out of its introduction stage and moving into its growth stage?
- *Research other ministries.* Churches around the country are conducting many great ministries and outreach initiatives. A few hours on the internet will gather all kinds of ideas and information on people, books, websites, churches, and organizations that will help in starting the new ministry.
- *Define the purpose.* A good ministry needs a reason to exist and a target group for whom to exist. A clear definition of this purpose is important from day one.
- *Draw up the plans.* To get from a dream to a fully functioning ministry requires specific goals, a time line, people, and money. Carefully and prayerfully identify them.

- *Plan the first meeting.* Prospective attendees will be asking, Why should I change my schedule to be a part of your meeting? Provide a good answer, and they will come.
- *Promotion.* Personal invitations and public announcements are the two ways to get the word out. The first is much more cost-effective, but the second can supplement it. Invite both members and nonmembers.
- *Evaluation.* What was learned from the first gathering that will make the next one even better? Go back to your plans and time line to take the next steps in pursing the dream.

#56 THE GOAL SETTING RULE

Every program area in the church should set specific goals each year.

■ Introduction

Your church is far more likely to achieve something significant if each program and ministry area has specific goals and plans.

■ Explanation

Goals are like gold! With them your church will become a better steward of the ministry God has left in your care. Without goals your ministry leaders are like basketball players without a hoop—they don't know what they are supposed to do with the ball you have given them. Specific goals in your church provide the following important benefits:

- They give ministry volunteers a clear sense of direction.
- They provide a performance standard to determine success.
- They provide a tool to measure progress.
- They are a source of motivation and encouragement for those involved.
- They are a tool to aid in the stewardship of resources.

So what is a good goal? Here are some ingredients that should be in each of the goal statements throughout your church:

1. It is *measurable*—there is no doubt when it has been accomplished.
2. It is *consistent with the church's purpose*—it contributes to, rather than detracts from, accomplishing your mission.
3. It is *feasible and attainable*—a good goal requires faith, but is not obviously impossible.
4. It is *an action verb with a deadline*—it identifies exactly what will happen and by when.
5. It is *controllable*—it addresses a result that you can actually make happen, rather than something you hope will happen.

Consider these sample goal statements. Identify the goals that include each of the above characteristics and those that do not. For the ones that are not good goals, which elements are missing?

A. Receive thirty adult members by letter of transfer.
B. Have each teacher attend one workshop in Christian education.
C. Convert ten non-Christian people in a direct mail campaign next year.
D. Establish a worship task force by the end of this month.
E. Acquaint our congregation with the church's mission statement.
F. Start two new adult classes in the next six months.

Here's our opinion about which of these goals meet the criteria for good goals.

	Measurable	Consistent	Feasible	Action	Controllable
A	Y	Y	?	N*	N
B	Y	Y	Y	N*	Y
C	Y	Y	N	Y	N
D	Y	Y	Y	Y	Y
E	N	Y	?	N*	?
F	Y	Y	Y	Y	Y

includes action verb but no deadline

■ What You Can Do about It

Discuss with your leadership team whether it would be helpful to include the process of goal setting at an upcoming leadership training event. If so, how will it be introduced and how will participants develop a sense of ownership of the idea? Remember how people think: *Good goals are my goals; bad goals are your goals.*

If this first step meets with success, decide whether you want to incorporate goal setting into the normal structure of all your program and ministry areas. If so, leaders should receive training in how to write good goals. Then review the goals in each ministry area with program leaders before they are set in stone. Doing so will assure that the direction of all programs in the church is in sync with the direction of the overall ministry. And because good goals have specific dates and deadlines, track their progress with your program leadership.

Consider the first year of this implementation to be a learning process. At the end of the year, gather your program leaders and review the benefits, problems, and changes that would help the goal-setting process be even more effective in the following year.

#57 THE LASER FOCUS RULE

Growing churches do a few things well.

■ Introduction

One of the differences we've observed between churches that are distinctive and creative versus those that are commonplace and predictable is the "size of their bite." That is, how much are they trying to be and do. The process is actually counterintuitive. The alive, growing churches are doing *less*, while the plateaued and declining churches are trying to do everything. The big difference is that the churches doing less are committed to doing it exceptionally well. The churches doing more find they can't do it all and end up not doing any of it very well. It is the difference between a narrow focus with excellence and a wide focus with mediocrity.

■ Explanation

Do you have Sunday school classes for nursery and preschoolers as well as for kindergarten, primary, elementary, and junior high? Do you have classes for high school and college kids, young adults, young marrieds, empty nesters, singles, middle adults, and senior adults? Have you dreamed about small groups in your church for any or all of the above groups? How about midweek Bible study and kids programs? Do you have women's circles, men's prayer breakfasts, sports leagues, and programs for young moms? If you have or desire to have all these groups, this rule is for you!

The Laser Focus Rule speaks to church leaders of most congregations today. Basically it says: Do a few things very well, rather than everything not so well. This may sound like a contradiction with #51, The Ministry Positions Rule, but it's not. That rule rightly states that an effective church should have 60 ministry roles and tasks for every 100 constituents. The Laser Focus Rule says that these 60+ roles should be laser-focused on important and productive kingdom work, not an institutional perpetuation of busywork.

Many churches could reduce the number of their institutional programs by 25 percent without doing any damage to their ministry. (Remember #53, The 80/20 Rule?) Such a strategic reduction could allow the church to focus on a few ministries that would likely put its quality head and shoulders above other churches in the community. These are called *signature ministries*—exceptional church-sponsored programs for which the church is known throughout the community.

Churches are not called to start new programs or add new ministries or begin new services. They are called to make new disciples. Too many programs may actually hurt a church's ability to do this very well. When it comes to effective programming, we recommend narrow and deep rather than wide and shallow.

■ What You Can Do about It

First, evaluate your current ministries and programs. Which ones contribute the most to the ministry and influence of your church in the community? Which ones establish the most connections with unchurched people? Which ones bring the most newcomers into the life of your church? Which are the ministries where "the action" is? In other words, identify the strong ministries of your church. It is likely that those programs are strong because the people involved in them are strong, passionate, creative, and dedicated. And this highlights an important point—*the strengths of your church are the people and passions in your church.*

After evaluating your ministries, identify the programs that struggle year after year, the ones for which it is extremely difficult to find people to serve. What are the programs where volunteers seem to either drop out or burn out? Are these activities a part of the church's programming only because they have always been a part of the church's programming?

Ask yourself (and others), "If we were starting our church today, which of our present ministry programs would we do? Which would we likely not do?" Make some hard decisions to either terminate ineffective programs or seek a way to redevelop them into more fruitful forms. Seek to eliminate or redesign at least 10 percent of your ministries for the coming year.

One church we know introduced a creative approach to keeping their ministry activities lean and mean. They call it "zero-based programming." The idea was based on an approach many creative businesses use called zero-based budgeting. In businesses this is where every department must annually justify its existence and its contribution to the greater mission of the company in order to receive funding for the coming year. In the same way zero-based programming requires that the leader of every church program justify the existence of that program and its activities based on its contribution to the greater mission of the church. If the leader can't do it, no money. For this particular church, it has proven to keep their leaders sharp about finding the best use of their funds, time, and people for the greatest contribution to the church.

10

Ministry Rules
for Staff and Leadership

The organization chart of most American congregations is far removed from the structure of the first-century church. In fact, church scholars tell us that for years there was not even a distinction between clergy and laity. But influenced by the Greco-Roman political environment in the second century, the church began to divide its people into two classes. The *kleros* (the Greek root word for "clergy") were those believers who were trained, who possessed wisdom, and who had the power to act. The *laos* were those who were untrained and expected to submit to authority. This distinction was a departure from the biblical concept of all believers as the chosen people of God. In the New Testament the words *kleros* and *laos* refer to the same people—the people of God. There is no shimmer of biblical foundation for a distinct group called clergy.[1]

The modern church, however, is not likely to soon divest itself of this structural duality. The business model with its CEO, board of directors, shareholders, assets, and liabilities has influenced the organizational structure of most Western churches. But this may not be entirely ill-advised. Scripture does not present the way for a church to be organized. It does, however, call Christ's followers to be about sharing the *way* to a lost world. So the question is not so much, How do we organize? as it is, How do we organize to best achieve Christ's mission?

This chapter presents what we hope are helpful rules of thumb concerning staff and church leadership (paid or volunteer). We will consider how many staff a church should have, what they should do, and how long they should stay. Given that the roles of clergy and staff seem to be here to stay in most churches, how can we maximize their productivity and leadership for effective ministry?

#58 THE PASTORAL STAFF RULE

A church should have one full-time pastoral staff member for every 150 constituents.

■ Introduction

"What do you think about the board's decision to build a gymnasium?" Carrie asked her husband, Rick, as they drove into the parking lot of their favorite restaurant.

"Well," the twenty-six-year-old father of two preschoolers said, "I think we'd be better off hiring a pastor to oversee the children's ministry. Did you see how unorganized the toddler class was this morning? If the church doesn't hire someone to lead the children's ministry, I don't think we'll ever attract a lot of young families."

"I agree," replied Carrie. "Last Sunday I spoke with Sid Williams about my concerns for the children's program. As a board member, I thought he'd understand. He told me the gymnasium has been a dream of one of the board members for the last decade. Apparently the board feels we need to increase our facilities before adding more staff."

"The rumor I've heard," Rick continued as he closed the car door, "is that the board thinks we're already overstaffed."

"All I know," added Carrie, "is that a lot of things seem to be falling through the cracks."

These comments highlight an ongoing debate that can best be summarized by asking, Which should come first: staff, programs, or facilities? Research in the last half century has found that the way a church answers this question significantly affects its future ministry.

■ Explanation

As a rule, your church may need to add staff if you answer yes to any of the following questions:

1. Is our church experiencing numerical growth?
2. Is our church on a plateau?
3. Do we have an assimilation problem with new members?
4. Are there ministry opportunities we would like to respond to but don't have the personnel?

5. Does it seem to take an increasing amount of time to accomplish things?

6. Do a lot of things that should be done get left undone?

Based on the evaluation of growing churches with multiple staff, a realistic ratio of pastoral staff to worship attendance should be no more than 1:150. That is, a church should have at least one full-time pastoral staff for every 150 in worship attendance. Actually, over the last 25+ years the ratio has been decreasing and some growing churches are finding their ratio is now closer to 1:120. While it is difficult to financially support a ratio smaller than 1:100, it is unwise to allow the ratio to go beyond 1:150.

Using this ratio as a guideline, consider the following recommendations for staff:

Professional Staff Positions

Average Worship Attendance	Full-Time Program Staff
up to 150	1
150–300	2
300–450	3
450–600	4
600–750	5
750–900	6

Add one staff member for each additional 150 persons in worship attendance.

What does this 1:150 ratio tell us? It indicates that each staff person tends to provide for a growth potential of 125 to 150 people. (It is common to see stagnant churches with a pastoral staff ratio of 1:200 or higher.) The addition of a second pastoral staff person does not actually double the productive capability of the senior pastor. A second pastor increases the overall productivity by approximately 80 percent; a third full-time pastoral staff person increases overall productivity by another 75 percent.

The ratio suggests that a church desiring to grow to the next level should add a new staff person *before* reaching the projected growth level. This is a critical aspect of staffing that churches often don't anticipate.

Using only the table above, leaders typically wait to reach the next numerical level before adding the new staff person. For example, a church may decide to wait until it reaches 300 people before adding the second staff person or wait until it reaches 450 before adding the third staff. By so doing, however, the church is significantly lengthening the amount of time it will take to reach the next level, if it ever does. This is not how the table should be used. A more useful table is seen below:

Professional Staff Positions

Full-Time Staff Position	Increases Church Size To:
1 pastor	150 people
1+1	300
2+1	450
3+1	600
4+1	750
5+1	900

Each additional full-time staff person allows the church to increase by 150 people.

As this table illustrates, it is the addition of the next staff person that actually helps a church grow to the next level. The congregation averaging 150 to 175 in worship attendance should be in the process of looking for a new staff member and not wait to reach 300.

In addition to *when* you take on a new staff member, seriously consider *what* he or she will do. Recall our discussion about Class I and Class II ministry roles for laypersons. The principle of inward-focused and outward-focused activity applies equally to staff. Will this person be spending all of his or her time on inward-focused activity, or will there be a good portion of time spent in outward-focused leadership and equipping members and attendees in Class II activities?

A regional district in the Southern Baptist denomination conducted a fascinating study on what happens when a church adds a new staff person who concentrates primarily on Class II activities. They found when the new staff person concentrated primarily on activities like connecting with unchurched people, overseeing visitor follow-up, assimilating new members, and other outward-focused concerns, they actually paid for their salary through new giving units added to the church within nine to eighteen months. And the addition of those new giving units provided the funds to add additional staff (when the time was right) in music, youth, education, or recreation.

■ What You Can Do about It

The obvious first step is to calculate your church's pastoral staff ratio. In fact, you might find it helpful to go back over the past twenty or thirty years (assuming your church is that old) and determine whether there has been any relationship between the number of pastoral staff and the worship attendance. If you believe the church has the need for an additional staff person, prepare a proposal for such an addition. (The job may be part-time if finances are a major issue.) The best outline would use the approach of what, why, and when.

Our recommendation is that the job description for your next staff hire include at least a half-time focus on Class II activities. Below is a collection of various responsibilities we have seen in the job descriptions of such positions:

- Create new groups in the church that involve both newcomers and nonmembers.
- Nurture a "Great Commission conscience" within the congregation through a variety of activities and emphases (see #4, The Side-Door Ministry Rule).
- Monitor involvement levels of new members for the first year of their membership.
- Identify "people groups" of potential new disciples.
- Develop and oversee a process for assimilating new believers into the life of the church.
- Equip church members in various methods of outreach and evangelism.
- Plan, coordinate, and assume an active role in the new member orientation classes.
- Seek to make every church organization and activity an opportunity for outreach.
- Assist the congregation in developing a sensitivity to and increased participation in world missions.
- Utilize mailings and mass media to present an accurate and inviting congregational image to the community.
- Evaluate community needs and church programs from the standpoint of stewardship of resources, and recommend program revisions as needed.
- Develop a process to help members identify their spiritual gifts and use their gifts in meaningful ministries.
- Identify receptive people in the community and build relational connections to them.
- Lead the church in reaching people in the community who are unreached by any other church.
- Lead in developing discipleship programs that will help new believers grow in their faith.

Imagine the positive effect a qualified person on your church staff would have if he or she were focusing on these Class II concerns! The result would be—and will be—an entirely new understanding of mission and purpose in your church and resulting growth in the body of Christ.

#59 THE SABBATICAL RULE

A full-time pastor should receive a three-month paid sabbatical every six or seven years.

■ Introduction

The role of pastor is extremely stressful. In effect a pastor is never off duty. This long-term stress takes a toll emotionally, spiritually, and physically. If a church desires to keep a pastor for many years, they must provide their pastor with seasons of rest.

■ Explanation

Consider the following statistics concerning pastors:[2]

- 23 percent have been fired or pressured to resign at least once in their careers
- 25 percent don't know where to turn when they have a family or personal issue
- 45 percent say that they've experienced depression or burnout to the extent that they needed a leave of absence
- 56 percent of pastors' wives say they have no close friends
- 70 percent of pastors don't have any close friends
- 75 percent report severe stress causing anguish, worry, bewilderment, anger, depression, fear, and alienation
- 80 percent say they have insufficient time with their spouse
- 80 percent believe that pastoral ministry negatively affects their family
- 90 percent work more than 50 hours a week
- 94 percent feel under pressure to have a perfect family
- 1,500 pastors leave their ministry each month due to burnout, conflict, or moral failure

Universities and colleges have given professors a sabbatical for many years. Originally modeled on the biblical cycle of work and rest, university professors receive a sabbatical for research, writing, travel, and rest every seven years.

Today many churches find that by providing a regular sabbatical they are able to keep their pastoral staff for a longer period of time. And, as you will see in #62, The Pastoral Tenure Rule, there is a direct relationship between pastoral longevity and the growth of a church.

■ What You Can Do about It

Establish a sabbatical leave policy for the pastoral staff of your church. There are a number of books, articles, and examples available to help you develop a workable policy. Google the phrase "pastoral sabbatical policy" and you will find nearly one thousand hits. Here are examples from two churches of a sabbatical policy.

Example 1. Personal development leave is for professional growth that will benefit our church and will be based on the following:

1. Leave will accrue at 1.5 weeks per year of service at the church.
2. A pastor must serve a minimum of two years before scheduling any leave.
3. All personal development leave must be scheduled and approved by the church council. The administrative committee will make a recommendation based on a review of all the pastor's schedules and the purpose of the leave with the assurance that all ministries will be properly carried on.
4. A pastor will serve a minimum of six months following the use of any personal development leave.
5. Accrued personal development leave is forfeited when a pastor resigns. The church council may waive this in the case of a tendered resignation.

Example 2. Sabbatical leave may be granted to full-time pastoral staff members of the church for the pursuit of activities as approved by the council of elders. The following stipulations and requirements will apply:

1. Sabbaticals may be approved for six months at the culmination of each seven years of full-time ministry at the church. Each staff member may apply vacation time earned to extend his or her leave to a maximum of one month.
2. Full salary and benefits will be paid during the leave.
3. A detailed proposal for the use of a sabbatical leave will be presented to the council of elders at the time of application for leave. Applications should be presented at least six months prior to expected leave. The council has the right to deny leave for sabbaticals it feels do not meet with its approval.
4. The intent of sabbatical leave is to further the ministry of our church.
5. On returning, the staff member will give a report to the council of elders on what was achieved during the sabbatical leave.

We recommend each year your church put aside an amount equivalent to one-twelfth of the pastor's annual salary to cover salary during the sabbatical leave.

It is important to provide at least three months sabbatical leave in the sixth or seventh year of a pastor's tenure. The seventh year of a pastor's tenure is often one of mental and spiritual fatigue. By allowing a pastor to take a three-month sabbatical at this time, the pastor's life and ministry will be reenergized, which will most likely have a positive impact on the church's ministry as well.

#60 THE SUPPORT STAFF RULE

A church should have at least one full-time support person for every pastoral staff member.

■ Introduction

The number of support staff needed in a church depends on a number of factors, but a good rule of thumb is one full-time administrative/secretarial staff person for each full-time program staff member. More support staff are needed if the church is program-based, or if a large number of full-time professional staff are employed, or the pastoral staff are specialists. Fewer support staff are required if the church is cell-based, if there is a large number of part-time staff, or if the pastoral staff are generalists.

■ Explanation

Historically, churches have understaffed secretaries, administrative assistants, custodians, and other support roles. In reality this makes the pastor a secretary, assistant, and custodian and obviously diverts his or her time and energy from the pastor's unique role of leader, vision-caster, and initiator.

The number of support staff closely correlates to the growth or decline of a church. Here are pastoral and support staff ratios we commonly find in growing, plateaued, and declining churches per 150 in worship:

	Pastoral Staff	Support Staff
Growing Church	1:150	2:150
Plateaued Church	¾:150	1:150
Declining Church	½:150	¼:150

Today many smaller, declining churches are in a survival mode with only a part-time pastor or perhaps a full-time pastor but little or no support staff. Larger churches, though they have enough pastoral staff, may be weakened by less than adequate support staff.

The Support Staff Rule is spelled out in the chart below. (Note that we are not suggesting that every support staff position must be a paid position.)

Ideal Number of Support Staff Roles

Average Attendance	Pastoral Staff	Support Staff
150	1	1–2
300	2	3–4
450	3	5–6
600	4	7–8
750	5	9–10
900	6	11–12
1050	7	13–14
1200	8	15–16

■ What You Can Do about It

As with #58, The Church Staff Rule, the obvious response to this chart should be to add support staff if you are understaffed. Here are some examples of support staff titles, in no particular order. These are support positions you may want to consider adding if you are understaffed. Note that each one need not be a full-time position and that several support positions could be covered by one person.

- Assistant to the Pastor
- Assistant to Worship Leader
- Accountant
- Head Custodian
- Administrative Secretary
- Business Manager
- Receptionist
- Bookkeeper
- Assistant to Student Ministries
- Technology Specialist
- Worship Leader
- Publications Administrator
- Missions Administrative Assistant
- Librarian
- Early Childhood Learning Center Manager
- Music Associate
- Mail and Copy Center Manager
- Educational Ministry Assistant
- Information Manager
- Financial Assistant

- Office Manager
- Resource Coordinator
- Database Specialist
- Graphics/Web Designer
- Care and Prayer Coordinator

#61 THE APPRENTICE RULE

A growing church needs one leader-apprentice for every existing leader in the church.

■ Introduction

Churches grow as they develop leaders. Unfortunately 90 percent of churches in North America do not have any intentional leadership development and training plan. Most churches just pray that God will send new leaders, which of course means they are hoping a leader transfers from another church.

There is a simple yet effective way to train leaders in your church—mentor an apprentice. If each leader in your church were to mentor an apprentice, your leadership potential would double very quickly.

■ Explanation

Lack of leadership development in a church can be most disheartening for the pastor, to say nothing of the effects on the church. Consequences of a lack of leader training include the following:

- Existing leaders become burned out by being stretched too far and wide.
- The congregation lacks a shared vision because there are not enough leaders to communicate it.
- A church has fewer ministries than are needed, due to lack of leaders to take responsibility for them.
- There is a lack of teamwork between people involved in ministry, since leaders have not been trained.
- Little time or attention is given throughout the church to seeking God's vision and guidance.

- There is reticence to recruit new people for leadership positions for fear of giving authority to untested individuals.

One reason churches do not consider leadership development a priority is that it may appear there is an adequate number of leaders to meet current needs. Most churches have 10 to 20 percent of the people involved in ministry, which does not create a sense of urgency to identify and train more leaders. But if there is an increase in the number of members who come under the influence of the church's ministry, the church will be caught by surprise. The first response will be to try to handle the new situation with existing programs and leaders. But this works only temporarily. Soon leaders start feeling overworked, ill-prepared, and underappreciated. As a result, the number of people involved drops off, the number who are uninvolved grows, and the church has missed a great opportunity to increase the number and percentage of "ministers." A better scenario, of course, is that the new involvement level spurs the church to recruit and train more leaders. But the tendency for most churches is to rely on their present tried-and-true nucleus.

Actually the entire idea of increasing member involvement before training new leaders is backward. If your goal is to increase member involvement levels (which hopefully it is), a far better strategy is to increase leadership levels *before* it seems necessary. Leaders precede followers. This is another application of the proven principle: *new units = new growth*. In other words, be proactive rather than reactive. A new Sunday school class will attract new people. A new small group will attract new people. A new church will attract new people. Likewise, training and deploying new leaders will attract new people into church involvement.

So the question is, How do you train new leaders? One of the best ways we have seen is the mentor-apprentice model. Paul Stanley defines mentoring as "a relational process in which a mentor, who knows or has experienced something, transfers that something (wisdom, advice, information, experience, confidence, emotional support) to a mentee at an appropriate time and manner so that it facilitates development and empowerment."[3]

There are numerous examples of mentoring in Scripture: Jesus and his disciples, Barnabas and Paul, Paul and Timothy, Naomi and Ruth, Elijah and Elisha, Moses and Joshua, Deborah and Barak, Elizabeth and Mary. According to Dr. Brian Jones, the model of Moses and Joshua (mentor and mentee) illustrates a successful mentoring partnership and provides a "how-to" for mentoring future leaders, as seen in the points below:[4]

- Make assignments requiring new skills and responsibilities (Exod. 17:9).
- Invite him or her to key events (24:13–14).
- Allow the mentee to observe the mentor in action (33:7–11).
- Affirm the mentee for his or her achievements (Deut. 31:7–8).
- Step aside to let the mentee succeed (Num. 27:15–23).

Mentoring leaders should actually be described as mentoring *potential* leaders. When someone is invited to be a mentee, there is no guarantee that he or she will serve on the church board or teach an adult class or serve in any position. Nor is the mentoring process an assembly-line kind of leadership creation machine. Rather, it is an opportunity for both the mentor and mentee to share a more intimate experience of life together and for each to grow in the process. If the mentee seems to be growing in his or her leadership skills, the person may be considered for a leadership position in the church.

■ What You Can Do about It

There are different models and methods for Christian mentoring. Do some homework to find the philosophy that fits your church best. An internet search will yield many excellent books, websites, videos, blogs, and other resources on mentoring leaders in the church. Select one or more of these resources to train your leaders to be good mentors.

How do you get started in developing new leaders? The first step is to use the approach of church consultant Carl George. He simply asks church leaders two questions: "Who is your apprentice?" and "When did you last meet with him or her?" As simple as it sounds, these two questions contain the genesis of a solid leadership development plan for any size church in any location and denomination.

The first question is, Who is your apprentice? Any church can begin to double its total number of leaders just by expecting each current leader to find an apprentice. There is one catch. An apprentice must be selected from among people who are not presently in leadership. If ten leaders recruit ten apprentices to work alongside them, the leadership potential will double.

The second question is also important: When did you last meet with your apprentice? Regular engagement between the mentor/leader and the mentee/apprentice is essential. A weekly or biweekly meeting works best. Formal teaching is not as important as mutual sharing between the leader and apprentice. These sessions, plus on-the-job-training, make for a solid leadership development process. So . . . Who is *your* apprentice? When was the last time you met with him or her?

#**62** THE PASTORAL TENURE RULE

Growing churches generally have pastors who have
been at the church for over seven years.

■ Introduction

Some years ago, a denominational study found a striking relationship between the length of time their pastors had been in their church and the likelihood of that church growing or declining. They found that approximately three-quarters of the growing churches were led by pastors who had been at their church *more* than four years, while two-thirds of the declining churches were led by pastors who had been at their church *less* than four years. The conclusion—and our experience causes us to agree—was that while long-term pastorates do not guarantee that a church will grow, short-term pastorates essentially guarantee that a church will not grow.

■ Explanation

Imagine a doctor completing her final year of residency and beginning her practice in a suburb in the Baltimore area. She finds a good location for her office, networks with her friends, creates a business card, puts an ad in the yellow pages, joins a local service club, gets involved in community activities, and begins the fulfillment of her Hippocratic oath. Her medical practice and reputation grow.

Then four years after she opened her practice, she decides her time in Baltimore is over and moves her practice to Albuquerque. She says good-bye to friends and clients, packs, and moves two thousand miles away where she starts building her new practice, with new clientele and a new network.

Then three and a half years later, she feels the call again. This time to Seattle. It's a bigger city and better opportunity. Off she goes.

Thirty-eight years later this well-intentioned and very qualified physician retires. She has moved eleven times. Her practice was good, but her productivity and influence in the communities she served were set back with every move.

An observer might think this physician had some kind of psychological disorder. And perhaps this is correct. But guess what? Pastors do this all the time. And, frankly, we think a pastor's decision to move every four years makes about as much sense as the physician's decision in this imaginary scenario.

The average pastoral tenure in Protestant churches today is just under four years. This, despite the fact that multiple studies and authorities have determined that a pastor's most productive and influential time in a church is between the 5th and 14th year.[5] It's sad that the vast majority of pastors miss out on the potential for their most fruitful years of ministry. Maybe there is a relationship between this short pastoral tenure and the high pastoral burnout rate noted in #59, The Sabbatical Rule.

Why do pastors leave their churches? Here are the results of one study[6] in which pastors were asked this question:

Reason	Percent of Total Responses
Desire to serve in a different type of community or region of the country	27%
Getting promoted to a higher position	20%
Wanting to pastor a larger church	16%
Leaving to start a new church	15%
Being transferred by their denomination	15%
Being called by God to another church	12%
Better pay and/or benefits	11%
Fired or asked to leave	10%
Switching to a different denomination	9%
Wanting to pastor a smaller church	4%
Church closed	2%
Other (family needs, job frustration, new challenge, etc.)	18%

(Respondents were allowed to identify more than one reason.)

A strong correlation exists between the length of time a pastor has been in a church and the growth or decline of that church. Churches that experience a pastoral change every three to four years never come to trust that their pastor will be around long enough for them to follow his or her leadership or commit to long-term plans. Most pastors simply don't have the leadership equity that comes with a long-term commitment.

■ What You Can Do about It

If you are a pastor, commit to staying in this or your next pastorate a minimum of seven years. You may find that you develop an itch to move on in the fourth and fifth years. But if you stay into the sixth or seventh year, you will begin to experience unsurpassed effectiveness and fruitfulness. Once you get past seven, there's a good chance you'll want to stay much longer. Frankly, we agree with Roger Parrot, who says, "Lead as if you'll be there forever! Imagine that the organization and position you are in right now is what God wants you to do for the rest of your professional life."[7] Of course it may be demotivating to imagine a place where there is no possibility of enhanced ministry or influence. But why not anticipate that ministry enhancement is happening right where you are? Don't fall for the myth that increased ministry and influence can only be found elsewhere! When you plan to be where you are for the next twenty years, you will approach your ministry with a commitment that the winds of change, challenge, and time will not be able to shake.

Here are some nonstarters for changing positions:

- *More money.* People tend to be financially dissatisfied, whatever they make.
- *Conflict.* There will be at least as much conflict in your next church, unless there's no one there.

- *You're out of sermons.* If that's your reason, you're just lazy and shouldn't be in the ministry at all.
- *You're getting stale.* Commit to being a lifetime learner. It will keep you and your church's ministry in touch with today's issues.
- *Greener pastures.* See Philippians 4:12.
- *Boredom.* To quote Rick Warren, "It's not about you."[8]
- *Burnout.* Whether you have reached the point of burnout or not, take time to retreat and renew. Note #59, The Sabbatical Rule, which says to take a sabbatical every six or seven years.
- *An exploratory call.* We all like to be liked. But just because a church is calling doesn't mean God is.
- *Too much pressure.* What makes you think the next church will be without pressure? And if your motivation is to avoid pressure, see our response to "boredom" above.

If you are a lay church leader, the next time you are looking for a new pastor, make longevity a requirement. When you call or accept a pastor, commit to supporting him or her spiritually, emotionally, and financially. Do everything you can to get your new pastor to stay at least seven years.

If you are a denominational leader, support longer-term pastorates. Encourage pastors already in churches to stay where they are rather than jumping from one place to another in search of a better situation. (Just to test whether it's really God's call, why not approve transfers only if the new pastors receive *less* money in their new church?) Reorganize your calling or appointment system to allow (or require) pastors and churches to stay together for longer periods of time.

11

Ministry Rules for Facilities

Both research and experience have shown that the number of pastoral failures (physical, mental, moral, relational) increases dramatically during and within a year of a major church building program.[1] Pastors and church facilities are not a match made in heaven. Few seminaries even brush the surface of the topic, let alone focus on it in detail. Nor do bricks and mortar hold much appeal to most pastors who feel called to minister to people and families. This presents a perplexing dilemma—buildings play an important role in accommodating (and anticipating) increased congregational ministry. And facility construction and maintenance certainly account for a huge part of the overall church budget. So can pastors be good stewards of their church's resources in this area when most know very little about it? Perhaps some rules of thumb will help.

#63 THE WORSHIP CAPACITY RULE

Worship attendance should be 65 to 80 percent of
room capacity to encourage optimal growth.

■ Introduction

There's a sweet spot in the ratio of people to room capacity. If you're in this range, you'll have one more factor for worship attendance growth in your favor. Of course there are other factors that influence attendance growth, such as the number of visitors, quality of the music, attractiveness of the facilities, and relevance of the sermon. But the relationship between the number of people in the room and room capacity is one dynamic that often goes overlooked. The ideal situation is when your sanctuary, worship center, or meeting room is around 70 percent full. Fewer than 65 percent in the room limits your growth potential, as does an attendance of more than 80 percent capacity.

■ Explanation

The "Too Empty" Phenomenon. When a newcomer or visitor enters a sanctuary that is less than 65 percent full (and the service has begun), the message that comes through loud and clear is that the meeting must be irrelevant since no one bothered to show up. Of course the actual number of people in a room has little to do with whether or not the meeting is relevant. But to the newcomer or visitor, that's the message they get before hearing a single word. And it's nearly impossible to salvage that first impression.

The "Too Full" Phenomenon. When visitors enter a sanctuary or worship center (perhaps at the last minute), and it appears full, many will conclude that the benefit of staying is not worth the discomfort of having to look for a place or sit too close to people they don't know.

The following table can help you determine the message that your facility is sending, based on the number of people who are present and the number of people the room will hold. By the way, your regular attendees receive the same message.

Room Capacity	Unspoken Message	Growth Potential
30–40%	awkwardly empty	low
40–60%	comfortably empty	fair
60–80%	comfortably full	ideal
85–100%	uncomfortably full	low

If you have pews, you may be wondering how to accurately calculate your room capacity, since there is no clear demarcation of where one person's space ends and the next person's begins. Using building codes to determine room capacity is not the best approach, since "physical space" is different from "psychological space." And psychological space is what determines psychological capacity. Most state building codes require eighteen inches per person. But this figure relates only to getting people out of a building safely in an emergency. In reality, people don't sit that close. Some architects figure twenty-two to twenty-six inches per person. Our experience would confirm Alice Mann's observation in *Raising the Roof*: "When your main worship service reaches 80 percent of comfortable capacity (measured at thirty to thirty-six inches per person), you may be pretty certain that you are discouraging frequent attendance by current members and presenting a 'no vacancy' sign to newcomers."[2]

The phenomenon of "too full" is well-known in church consulting circles. When a room has theater seating, some issues are eliminated, such as the challenge of determining room capacity and how many seats are still available. But "a sufficient number of empty seats in desirable locations must still be available if growth is to be facilitated."[3]

■ What You Can Do about It

First, obviously, it is necessary to determine the capacity of your worship center. Counting chairs is easy. If you have pews, figure 30 to 36 inches per person.

Next, compare this capacity to your average attendance over the previous year. Simply divide your average attendance by your room capacity and you will get a percentage somewhere between 1 and 100 percent. Find that number on the chart above. If you are between 40 and 80 percent, you are in the "comfortable" range (with 60 to 80 percent being ideal).

Remember that an empty meeting room communicates an unspoken message that the service is irrelevant. If you average below 50 percent capacity, do some rearranging. A room can have different seating capacities, and an "empty" or "full" service is based more on the seats available than the size of the room. Remove chairs or pews, widen the space between rows, add more space between chairs, enlarge the aisles. A good goal is to have your chairs or seating area approximately 70 percent full.

If you average at or above 85 percent on a consistent basis, your options are to:

- rearrange the furniture to provide more available seating (doing the opposite of what is described above)
- enlarge your existing facility by knocking out walls
- add another worship location in another room on campus with a large screen and video feed
- add an additional service
- construct a new facility
- do a combination of the above

You will have a few Sundays when attendance is significantly above average (Christmas, Easter, Mother's Day). But don't set up your permanent facilities for these exceptions. Better to bring in additional chairs than have the room uncomfortably empty the rest of the year.

#64 THE FELLOWSHIP CAPACITY RULE

The capacity of the lobby should be 60 to 70 percent of the worship center capacity.

■ Introduction

Fellowship has been an important part of Christian gatherings since the first century. Scripture tells us that the early believers "devoted themselves to the apostles' teaching and to fellowship, to the breaking of bread and to prayer" (Acts 2:42). Today's effective churches continue to encourage and prioritize fellowship as an important part of the gathering of the saints.

Much of the fellowship in churches occurs after the Sunday worship service—if there is enough room. The space available near your worship facility for people to gather following the service is key to whether this vital function actually happens in the life of your church.

■ Explanation

There are several reasons to be concerned with the amount of fellowship space accessible from your sanctuary:

1. Those we have interviewed after their first visit to a church tell us that the number one factor influencing their decision to return was "the friendliness of the people." When we asked *when* they determined whether the church was friendly, most told us that it was immediately following the conclusion of the service. This is when most of the fellowship occurs in a church. If you have a place where such fellowship can occur, it is much more likely that it will occur. If you have no facility for such fellowship, it is likely that most attendees (including visitors) will head for the exit. And it's less likely that these visitors will return.

2. Fellowship is what keeps relationships in the church growing. As we saw in chapter 4, the average new member who joins a church and stays has made seven friends in the church during that first year. The average dropout made just two. Of course there is much more to developing meaningful friendships

than a few minutes spent in casual conversation after the service. At the same time, it's one predictable place to connect and nurture those relationships.

3. The farther away fellowship space is from your worship center's exit, the less likely people will seek it out. In fact, if the visitors are ignored during that critical ten minutes following the conclusion of the service, be assured that they won't go out of their way to seek out the "fellowship" place on their own. However, if someone in the church approaches and invites the visitor to coffee and refreshments in the fellowship area, chances are good the guest will go, even if he or she wouldn't have gone alone.

■ What You Can Do about It

First, determine whether you have any fellowship space available. This does not mean any space anywhere in the church. The fellowship space must be very close, and easily accessible, to the worship center. Your basement doesn't count. A distant classroom doesn't count. Space for the postservice fellowship must be in the natural path people take on their way to and from the service.

To calculate necessary fellowship area, figure 6 to 8 square feet per person. So, if you have 200 people in the service, and you want fellowship space for 60 percent of them (120), you need a room between 720 and 960 square feet.

If you don't have a room already available and/or accessible, what to do? Obviously, choices depend on your church size, average number in worship, finances, and available space. Options include knocking out a wall, constructing additional space, purchasing one or more mobile classrooms to locate near the sanctuary entrance, or remodeling your existing facilities. Some churches in warmer climates can use outdoor space for hospitality.

If you have adequate space for after-service fellowship, determine whether it is being well utilized. Here are a few suggestions for inviting people in:

1. At the end of the service, encourage members and regular attendees to introduce themselves to anyone near them whom they do not know. If they turn out to be visitors, the regulars should invite the guests to the fellowship area and introduce them to friends and church staff.

2. If you have gifts for guests (a good idea, by the way), put them in the fellowship and refreshment area or in your nearby information center. Portable freestanding signs should point the way to the fellowship area if it's not obvious when leaving the sanctuary.

3. Give people a good reason to drop in. Cookies, donuts, or pastries are nice. For healthier options add an assortment of fresh fruit, veggie sticks, health bars, popcorn, or cheese sticks. Include a coffee bar with various coffee options, plus hot chocolate, lemonade, hot water and tea bags, ice water, and other creative concoctions. It's okay to charge a nominal fee for some of

the goodies, but some should be free. If you do charge, be sure visitors and guests know they need only introduce themselves as new and the goodies are on the house. (Some churches include a coupon in their guest bags for free drinks and snacks.)

4. Appoint fellowship area hosts. Their responsibility is to circulate and be on the lookout for people standing alone, particularly newcomers. A good host will be skilled in social exchange and engage the person(s) in casual conversation. Introducing the guests to the pastor and other members is good hospitality.

5. If your fellowship area is a separate room, have more than one door. A normal three-by-seven-foot door is too small, restricting the ability of people to come and go. Double doors are better. An open space without walls is best. You may need to knock out some walls to create more open space, but it's a worthwhile expense.

An investment in fellowship space may seem pointless to some. It is, however, one of the best investments a church can make in its future growth. There is a very direct correlation between the sense of community in a church and the attractiveness of that fellowship to outsiders. Churches with members who simply come and go without much interaction don't attract or hold guests and have a low level of fellowship among those who do attend. Just as the gears of your car need regular lube and service, the gears of your church need to be lubricated through fellowship and community. It's just good preventative maintenance.

#65 THE FACILITY BALANCE RULE

A church's total facility should be strategically balanced in size and capacity.

■ Introduction

Church facilities can be in or out of balance. When a church's overall spaces—parking, seating, child care, education, fellowship, lobby, and so on—are in balance, they complement each other and encourage growth. But facilities that are out of balance can be the reason for otherwise inexplicable lack of growth.

■ Explanation

The exact ratios will vary with the location, demographics, and program strengths of a particular church. However, here are a few rules of thumb to use in evaluating the "facility balance" in your church. We will expand on several of the rules later in this chapter.

Parking to seating space balance. A worship center may have enough seats, but if the number of parking spaces is not balanced, the auditorium will never be filled. A church with 500 seats in the worship center but only 150 parking spaces in its parking lot is out of balance, since the number of spaces allow for only 300 to 400 people to attend at one time. The sanctuary will rarely, if ever, be filled.

Child care space to worship attendance balance. The total childcare and children's Sunday school space should accommodate 25 percent more people than your average worship attendance. Thus a church seating 200 in worship is balanced if it has room for 250 in its educational areas.

Parking to people balance. The available off-street parking should be equal to one-half of the total number on campus at one time. Thus if there are 300 people on campus (attending worship or in classes, for example), then 150 parking spaces are needed.

Fellowship space to worship attendance balance. The total space for corporate gathering should accommodate 25 percent more people than the average worship attendance. Thus a church with 150 people in worship needs enough space for 190 people to gather in groups for fellowship.

■ What You Can Do about It

Based on the above discussion, evaluate your available space relationship and circle one of the following:

Our parking to seating space is	excellent	fair	poor
Our child-care space to worship attendance is	excellent	fair	poor
Our parking to people on campus is	excellent	fair	poor
Our fellowship space to worship attendance is	excellent	fair	poor

For any area that you marked as fair or poor, brainstorm with leaders and come up with three or four ideas that could overcome these growth-restricting obstacles. Then develop a strategic plan, including a time line, to bring the fair and poor areas into compliance with these rules of thumb.

#66 THE MINIMUM ACREAGE RULE

For every one acre of land, a church will have
100 people in worship attendance.

■ Introduction

As any church leader knows, ministry requires space. And more ministry requires more people, which requires more space. Ministry space is required for worship, educational classes, fellowship, parking, and facility development. The standard guideline is that a church can grow to a maximum of 100 to 125 people per acre.

■ Explanation

Building regulations require that public organizations, including churches, provide adequate parking space and landscaping. This means that a growing church must think about not only how much space the building footprint will occupy, but also about how much space must be dedicated to parking and landscaping. Most cities require that churches provide one parking space for every 4 or 5 worshipers. However, in reality churches should have 1 parking space for every 2 worshipers. Add to this the requirement that public parking be landscaped with trees and other green space, and it is easy to understand that more acreage is needed by churches today than several generations ago.

This rule of thumb states that a church with one worship service will reach an attendance plateau once it reaches 100 to 125 people per acre of land. Churches that were built in the last century on 2 or 3 acres of land can expect to be landlocked and will need to find options to revitalize their growth.

■ What You Can Do about It

So what are the options? Here are a few; perhaps you can think of more.

- *Relocate.* Approximately 10 percent of the churches in the United States will not grow due simply to their present location. This may be the result of inadequate parking, insufficient meeting space, or simply a mismatch between the congregational makeup and the surrounding community.
- *Repeat.* Adding a second service at an earlier or later time or on a different day can ease the pressure on parking and other meeting facilities. The new service can be a second identical service, which allows more people to attend the kind of service they have come to enjoy. Or the new service can be a new style, which will reach out to new people groups in your community.
- *Reproduce.* Starting a new church or worship service in another location can offer choices to people who connect to your church but do not meet on your campus. The multisite phenomenon is increasingly popular for churches that are landlocked and/or want to reach new areas of the community.

#67 THE ADEQUATE PARKING RULE

A church will grow only to the size of its parking capacity.

■ Introduction

While adequate seating capacity is rightly emphasized as a necessity for growth, parking capacity can be even more important. If people can't park, they will never make it to the worship center or any other part of the campus. So it's important to know how much parking you need.

■ Explanation

The rule of thumb is one parking space for every two worship attendees. This will vary if you are in an urban location with a high percentage of congregants using mass transit. These days, however, the large majority of people drive to church and they need a place to park. Most city regulations require one parking space for every three to five seats in the main place of assembly. Don't count on this as a growth ratio, however. More likely it will be a growth inhibitor.

With our rule of thumb, a church with 50 off-street parking spaces can provide for about 100 worshipers; a church with 150 off-street spaces can have a maximum of 300 worshipers. If a church wants to break the proverbial 200 barrier, it must have at least 125 spaces (125 spaces x 2 people = 250 worshipers). If a church wishes to break the 400 barrier, it needs at least 225 off-street parking spaces. The importance of adequate parking cannot be overemphasized.

■ What You Can Do about It

Calculate your present parking ratio and then graph your worship attendance (by monthly average) for the past five to eight years. Look for a relationship between worship attendance trends and number of parking spaces available at the time. Some churches discover that their attendance growth was actually being limited by their parking capacity in the same way a plant's growth is limited by the pot size. If your parking capacity seems to be affecting your attendance, do some creative problem solving. Here are a few ideas:

- *Offer valet parking.* Wouldn't it be nice to drive up to the front of the church, give your keys to the nicely dressed young man, take a claim check, and walk into church? In addition to convenience, think of the benefit to your visitors, when parking is at a premium; older adults, who don't thrive on long walks; the disabled or handicapped, who deserve our most courteous efforts; parents, with kids who love to run in parking areas; Easter and Mother's Day attendees, when the family likes to be together; anyone who doesn't like getting wet in a rainstorm.

- *Arrange for off-site parking and provide a shuttle.* If there are nearby parking lots for movie theaters, malls, schools, or offices, it's easy to work out an arrangement with the owners to use their space on Sunday morning. If the church already owns a van or bus, that's a natural way to move people around. Used golf carts, which can be found on eBay for several thousand dollars, could be used to shuttle people to the church building. Regular members should be encouraged to park off-campus to provide room for visitors. A rotation system can be organized to keep the parking arrangement equitable for everyone.

- *Organize carpooling.* Riding to church together is a great way for members to get to know each other, while doing a small part in stewarding God's creation. Setting up a car pool system involves:

  1. Signing up. Ask interested members to sign up on a sheet that includes contact information, street address, which worship service they attend, how many available seats are in their vehicle, how many household members will need a ride, and whether they would be willing to be the neighborhood's car pool organizer.

  2. Mapping it. Use MapQuest or Google Maps to identify clusters where volunteers live. Contact those willing to be car pool organizers and provide them with the locations, vehicle availability, and number of drivers in their neighborhood. Car pool clusters can be organized into actual routes, times, and volunteer schedules.

  3. Valuing it. Carpoolers get perks at work, so why not at church as well. Perhaps free tickets to a concert or special event at the church, including reserved seating. Print the names of carpooling participants on brochures that describe the service.

- *Add additional parking.* It may not be difficult to add parking spaces in your existing lot. The width of angled and perpendicular parking spaces range from 7.5 to 9 feet. If your spaces are 9+ feet, make some 8.5 feet and create compact spaces that are 7.5 feet. You might also rearrange spaces for less length. Many existing spaces may be up to 18 feet long, whereas angled and perpendicular spaces can be 10 feet long.

- *Purchase additional land.* To determine if purchasing more land for parking is a good idea, divide the current number of parking spaces into your total church budget. For example, a church with a budget of $455,000 and 125 parking spaces would mean that each space equals $3,640 per year. Once the income per parking space is known, then multiply that amount by the number of new parking spaces that could be added to the potential property. Using the above example, if the property for purchase can support 50 new parking spaces, the potential income for one year would be $182,000 ($3,640 per space x 50 new spaces). Now multiply the total potential income from the new spaces by 10 years; in our example, this is $1,820,000. If the property costs less than that, it should be considered. If more, you might be wise to look at other options.

- *Add a new worship service.* With two worship services, expect 100 percent of available parking to be used in the first service and about 80 percent in the second. A third Sunday morning service would use around 70 percent of available parking. (There is not a 100 percent turnover of each space from one service to the next.) Thus a church with 100 spaces in three services can serve approximately 500 people:

> Service 1—100 spaces x 2 people = 200 worshipers
> Service 2— 80 spaces x 2 people = 160 worshipers
> Service 3— 70 spaces x 2 people = 140 worshipers
> Total = 500 worshipers

- *Begin an off-campus worship service.* We have previously mentioned that multisite services are an increasingly popular strategy of growth, and that they have numerous benefits. Obviously one is reducing parking problems. A few churches experimented with the multisite model in the mid-1980s. But since the year 2000, the idea has gained such momentum that entire books, websites, and conferences are now devoted to this creative strategy. Approaches will vary. Some churches record the first sermon and then replay it in a later service at a different location. Other churches schedule their services at different times so the pastor can deliver the sermon in each location. Some churches have an entirely different set of personnel at the two locations.

#68 THE RESTROOM CAPACITY RULE

A church needs enough restrooms so that every attendee can be accommodated within fifteen minutes.

■ Introduction

One of the first questions visitors ask themselves is, "Where are the restrooms?" Some may not feel comfortable asking, but it's on everyone's mind sometime during their visit to your church. In fact, Lyle Schaller goes so far as to suggest that the women's restroom is *the most important* room in your church!

■ Explanation

There are several issues that churches should consider when it comes to adequate restroom facilities. First, are there enough? A church has enough restrooms when everyone in a worship service can come and go within fifteen minutes. (No pun intended.) If the capacity of your restrooms cannot serve your worshipers in that amount of time, you need more restrooms or more facilities within your existing restrooms.

A second question is, Are there enough restrooms for the total number of women in attendance? Like malls, airports, stadiums, and other public buildings, churches should consider having twice as many women's restrooms as men's.

Also the restrooms should be nicely furnished. Paint, wallpaper, floors, and sinks should be of the same quality and cleanliness that you would expect in a modern office or other public facility.

And restrooms should be handicap accessible. Older churches built before the current regulations may find their facilities inadequate. Even if you are not required by law to update your facilities, the existence—or lack—of handicapped facilities says much about your thoughtfulness of others.

■ What You Can Do about It

Familiarity breeds oversight. Those who have been regular attendees at your church for more than a few years are not likely to notice the watermarks in the ceiling or stains on the restroom walls. If you are interested in the first impressions that your restroom (and other areas on your campus) make on newcomers, invite some friends or relatives who have never been to your church to do a "walk-through." In addition to the restrooms, see the checklist under #71, The Building Age Rule on what to look for.

We have conducted "secret visitor" evaluations of churches and found that a consistently overlooked area is maintenance of the restrooms *during* the Sunday services. Many churches will check the restrooms Saturday night or before people arrive on Sunday. But then the restrooms are ignored from 9 a.m. to noon on Sunday morning. Chances are good that people will inadvertently miss the trash can or splash on the counter and mirrors. A system to check and clean restrooms every 20 to 30 minutes during the morning service(s) will avoid a poor first impression in this important area. People won't notice a clean restroom but they will notice a dirty one.

#69 THE BUILDING STRESS RULE

Pastors are at risk during a church building program.

■ Introduction

The number of pastoral failures (mental, physical, moral, spiritual) increases dramatically during, and in the year following, a major church building program. This fact raises the question, Is the benefit of building worth the risk? We think so, but pastors are wise to prepare themselves and their congregation by being aware of the potential problems and implementing preventative measures.

■ Explanation

There are a number of important dynamics that arise in a church moving through the stages of major renovation or relocation:

1. *The problem of psychological displacement.* "Place" involves more than a pew where a person sat for years. It has a great deal to do with identity. "Place is space which has historical meaning, where things have happened which are now remembered and which provide continuity and identity across generations."[4] There will be an uneasiness caused by major renovation of facilities or relocation that can breed tension, depression, and hostility.

2. *The problem of anticipation letdown.* The average church building program lasts three years, from inception to dedication. During that time, fantasies of the pastor and church leaders see the new building to be the savior for all the congregation's ills. Unresolved conflicts, put on hold during the building program, wait for the first sign of emotional letdown before they raise their ugly heads.

3. *The problem of assumed authority.* If there is anything that a building program evokes, it is a seemingly endless series of decisions. Because the pastor is usually the most readily available, he or she may be called on to make decisions for which he or she is either unauthorized or unqualified. It is just a matter of time before the pastor is confronted by a challenge to this assumed authority, which provides the setting for resentment, antagonism, and conflict.

4. *The problem of program lag.* With the intense involvement of church leaders in the building program, thoughts of new mission and ministry are often set aside. Then suddenly the building is finished! If appropriate planning has not taken place, the former programs may seem obsolete and inadequate in the new structure. The lack of dynamic new activities to go along with the new facility may be seen as an indication of the pastor's inadequate leadership.

5. *The problem of transition grief.* Old buildings hold many memories. This is where members spoke to God, and God to them. It is where life's turning points occurred—spiritual commitment, baptism, communion, weddings,

funerals. Often the "abandonment" of such a sacred place brings grief, which can lead to guilt, which can lead to anger. As irrational as it may be, both the new building and the pastor are likely targets for that anger. As a result, the pastor may feel isolated, disappointed, angry, frustrated, useless, and abandoned.

■ What You Can Do about It

There are a number of things you can do to avoid these problems, or at least anticipate them so you can handle them with wisdom:

- Be aware of the added stress that is inevitable during a building program. As much as possible, delegate the responsibility for planning and overseeing projects to lay leaders.
- Don't begin a building program without an overarching church purpose statement in which the new building fits. Winston Churchill said, "We shape our buildings; thereafter, they shape us." Your purpose statement (see #84, The Means to the End Rule) should strongly influence your building design and utilization.
- A building program will significantly increase your contacts with committees, banks, community officials, architects, contractors, and denominational personnel. Your established routines will be upset and personal life disrupted. Especially during a building program, use your time wisely.
- Establish proper decision-making procedures. The question, Who has the authority? will be asked many times during the typical building program. Failure to determine the answer in advance will open the door for conflict, power struggles, and political maneuvering, not to mention hurt feelings and poor decisions.
- Be sensitive to the unexpressed feelings of people who may appear to be dragging their feet, particularly long-term members. Validate their feelings and affirm their value.
- Bring parts of the old church into the new. It may be a cornerstone, a stained-glass window, a picture, a pew, a church bell. Carl Dudley has wisely said, "By honoring our history, we can satisfy our need to say thanks to the past. When we have recognized the meaning that some places have for some people, then we can liberate those rooms for other uses"[5] and liberate those people for other purposes.
- Neither ignore nor internalize negative remarks about the new building or about yourself. In leadership, criticism is unavoidable. If a critical remark is valid, the effective leader will gain by paying attention to it, and the speaker will feel satisfied for having been heard. If the criticism is invalid or the matter

cannot be corrected, treat the critic with kindness and thank him or her for trusting you enough to share their thoughts with you.

- Avoid the temptation to create a monument to your own ministry. One of the greatest dangers of a church building program is that the pastor may unconsciously seek a memorial and, in a subtle way, the building can become the possessor of the pastor!

Above all else, the pastor and congregation must remember that "in him the whole building is joined together and rises to become a holy temple in the Lord" (Eph. 2:21).

#70 THE FIRST BUILDING RULE

The size and shape of the first building defines the future of a church's ministry.

■ Introduction

It is always an exciting time when churches construct or purchase their first permanent facility. However, most new churches build too soon, and many build the wrong thing. The first building or unit that is constructed has a long-term influence on the church's future ministry, for better or worse.

■ Explanation

If a church wants to grow, it is best to put property acquisition and building construction as the last priority. Here is the best sequence:

Priority 1: Programming. New groups created for men, women, children, couples, special interests, and special needs will greatly enlarge the church's influence and magnetism. And they don't need a permanent building to meet.

Priority 2: Staffing. Additional program and support staff will allow the church to enlarge its ministry in more areas, more quickly. And they don't need a permanent building to work.

Priority 3: Building. Eventually most churches feel that ministry efficiency warrants more permanent facilities. But the ensuing financial drain may mark the onset of institutionalization. "The church" now becomes the *building* rather than the *people*. The mortgage becomes the first bill to be paid if funds are limited. Committee meetings are now in the new building rather than members' homes. One well-known congregation grew into a mega-church unencumbered by the burden of facilities for its first fifteen years. By the time they constructed their first building, they had moved seventeen different times. You don't need a building to grow!

■ What You Can Do about It

Our advice is to delay building as long as possible. If you feel like you can't go any longer without building, consider the following:

- If and when you do build, build for growth. If you are leading a new church, assume that you will grow to be much larger than you are at present.
- Purchase land that has good visibility and accessibility. Turn down a location that people will have difficulty finding. Since people tend to drive to church in the same direction that they travel to work, look for land that is in the general direction of the main traffic flow in your community.
- It is usually wise to build a multipurpose facility before a sanctuary or other worship venue. Worship facilities are more expensive to build, and if people get too comfortable, they may not be motivated to build additional facilities necessary to support continued growth.
- Hire a good architect to develop a master plan of the *entire* church property before building any units. By so doing, the first unit will fit into an overall plan, it will continue the vision, and it will allow for a balanced facility to provide the greatest potential for maximum growth.

#71 THE BUILDING AGE RULE

If your church interior is more than fifteen years old, it is probably a growth-restricting obstacle.

■ Introduction

Check out the interior of national chain retail stores in your neighborhood (grocery, pharmacy, clothing, and restaurants). On average, retail businesses remodel their facilities every five to seven years, and with good reason. "New" attracts people—new toothpaste additive to whiten teeth, new vitamin potency in cereal, new and improved mileage for cars. New attracts.

In contrast with retail businesses, we find that churches renovate their interior facilities about every twenty-five to forty years; some go even longer without a makeover.

■ Explanation

When it comes to church visitors, you don't have a second chance for a good first impression. And your building will be one of those first impressions—first the outside, then the inside. People don't need to be professional architects to sense that the ceiling is too low, the halls are too narrow, the windows are outdated, or the paint is a color that was popular twenty-five years ago. As Marshall McLuhan said, "The medium is the message." In this case, your building is the medium.

The design and architecture of your church building will have more influence on your visitors than on your longtime attendees. The longer people have been attending your church, the less able they are to see it through the eyes of a newcomer. They don't notice the rain marks in the ceiling, the chipped paint on the wall, the hole in the carpet. And for longtime attendees, it doesn't really matter anyway. They come to church because of the people, the relationships, the fellowship, and the spiritual growth, not the facilities.

But to newcomers who don't know anyone, other things (including facilities) shape their initial attitude and decision to come back. If they do come back, relationships grow in importance and facilities decline in importance.

Also facilities have an effect on congregational self-esteem in a similar way that your house affects your personal self-esteem. If you live with junk in your backyard, unwashed dishes in your sink, dirty clothes around the house, and rooms in need of paint, it can't help but affect your sense of self-worth. And do you want company to drop in unexpectedly? Probably not. When you know special guests will be arriving, you pick up the clothes, wash the windows, clean the dishes, and put on your house's best face. Why not take the same attitude about your facility and the special guests who are coming to visit your church?

While nice facilities don't cause churches to grow, poor facilities often keep churches from growing.

■ What You Can Do about It

As we suggested in #68, The Restroom Capacity Rule, an outsider's perspective is quite valuable. Invite a friend, an out-of-town guest, or a next-door neighbor to walk through your church building with you sometime in the next few weeks. We suggest one or more women be invited since women tend to be more observant of a room or building's appearance. The walk-through need not be on Sunday. The person you invite should not be familiar with your church or have ever attended. First, drive by and around the church. Then park and walk toward, and eventually into, the building. Ask the person to speak freely about her impressions, sharing what catches her attention, what she likes and dislikes. Either take notes or use a recorder to be sure you get all the comments. Tell her not to be worried about any hurt feelings. Of utmost importance are the person's honest first impressions.

We suggest doing this exercise three times with at least three people. That way you won't make decisions based on only one person's perceptions. See if the different people notice the same things. Finally, compile your notes into categories and analyze them. As you consider the comments, remember that you don't need to make *all* the changes suggested. But you do want to know how visitors and newcomers see your facilities. And, if there are obvious issues that come up consistently, make the improvements as soon as you can.

Here's an interesting thought we picked up from a Christian architect. The more the inside of a church looks and feels like the facilities people are used to seeing during the week (lights, interior decoration, restrooms, classrooms, and so on), the more likely the facility will present a positive first impression. Conversely, the more out-of-date your facilities are, the more negative will be the first impression. When a newcomer enters a church building that is fifty-plus years old—and looks it—he or she will subconsciously wonder whether the message of the church is as outdated as its facilities.

Here's a checklist we use in our consultations to evaluate a church's facilities. Each item is graded on a 1 to 7 scale (1 = poor; 7 = excellent). Perhaps it will be helpful as you think about your own facilities and whether they are an asset or a liability.

Building

Ease in finding the location

First impressions from the outside

First impressions of inside (immediately upon entering)

Impressions after walking around

Parking

Appearance

Adequacy of spaces

Proximity to entrance

Signs

Directions from parking area to appropriate building entrance

Where to get general information

Directions to sanctuary/worship center
Directions to fellowship hall
Directions to restrooms
Directions to nursery

Nursery
First impressions on entering
Confidence in security
Confidence in nursery staff

Sanctuary/Worship Center
First impressions on entering
Ease of visibility
Sound/acoustics
Video capability
Ease in finding a seat (during a service)
Seating comfort

Restrooms
First impressions on entering
Impression on entering the stalls
Adequate supply of soap and towels
Cleanliness of sinks and counters
Toilets and faucets working properly

Classrooms
First impressions on entering the room
Appropriate facilities for age groups (size and comfort of furniture, etc.)
Up-to-date audiovisual equipment

 THE PLAYGROUND RULE

There should be eighty square feet of space
for each child on a playground.

■ Introduction

Unless your church's target audience is exclusively adults and seniors, we recommend a designated play area for kids. As you think about your church's play area, ask the three following questions:

1. Why do we have a playground?
2. Does our playground encourage physical and emotional development?
3. Is our playground safe?

Too often churches give little consideration to their playground. But to parents, your "kid priority" will come through loud and clear when they look at your playground. Their decision to become more involved in your church will be determined more by your facilities for their kids than your facilities for adults.

■ Explanation

The primary purpose of a playground is to stimulate educational play, not just to be a babysitting facility for the church. A close second is to provide a *safe* play area for children. As a general rule, a playground should have at least eighty square feet of space for each child playing with a group of children, a four-foot high-fence, two gates with latches that work, safe access routes, and appropriate ground material to absorb impact.

■ What You Can Do about It

The first thing to do is to develop a playground philosophy of ministry. Determine why you have a playground in the first place. Is it to promote learning development, nurture peer interaction, care for children (babysit) during services?

Observe other public and private play areas in your community. Talk with your city recreation director about local requirements that affect churches. Look at exceptional models of children's recreational areas. Research play equipment and articles on the Internet. Identify safety issues that should guide the overall development of your playground.

Next, analyze your present playground and answer the following questions:

1. How many children use the playground at the same time?
2. How many square feet does your playground provide per child at the busiest time?
3. Is the playground free of hazards (rocks, concrete, exposed wood, wires, sharp objects)?

4. Is the surface of the playground covered with approved impact material? (Most injuries on playgrounds come from falls.)

5. Is there adequate drainage of the playground?

6. Is the play area set up to distribute children by age group?

7. Is there adequate space between play centers to avoid overcrowding?

8. Is there an adequate safety fence to separate children from traffic or intruders?

9. Is there a safe and protected route into and out of the playground area?

10. Is moving play equipment—teeter-totters, swings—located away from where most of the children would be playing?

Finally, take what you learn from your study and begin to make changes to improve the safety of your playground area. Involve parents in the process and use it as a friendship-building experience. And, as always, don't limit your invitations for help just to church members.

#73 THE RELOCATION RULE

Consider relocating if your church's ministry is being stunted in its present location.

■ Introduction

It used to be common practice to plant churches in quiet neighborhoods away from major traffic arteries. Today's approach actually seeks to place churches as close to the flow of traffic as possible. Busy streets are better than quiet lanes, for out of sight is out of mind.

■ Explanation

There are some churches today that simply cannot grow in their present location. If your church has been in the same location for more than thirty years, it is likely that the immediate neighborhood for which your church was originally begun has changed. Some resilient churches are able to change with the times; others are not. Because the church is people, not buildings, it is possible that to continue serving people most effectively, you should consider moving. Often biological families need to move. Sometimes church families need to move as well.

Reasons for relocating a church so that it can minister more effectively include items such as these:

- need for more facilities and acreage
- attendance decline
- desire to reach a new target audience
- desire to minister to the present target audience, which has moved
- desire to create a new vision
- industrialization or commercialization of the community
- deterioration of the immediate neighborhood

The average church relocates 5.5 miles from its former location. Most (40 percent) locate less than one mile away, 30 percent relocate two to nine miles away, and 30 percent relocate ten or more miles away.

Most churches experience a measure of new growth—spiritual and numerical—soon after relocating. In our experience we have observed the following:

- 70 percent of churches that relocate experience some degree of numerical growth
- 20 percent of churches remain the same size
- 10 percent of churches experience some decline

Other benefits following relocation include the following:

- the challenge and rewards of reaching new people
- newer facilities provide positive self-esteem
- increased ability to accommodate growth
- new vision and enthusiasm among the people
- renewed hope for future ministry
- greater opportunities for evangelism

Interestingly, a move within one mile of the present facility results in the lowest subsequent growth in attendance and participation. Moving farther away results in greater growth, since there is both new opportunity and new motivation to reach new groups of people. But there is a point where moving too far away from the original location can prove problematic. Beyond twelve to fifteen miles seems to be that point. Relocation will be most helpful in stimulating renewed growth when the move is between three and ten miles from the former location.

▪ What You Can Do about It

Churches that have successfully relocated found these steps to be helpful:

1. *Seek God's will through fervent prayer.* Don't decide to relocate just on a hunch or a momentary frustration. God must be directing your move based on his eternal purposes.

2. *Involve key leaders.* Include formal and informal leaders in prayer, research, and exploration of options in the relocation process. Their involvement will create a sense of ownership that will be important in the long-term process.

3. *Interview other church leaders who have relocated.* Learn from the experience of others. What would they do differently or the same? What surprised them?

4. *Conduct a feasibility study.* Clearly identify the advantages and disadvantages of a move. What are the costs versus the benefits? A facilities consulting firm that specializes in churches can be most helpful.

5. *Conduct a demographic study.* What is the best location for your church where it would most likely prosper and grow?

6. *Develop a relocation plan.* A time line of events will be very useful. In your planning, remember that things almost always take longer than you expect. Share this time line with others and seek their input.

7. *Be available to your people.* There will be a sense of loss for many who have spent years in the old location. To them, the building is not just wood and tile; it is a sacred place. Love and nurture them through the transition. Listen to their hurts and concerns.

8. *Find a place to hold services in the interim.* You most likely will need a temporary location for one or two years. Find a meeting place as close to your eventual permanent location as possible.

9. *Plan and organize.* Most disappointments in the relocation process come through poor planning. Take nothing for granted.

10. *Make your move.* If at all possible, move in less than one year. The longer you wait, the greater the likelihood of problems.

Experienced real estate salespeople know the top three concerns for a good home are location, location, location. The same could be said about your church home.

12

Ministry Rules for Finances

The man who had received five thousand pounds went out at once and by doing business with this sum made another five thousand. Similarly the man with two thousand pounds made another two thousand. But the man who had received one thousand pounds went off and dug a hole in the ground and hid his master's money.

Matthew 25:16–18 Phillips

The parable of the talents provides a wonderful variety of lessons on how the Lord wants us to invest our resources. One of the lessons is that the Master expects a return on the investment of what he left us. Jesus left us the Holy Spirit as our strength to build his church. When the Master returns, this parable of the talents suggests that we will be accountable for what he has left in our trust. The "talents" Christ has given the church are people, people who are followers of the Way. So what is the best strategy for increasing the talents—the people—that we have been given, so that when the Master returns, he will respond, "Well done, good and faithful servant"? The best strategy is to invest our church's finances in ways that will reach new people.

Finances are not the definition of a church's success, but lack of finances can be the cause of a church's failure. It is important to understand and use money carefully. Hence, a few rules of thumb.

#74 THE EVANGELISM BUDGET RULE

One dollar of every ten should be spent on local community outreach.

■ Introduction

Usually the amount of money allocated for evangelism and outreach represents the lowest percentage of a church's budget line items. This is unfortunate since investment in this category is most likely to bring new people to Christ. And, from even just a purely financial perspective, new people become new giving units added to the church.

■ Explanation

Investing the financial resources of the church calls for good stewardship. The goal of your financial investing should be to make the greatest number of disciples. Of course, like the different servants in the parable of Matthew 25, different churches have been given differing amounts of resources. The mission is not so much to bring back the most as it is to bring to the Master more than what was originally provided.

The Evangelism Budget Rule says that one dollar of every ten (10 percent) in your church budget should be used in outreach and evangelism in your immediate community. Using this ratio, a small church with a budget of $100,000 would invest $10,000 in local outreach. A larger church with a budget of $1,000,000 would invest $100,000 in reaching out to its surrounding community. This is not money invested in overseas missions (although such an investment is also important in responding to our disciple-making mandate). It is money invested to reach people in your immediate ministry area. The money is used for anything that builds bridges to the community so that people outside of Christ and the church can learn of the hope, peace, and joy of life in him.

It may have occurred to you, while reading this 10 percent rule of thumb, that 10 percent is also the amount that churches have long taught their members is a tithe. It is not inappropriate to consider the relationship between these two 10 percent figures and the idea that your church is also called to give a tithe to God. What better way to invest God's money than in the reproduction of new disciples reached for Christ's church?

■ What You Can Do about It

Begin by determining the amount, as well as the percentage, of your last year's budget that was spent on local community outreach and evangelism. If you are like most churches, you will find that it makes up less than 1 percent of the budget. With that percentage, it is easy to see the reason most churches are not growing through conversion growth.

Determine whether it is possible to designate 5 percent of your total budget for outreach next year. From what other parts of the budget might the money come? If it is not possible to allocate that much in one year, consider doubling the amount from this year. Then add an equal amount the following year. Keep increasing your evangelism budget each year until you get to 10 percent.

How would you spend a 10 percent tithe of your church's budget to reach your community? Churches can burn through a great deal of money very quickly by purchasing billboards around town, mailing brochures to everyone in the immediate zip code, and buying television and radio time for catchy commercials. Research has clearly shown, however, that such expenditures are usually a near total waste of God's money.

We suggest that the best use of your funds is in activities that will build and nurture relationships between members and nonmembers in your community. Here are a few ideas:

> *Entry events, such as a community Halloween festival, Easter egg hunt, Memorial Day service, Cinco de Mayo festival, or special topic seminar.* Be sure to obtain participants' names and contact information for subsequent follow-up and invitations to future events.
>
> *Entry paths, such as a single-parent support group, walking club, after-school homework club.* These are smaller groups that meet initially for six to ten weeks and may be extended if the participants desire. The purpose is to encourage closer relationships between members and nonmembers.
>
> *Staff, such as a recreation director, evangelism/assimilation coordinator, visitor follow-up director.* Too often staff are hired and evaluated based on the programs they provide for church members. This person, however, should focus on strategies and events that nurture new relationships between members and nonmembers.
>
> *Facilities, such as a skateboard park, softball field, family life center.* The facilities should be used to create relationships, not just for participants to come and go independently.
>
> *Publicity, such as flyers for your upcoming events, postage, design, website.* Publicity brochures are best distributed to church members' friends and acquaintances, previous church visitors, parents of VBS kids, and the like. Don't mail them randomly to a phone book list of names.

Does 10 percent of your total budget seem too large? Most growing churches invest at least that in local evangelism and outreach. Such an investment results in people coming to Christ and into the church. (At least, it *should* produce results if the money is well spent. If you are spending that much money and not seeing results, review and redirect your expenditures into other outreach activities.)

As new people are added to the church family, they bring additional funds into the church as new giving units, which means your 10 percent for outreach next year will be more than your 10 percent last year.

#75 THE SALARY AND BENEFITS RULE

Between 40 and 60 percent of a church's overall budget should go to staff salaries and benefits.

■ Introduction

Salaries and benefits together make up one of the largest parts of a church budget. This includes cash salaries for pastors and staff, retirement, housing allowance, medical insurance, and tuition and continuing education assistance. Typically, larger churches spend between 40 and 50 percent of their overall budget on salaries and benefits. Smaller churches may spend 50 to 60 percent of their budget on staff. It is not unusual to find some very small churches spending upwards of 80 percent of their budget for the pastor. If a church spends less than 40 percent for staff salaries and benefits, it is likely that either the church is a megachurch or it is taking advantage of the staff by asking them to carry the burden (through lower salary and benefits) of an extremely high mortgage or some other diversion of funds.

■ Explanation

Researcher John C. LaRue Jr. reports in *Your Church* magazine[1] the average number of ministry staff by church budget as follows:

Church Budget	Full-time	Part-time
Under 50,000	0.7	0.4
50,000–100,000	0.9	0.4
100,001–150,000	1.2	0.6
150,001–200,000	1.6	0.7
200,001–300,000	1.9	0.9
300,001–500,000	2.6	0.9

Church Budget	Full-time	Part-time
500,001–1 million	3.5	1.1
Over 1 million	4.8	1.5

LaRue goes on to report the percent of the total budget spent on ministry and support staff:

Church Budget	Percentage of Budget for Staff
Under 50,000	89%
50,000–100,000	56%
100,001–150,000	53%
150,001–200,000	51%
200,001–300,000	47%
300,001–500,000	40%
500,001–1 million	32%
Over 1 million	27%

■ What You Can Do about It

First, analyze your church's budget to determine the percentage being spent on staff salaries and benefits. Compare your percentages to those mentioned above. If you are not spending enough on personnel, determine if you are spending too much in other areas of ministry. Or if you are spending too much for staff, what has caused this to happen and is the church's ministry suffering for lack of funds in other areas? Finally, discuss whether, when, and how to bring the budget into alignment with the suggested ranges.

Next, determine if you have enough staff. Based on your total budgeted amount, how closely do you match the number of typical staff when compared to the LaRue study? Another way to evaluate the total number of staff needed is to determine the ratio of staff to worship attendees. As we have noted, the rule for growing churches is a ratio of one full-time pastor (or person in a pastoral-type role) for every 100 to 150 active members and attendees (see #58, The Pastoral Staff Rule). What ratio of staff-to-attendance does your church have in place? Do you have too many staff, not enough staff? Are they being effectively deployed?

Based on what you discover in your analysis, what steps do you need to take to improve your church's financial support and total number of staff in the coming years?

#76 THE MINISTRY BUDGET RULE

A good church budget will have a clear delineation of ministry areas and the percentage of the budget allotted to each.

■ Introduction

As churches experience economic ups and downs, a well-defined budget is extremely helpful. Elmer Towns, an authority in church ministry, recommends that expenses for church operations—and their percentage of the overall budget—be clearly identified and evaluated each year.[2] This, of course, raises the question of what are appropriate expenditures in the overall operations of a church.

■ Explanation

Expenses and percentages of the budget will vary from church to church and be affected by building size, church age, systemic complexity, and demographic profile. But our experience over the last three decades has provided some rules of thumb that financial managers may find helpful, in addition to the rules for budgeting for evangelism and staff we have given previously.

Education. Between 10 and 15 percent of a church's total budget should go to educational ministries and program support. This may be higher in a church with a large traditional Sunday school program, or lower in churches that emphasize small groups. This category may include expenditures for study materials, curriculum, teacher/leader training and materials, and equipment purchase.

International missions. Between 10 and 15 percent of a church's budget should go to international missions. Many churches that raise money for foreign missions through special offerings give between 15 and 20 percent of their total budget. A few passionate churches dedicate between 40 and 50 percent of the budget to missions but, by doing so, may encounter problems in funding their own local ministry.

Fixed costs. Between 10 and 15 percent of a church's total budget should go to fixed costs, such as insurance, maintenance, rent, telephone, taxes, and utilities.

Mortgage and debt reduction. Between 15 and 25 percent of a church's budget should be allocated to pay the mortgage and reduce debt. Ideally the cost of debt service does not take more than 15 percent of the total budget, but in today's economy 25 percent is not unusual. If the amount grows beyond 25 percent, it usually hampers church effectiveness by sapping funds from direct ministry.

■ What You Can Do about It

There are many similarities between a church budget and a family budget. The process of developing both reminds us that there is seldom enough money to do all that we would like. Yet a budget is the best way to be a wise steward of the money we do manage. When there is not enough to go around, it forces us to prioritize. What do we *need* to have, and what is just *nice* to have? What are creative ways we can save money? How can we increase our cash flow to carry out greater ministry?

One way to lower costs is to bring some services in-house. If you currently use a cleaning service, you could save money if members volunteered to clean the building. What about outside work—mowing, gardening, painting? Could volunteers do this work?

On the other hand, sometimes money can be saved by outsourcing work. If you pay someone to answer a few incoming calls, explore the possibility of an outside answering service whose professional attendant will connect incoming calls for a low fee. Or an electronic phone director may be an option. Are you being most efficient with your printing of weekly programs and/or bulletins? Explore whether duplication costs are less expensive when done in-house or when they are outsourced.

Installing motion-activated light switches in bathrooms, hallways, closets, and other rooms can save hundreds of dollars in a year's time. Programmable thermostats can efficiently control heat and air-conditioning. Compact fluorescent lights use one-fifth to one-third less power and last eight to fifteen times longer than incandescent bulbs. Ask your local utility company to send a representative to inspect your building and make suggestions for how to save money on the utility bill.

When planning to build, use a good fund-raising company that specializes in this area. If it's been at least three years since your initial fund-raising program, do a second one, dedicating all the money raised to paying off the current debt, showing how doing so will free up money for new ministry and outreach. Consider restructuring or refinancing your loans to reduce the monthly payments.

Be conservative when purchasing furniture, computer equipment, or vehicles; negotiating leases; and hiring staff. Remember, the less money you spend on expenses, the more money will be available for ministry.

#77   THE FIVE POCKETS RULE

Focus on the five motivations people have for giving to a local church.

■ Introduction

A helpful way to understand people's different motivations for financial giving is to think about their five different "pockets." With an understanding of these pockets you can focus your financial giving opportunities on one or more of these pockets, and thus provide members a chance to give to their passion rather than just to a budget.

■ Explanation

The first pocket people give from is the *bill pocket*. This represents money that is contributed to the general fund to help the church pay its regular bills. Utilities, mortgage, salaries, and maintenance are paid from this pocket. People in the Builder generation (those born before 1945) are more likely than younger people to support such institutional budgets and needs.

The second pocket is the *missions pocket*. People reach into this pocket to help support missionaries and mission agencies engaged in the Great Commission in foreign countries. People with firsthand experience, often former missionaries, are so motivated by foreign missions that they want most of their giving to go to this cause. Local community outreach can also be in this pocket.

The third pocket is the *education pocket*. Some people like to support universities, colleges, seminaries, and Christian schools. Their commitment to education motivates them to reach deeply into this pocket to help pay for tuition, scholarships, libraries, classrooms, computers, and a host of other educational endeavors.

The fourth pocket is the *benevolence pocket*. Caring for the poor and needy has been a long-term concern of Christians. Jesus required his followers to care for those with needs, and some people in your congregation have deep concerns in this area. They dig deep into the benevolence pocket to support food banks, women's shelters, and medical clinics.

The fifth pocket is the *building pocket*. Some people like to give to bricks and mortar. There is a sense of permanence in a building that can transcend changes in time and generations. People who are more task-oriented and institutionally oriented (versus people-oriented) are motivated to give larger amounts of money to a building fund.

■ What You Can Do about It

Sharing a need and providing an opportunity in all five of these areas gives people the chance to give out of desire rather than duty. Giving should be joyful. The more opportunities people have to give out of passion, the more likely their giving will be joyful.

Allowing and even encouraging people to give to multiple funds actually results in more money given to the overall mission of the church. Financial consultants have found that money in one pocket will not likely be given to a different pocket cause. For example, a person who finds fulfillment giving to a building project will not give that same amount to missions. Nor is a person who prefers giving to people in need going to find the same joy in giving to a building program.

Try balancing the giving opportunities presented to your members among these five pockets, thus connecting with all the motivations that cause people to give to the church. If you don't have well-balanced stewardship opportunities, you are probably losing money that could be used for greater ministry.

#78 THE FUNDING VISION RULE

People give more to pursue vision than to pay bills.

■ Introduction

It is an old, but still accurate, truism: Money follows great ideas. If a lack of financial resources seems to be a regular condition in your church, the chances are good that you don't have a money problem—you have a vision problem. This vision rule applies to each of the five areas described in #77, The Five Pockets Rule.

■ Explanation

Victor Frankl, noted Jewish psychologist and survivor of a German concentration camp, wrote the insightful book *Man's Search for Meaning*. In the book Frankl recalls those in the camp who did and those who did not make it out. While most had no choice of their destiny once they arrived at Auschwitz, some were kept alive to service the needs of the camp. Among those who lived through the terrible ordeal rather than commit suicide in those hellish conditions, Frankl found a common thread, a trait essential to their survival. All those who made it through had something significant yet to do in their future. "It is a peculiarity of mankind," Frankl later wrote, "that we can only live by looking to the future. This is our salvation, even in the most difficult moments of our existence."[3] A dream or vision keeps people focused on the future. Especially in the hard times, a dream is essential. And whether it is an individual, a family, a nation, or a church, without a vision the people perish (Prov. 29:18 KJV).

Leading a focused, effective, growing church is not easy. In fact, it is easier to lead a stagnant, ingrown, plateaued church. But the excitement and challenge of a pursued vision makes the journey worthwhile, and is far more likely to change lives and make disciples. The New Oxford Dictionary defines a vision as "a cherished ambition, aspiration, or ideal." "It is that vision," observes Donald McGavran, one of history's most noted missiologists, "that compels the pilgrimage."[4]

■ What You Can Do about It

The pursuit of a vision requires the *existence* of a vision. The first priority, therefore, is to identify a vision for your church. In reality you are not looking for just any vision. You are seeking to discover God's unique vision for your church. Make it a part of your regular prayer life that God reveal his unfolding vision to you and your church. Your attitude and prayer should reflect the prophet Balaam's words, who wished to be "one who hears the words of God, who sees a vision from the Almighty, who falls prostrate, and whose eyes are opened" (Num. 24:4).

Many authors in the field of spiritual gifts suggest there is a spiritual gift of vision. Others identify it as the gift of faith. In either case, the gift is "the special ability that God gives to certain members of the Body of Christ to discern with extraordinary confidence the will and purposes of God for the future of His work."[5] There are some people in your church with the gift of faith or vision. Do you know who they are? Are you tapping into their special giftedness to see God's purposes identified and then pursued in the future of your church? Serving on a "dream team," comprised of people with the gift of faith who are seeking God's vision, can be very inspiring. Following prayer, here are a few questions to spark the conversation in such a group about discovering God's vision:

- How does God want to express himself through this church in this community?
- If our church building burned down, would we rebuild it to be the same? If not, what would we change?
- If we were starting our church from scratch, what would we do differently?
- If our church lived up to God's expectation, in five years we would _____ [fill in the blank].

Or here's a different approach. Try this activity with different groups throughout the church (classes, small groups, boards, and committees). It's a great weekend leadership retreat activity.

- Begin by reviewing God's priorities as found in Scripture. The Great Commission in Matthew 28:19–20 is a great place to start. Check out Matthew 16:18; John 20:21, 23; Acts 1:8; and Ephesians 4:11–16. Ask participants for other verses or parables of Jesus that illustrate God's priorities.
- Then do some dreaming about your church. Take a few moments to have group members clear their mind. Ask each person to work independently and imagine their church five years from today. Have them think about some or all of the following areas, and then write down a dream about each one:

  worship

  education

  evangelism

membership size

facility

member involvement

other

- Once everyone is done, go around the room and have members share their dream for the first category (worship). If a person doesn't have a statement for that particular category, it's fine to pass. After everyone has finished, discuss common elements heard from participants and write down some of those vision ideas. Keep in mind God's purposes for the church (as studied earlier) and be sure the vision statement is related.
- Then go on to the next category and repeat the process.
- Finally, if people have dream ideas that were not mentioned in the above categories, encourage them to share these as well. Keep all the notes from this exercise and the various groups that participate in it.

No time line can be developed that says how long it will take to confidently grasp God's vision for your church. But major steps forward should not be taken without such confidence. When you have determined your vision, begin communicating it to the congregation. Resist the urge to preach a sermon on the vision as your first step. Instead develop a complete diffusion plan.

Start by sharing the vision with the main church board and then gradually fan out over the entire church, expanding the communication to every level of leadership. Recruit and train respected laypersons as "ambassadors of the vision" to go to every home in the church over a monthlong period to communicate the vision and seek input from every member. Develop signs, banners, letterhead, advertisements, and a church web page that communicate and explain the new vision. Reference the vision in sermons throughout the year. Plan on at least one year to completely share and sell the vision to your congregation. Then when you ask for people to give financially to the church, tie giving to some aspect of the vision. If the people of the church own the vision, money will not be a problem.

Effective, healthy, growing churches believe their best days are still ahead, because that's where the vision is.

#79 THE MORTGAGE AND DEBT REDUCTION RULE

Between 15 and 25 percent of a church's budget should be used to pay the mortgage and reduce debt.

■ Introduction

Having adequate facilities is a common prerequisite for church growth in the United States. Studies of growing churches point out the need for sufficient seating, parking, and meeting space. For most congregations, this means operating with some level of debt as church buildings are financed.

■ Explanation

The cost of borrowing money for land acquisition and building construction is substantial. The emphasis should always be to keep the amount allocated for debt servicing as low as possible and the amount allocated for ministry as high as possible. Ideally the cost of loan repayment should be no more than 15 percent of the total church budget. Yet in today's economy it is not unusual to see churches allocating 30 percent of their income simply to repay mortgage payments. Our experience is that if the amount of a church's budget for debt reduction rises beyond 25 percent, it hampers the ministry by siphoning funds that could be used for more direct ministry.

Often churches launch a capital funds campaign to reduce the amount of the loan and free up funds for ministry. If you are above 25 percent of your budget in loan repayment, such an effort should be seriously considered.

■ What You Can Do about It

To keep the amount spent on debt service lower than 25 percent of your total budget, only go into debt for real property—that is, property that tends to increase in value. For all other items save or raise the money and pay cash. Second, raise as much money as possible so that you borrow the smallest amount necessary.

#80 THE FINANCIAL STABILITY RULE

A church needs a minimum of twenty-five giving units to be financially stable and independent.

■ Introduction

This rule applies primarily to new churches and/or small churches. However, every church must obviously have some kind of financial base from which to provide the essentials of effective ministry. The variables of meeting space (owned, rented, or donated) and salary (full-time, part-time, or volunteer) are the two most financially significant items for newer congregations. But at some point, unless the paradigm of doing church dramatically changes from the traditional structure of most churches today, the rule of thumb is that at least twenty-five giving units are needed for the church to be financially stable.

■ Explanation

A giving unit is considered to be an individual, couple, or family who contributes 10 percent of their income to the church. It is wise to track your total number of giving units as a measure of your church's health and strength.

The rule of thumb of at least twenty-five giving—tithing—units is based on the assumption that a church desires the services of a full-time pastor. Normally it takes at least that many giving units to financially support a full-time pastor and still have enough money to finance a basic church program. For example, let's assume that each of the twenty-five giving units donates 10 percent of their income to the church each year. Let's also assume that the church desires to provide a salary package equal to the average income of the twenty-five giving units. Finally, let's assume that the pastor's financial package makes up 40 percent of the church's total budget. Based on these assumptions, one budget scenario would look like this:

> Average income per giving unit: $60,000
>
> 10 percent tithe per giving unit: $6,000
>
> Number of units needed for a pastor's salary package: 10 (10 x $6,000 = $60,000)
>
> Number of additional units needed for ministry budget: 14 (14 x $6,000 = $84,000)
>
> Total number of giving units needed to support a full ministry: 24

Of course this simplified example assumes each giving unit is a tithing unit. If some people are giving less than $6,000, more giving units would be needed. But you can begin to see how the minimum critical mass for most churches is around twenty-five tithing units. It simply takes that many dollars to finance a significant and growing ministry.

■ What You Can Do about It

Research the following about your church:

- How many giving units do you presently have? Tax receipts or giving reports mailed at the first of each year can be a start in collecting this information.

The average offering collection should be factored in, although it is difficult to tell where all the funds are coming from.

- Determine the average amount given to your church per giving unit. Divide the total income from contributions by the total number of giving units for a functional estimate.

- Determine how many *potential* giving units are in your church. To do this, cross-reference your list of giving units with your regular mailing list to see who has not given to your church in the past year.

- Add the number of potential giving units to the number of present giving units and multiply the total by the average amount given last year per giving unit. This is the potential income to your church *if* all giving units were contributing at the average giving rate. Of course there are many variables, but *any* figure is better than operating in the blind.

Once you have this basic information, you will have a better handle on your financial situation, how to track giving, how to do stewardship campaigns, and projections for future planning.

#81 THE FUND-RAISING POTENTIAL RULE

Churches using a well-designed fund-raising campaign can raise up to three times their annual income.

■ Introduction

Suppose your church has just completed a feasibility study on a two-million-dollar building initiative. Your present income is five hundred thousand dollars, the church is healthy, and congregational giving is good. But there are no spare funds to pay for the project up front. The congregation is willing and able to support a capital fund-raising campaign. You are now at a crossroads. The decisions you make from here on will have major impacts on the future of your church. Should you launch a capital funds campaign? Who should do it? How much can you expect to take in? What are the risks? And you're thinking, *They never taught us about this in seminary!*

■ Explanation

According to most financial authorities, a church's indebtedness for capital building should not exceed 2.5 times your previous year's undesignated income (funds taken in that are not designated for a specific purpose). As an example, if a church had undesignated income of $500,000 for the last year, it would not be wise to enter into an indebtedness greater than $1,250,000.

Thus most churches seek to raise as much money as possible before turning to loans to fund facility development. One of the ways to do this is a fund-raising campaign. Over a three-year period the average church can raise an amount equal to its annual giving income. Churches that conduct their own campaigns tend to produce results at about 50 percent of the professionally led campaigns. These churches do well to raise an amount equal to their annual budget. Churches that use consultants often raise two or even three times their annual income in three-year commitments.

■ What You Can Do about It

Start by gathering information on the need for capital investments and surveying the potential costs compared with the potential ways to pay for the project. Using the information in the paragraph above, determine how much money your church could possibly raise through a fund-raising campaign.

We recommend working with a capital fund-raising organization throughout the entire process. There are a number of good church capital fund-raising organizations available.

> *National firms.* These organizations have a large consulting staff (generally twenty or more) with diverse experience among a large number of clients across the country.
>
> *Regional firms.* These companies focus on a specific geographic region; some specialize in one or two denominational groups within a region.
>
> *Local firms.* These are small consulting groups that focus on a specific area or denominational group or both.
>
> *Denominational resources.* This will vary by denomination, but have the advantage of intimate knowledge of the churches in their denomination.

Selecting a firm is straightforward. First, create a selection committee. The committee will contact firms and request introductory information on the company. Contact any churches you know that have recently had a capital funds drive and find out their experience. Then invite several firms to your church for on-site interviews. Be sure to allow plenty of time for the interview.

Whether you hire a professional organization or do it yourself, all good fund-raising campaigns should include the following:

> *Participation.* Give everyone something to do! No job is too small. People are needed to serve on a committee, ask for a gift, stuff envelopes, serve food.

Timing. Every campaign needs a predetermined beginning, middle, and end.

Giving. Everyone's gift is important.

Information. People always have questions. Why are we doing this? How did we get here? What is the goal? Is this what we are called to do? Have ready answers.

A clear goal. Members need to know when they have made it! Good records help bring good news.

Enthusiasm and celebration. When you succeed, part of God's purpose is accomplished! Take time to give thanks to God and to the people who worked so hard.

13

Ministry Rules for Change

By nature, people resist change. So *how* you introduce a new idea in your church will have as much influence on its eventual acceptance (or rejection) as *what* the idea actually is. Don't assume that your idea will be immediately accepted on its obvious merits. It will not. People are allergic to change.

Why don't people like change? Here are a few reasons:

- Some people don't feel a need to change.
- Many people prefer the status quo.
- A few cling to vested interests.
- Some distrust leadership.
- Many find change stressful.
- Some things have become sacred in their own right.

We recommend that you carefully think through your strategy for introducing a new idea *before* you announce it. This chapter has some rules of thumb we think you will find helpful for seeing an idea become a reality.

#82 THE EARLY ADOPTERS RULE

Find and work with the people who are more open to change.

■ Introduction

One of the rude awakenings for many new seminary graduates is the response they receive after introducing their first inspired idea for improved ministry. Their assumption is that most members of the church will recognize the proposal as the obviously good idea that it is and support the idea on its merits. If only it were so.

Knowing how people respond to a new idea can be very helpful to any church leader who wants to see the dream come true.

■ Explanation

Business studies have examined the "diffusion of innovation" and discovered there are predictable responses when a group of people are confronted with a new idea. The following bell curve illustrates the five categories into which people (such as a congregation) can be expected to fall:

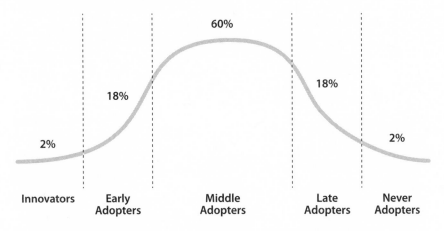

Innovators are the dreamers and visionaries in your church. They get more excited about future goals than past accomplishments. Innovators are not generally acknowledged as leaders or policy makers. Many have the spiritual gift of faith (1 Cor. 12:9).

Early adopters know a good idea when they see it. Their opinions are generally respected by others and they are influential in moving the church in new directions. Often early adopters receive credit for ideas that were not originally theirs. Many have the spiritual gift of wisdom (v. 8).

Middle adopters make up the majority of your congregation. They tend to react to the ideas of others rather than initiate their own. While these people are reasonable in their assessment of a new idea, they are more inclined to maintain the status quo and are more easily influenced by those opposing change than those supporting it.

Late adopters are the last in a church to support a new idea. In congregational and committee meetings, these people usually speak and vote against proposed changes. They may never acknowledge their acceptance of a new idea but will eventually go along if the majority supports it.

Never adopters seldom if ever accept a new idea. Their commitment is to the status quo and the past. If a change is adopted, they may sow discord and eventually leave the church if they don't get a following.

■ What You Can Do about It

There are several things to keep in mind when you introduce your next terrific idea:

Realize that not everyone will be happy. Innovators are on a collision course with never adopters. Early adopters are frustrated by late adopters. Middle adopters may even encourage disagreement so they can adequately consider both sides. Despite these differences, it is preferable to articulate opinions early, because if they're not expressed at the front end of a discussion, be assured you will hear them later (at a less favorable time).

Some members will leave. Don't think that avoiding controversy will avoid the loss of disenchanted members. David DeSelm, in the video *A Church for the 21st Century*, observes, "You're going to lose people even if you *don't* change."[1] He's right. If you add a new style worship service, for example, some stalwarts from the right side of the bell curve will leave. If you don't, some visionaries from the left side will leave. Don't ask the question "What can we do to avoid creating dissatisfied people who may leave?" because there is no answer. Rather, ask the question "Which dissatisfied people would we rather lose, the never adopters or the innovators?" If it's any consolation, neither group will drop out of church life when they leave your congregation. The visionaries go to more progressive churches, the stalwarts to more traditional ones. Whom would you rather keep?

The battle is for the middle adopters. You won't need to work very hard (if at all) to convince your innovators and early adopters of the value of your new idea. The late adopters will not be convinced before the idea actually becomes a reality. And the never adopters will never be convinced. But if you can sway the majority of middle adopters to support the initiative, the battle is won. Remember that middle adopters are more easily influenced by late adopters than by early adopters. Most middle adopters, while reasonable people, prefer the known to the unknown, the present certainty to the future's uncertainty. This does not mean middle adopters are closed to new ideas or can't catch the excitement of a new vision, but they're just normal people, with normal fears of the unknown. The majority of these people tend to vote for the status quo unless they are given a good reason to change or are assured that change will not result in the loss of something valued.

Make early adopters your allies. Generally early adopters are well respected in the church. (Often innovators are not.) Their words are given serious consideration and their leadership is usually followed. Make a list of these people and solicit their active support. Ask them to endorse the new idea in formal meetings and informal discussions. Explain that their conversations in the halls and on the telephone can influence (middle adopter) members more than anything else. And in board and committee meetings, let early adopters know that it will be their support that could make the difference between adoption or rejection.

Leading a church through the process of change is one of the great challenges pastors face in their career. Those who master the process find their ministry years to be much more fulfilling and rewarding. Eventually those who don't master the process of innovation conclude that the price of change is not worth the benefit and they remain in a stagnant and usually nongrowing church. We believe it is well worth your time to learn and apply the principles of successful change.

#83   THE SHORT-TERM CHANGE RULE

Introduce your idea as a short-term experiment rather than a long-term commitment.

■ Introduction

Funny how we humans can tolerate most anything if we know it will soon be over—giving blood, a giant roller coaster, exercise, jumping into a cold pool. But long-term commitment? Well, now it's time to go a little slower. Book club memberships are down. Magazine subscriptions are for shorter periods. Lease-option house contracts are increasing. Even the average age for marriage is rising. The modern mind-set is: Keep your options open. For better or worse, you can tap into this mind-set to increase the likelihood of your new idea being adopted.

■ Explanation

It's natural for people, including most church members, to be hesitant about long-term change. "Suppose the idea doesn't work?" they ask. "Why should we throw good money after bad?" But most would be willing to try a short-term experiment before they commit to an idea for the long term. We recommend that you don't introduce *long-term* change if you can help it. Regardless of what the change is, the more it is seen as having long-term implications, the less likely the congregation will adopt it.

Rather than long-term changes, introduce new ideas as short-term experiments with a beginning, an end, and an unbiased evaluation. Not only will this make it more likely the change will be adopted, it's just a lot safer for those introducing the change. Suppose your great new idea turns out to be a flop (impossible as that may seem). It's to your benefit, and all those who championed the new idea, to be able to cut your losses as soon as possible. And if the idea turns out to be a winner, then it will be much easier to make a case for extending the new program or activity for a longer term.

Another reason for the short-term approach is that we humans are more tolerant of change if it is a temporary situation. More members will support a provisional change than a permanent one. But usually over time people discover that the new way of doing things—that was once feared—has actually become more tolerable and perhaps even desirable. At that point the long-term change becomes both plausible and even preferable.

■ What You Can Do about It

When introducing your new idea, determine a trial period that will give the idea enough time to show its merits. Agree on a date at the end of that trial period to review and evaluate the results. Everyone who was affected by the change should be invited to this time of evaluation. Depending on the particular idea, three to four months is generally an adequate amount of time for the experiment.

Before you begin the trial, carefully document the present condition so that when the idea is eventually reviewed, you will have concrete measurements against which to compare and evaluate. The more factually and numerically the results can be described, the more objectively the results will be evaluated. You want to be able to say, "Look at the numbers; they clearly show what happened during the last four months." You don't want to be limited to, "I think it all went great," while someone else responds, "Well, I don't."

For example, suppose you have an idea of a new way to follow up with first-time visitors. Carefully research and document the visitor return rate *before* the new approach, and then track the figures for your visitor return rate *during* the four-month trial. Your evaluation of the new strategy at the end of the trial period should compare the numerical results. Did the visitor return rate change measurably? The more objective your evaluation can be, the less likely you will slip into subjective and unmeasurable opinions. If that does happen, innovators and early adopters will be in favor, while the middle, late, and never adopters (see #82, The Early Adopters Rule) will be against it.

#84 THE MEANS TO THE END RULE

Introduce the new idea as a way to reach an already agreed upon goal.

■ Introduction

One of the best reasons for a church to develop and adopt a mission (or purpose) statement is when it comes time for change. If previous thought, discussion, and prayer have gone into a church mission statement—and if the congregation has adopted it—then subsequent steps of change are more likely to be supported when they are positioned as a step toward this previously agreed-on purpose.

■ Explanation

Precedent makes a lot of decisions! Once you've "been there and done that," it's much easier to do it again the next time. So when your new idea becomes a way to achieve a goal that has already been agreed on, there will be less inclination for people to resist. The "what" has already been decided (in the church's purpose statement). Now it's just a matter of "how." If you introduce your new idea as a "how," it will be much easier to see the new idea adopted. For example, the bulletin of a church in Pasadena included a Q&A flyer about a new contemporary service the church was considering. The first question read: "Why are two worship service options being studied?" The answer was:

> Our Mission Statement states that we intend for ministry to be offered with a "diversity of options." This means any options consider the needs of our church family and those of our community. Both experience and research indicate that a more contemporary style of worship would allow us to have a significant impact on local people not presently a part of our church fellowship, nor of any other church fellowship.[2]

If your church does not have a purpose statement, you would do well to develop one. A good purpose statement defines the reason the church exists, and justifies the church's expenditure of time, money, and people. Without a mission or purpose statement, there is nothing to keep various groups and departments from simply doing their own thing and diverting the church's limited resources to activities that do not contribute to the church's unwritten purpose.

■ What You Can Do about It

First, become familiar with your church's purpose statement. Learn when it was created and the process by which the church developed and adopted it. Find the place(s) in the purpose statement that best supports the new idea you will be proposing. If you were not personally involved in the development and adoption of this purpose statement, speak with several people in the church who were. Find out all you can about how it was developed and who initiated the process. Learn about how the purpose statement was formally adopted and what the outcome of the vote was.

Next, write out your initial recommendation and generously quote the church's purpose statement. In the rationale for your new idea or proposal, describe how the recommendation is actually a means to an end, with the "end" having already been agreed upon in the church's purpose statement and, of course, in Scripture.

If the church does not have a purpose statement, you may want to suggest that creating one would be an important activity. Here are the elements and an example of a church's purpose statement:

Elements of a Purpose Statement

1. *Biblical understanding.* What you are seeking to accomplish must include God's priorities as expressed through his Word.
2. *Geographic area.* The early church, in response to the Lord's command, began in Jerusalem, then moved to Judea, then Samaria, and then "the uttermost part of the earth" (Acts 1:8 KJV). A purpose statement should define your Jerusalem, your Judea, and the world in which you are called to minister.
3. *Target audience.* A good purpose statement identifies the people groups that are the focus of your ministry. No church can be everything to everyone. Who are the specific people you feel God has equipped you to reach? That is, what are your strengths, and how will you be good stewards of the resources you have been given?
4. *Major activities.* From your understanding of Scripture, your geographic community, and the resources God has given you, what will be the means and methods through which God uses your church for his purpose?
5. *Expected results.* As a result of the above activities, with the target population you have defined, what are the results you trust God will provide?

A Sample Purpose Statement

Here's a sample of a church's well-written purpose statement. Look for the above five elements:

Believing that our church has been called of God to make disciples, and it is our greatest privilege and responsibility, it is our purpose to equip our members in the task of making disciples from among our family, friends, and business acquaintances in Centerville and throughout the world.

To accomplish this, we will focus our worship, our preaching, our teaching, our fellowship, and our outreach towards motivating, training, and deploying people in such a way as their full potential in making disciples will be achieved.

#85 THE GOOD MATH RULE

Introduce your new idea as an addition, not a substitution.

■ Introduction

Have you ever noticed how people in your worship service usually sit in the same place Sunday after Sunday, when any seat would be equally good? Before you smirk at those who act in such a habitual manner, ask yourself, *Do I drive to work the same way every day? Do I have the same routine every Saturday morning? Do family members sit in the same place around the dinner table?* We are all creatures of habit and we like the comfort and security of the familiar. When it comes time to introduce a new idea in your church, remember this phenomenon because it can be either your ally or your adversary.

■ Explanation

People often resist a new idea for fear of losing the comfort of the familiar. Because of this character trait of human nature, any change that is perceived to require giving up the known for the unknown will be uncomfortable and often resisted.

On the other hand, if you can honestly convince those middle and late adopters in your church that the new idea will not cause them to lose whatever it is they value, then their response will more likely be, "Okay, go ahead [as long as it doesn't bother me]." You are not necessarily looking for active support from all the middle or late adopters. From some, you just need their tolerance. And you're more likely to get it if the change doesn't rock their boat.

Let's suppose you want to introduce a more contemporary worship service to connect with new kinds of people. You have the choice of either adding a new service or changing the existing one. If you apply The Good Math Rule, the best approach will be to add a new service while assuring longtime members that their present, familiar service will not be changed. By choosing this approach, you have created more choices for more people groups, while avoiding a potential confrontation with those who know and love the original service and style.

▪ What You Can Do about It

Consider what ministry areas and people in the church your new idea will affect. Who is most likely to have a strong opinion about the change and why? Think about what loss they might feel if the new idea were to be implemented, and consider whether The Good Math Rule could be applied in a way that would avoid that perceived loss.

The best time and way to raise the topic of change with those who will be affected is through individual conversations *before* having public exchanges. Begin your conversations by affirming the person's contribution to the church and your assumption that they, like you, want to see the church provide the best possible opportunities for spiritual growth to all members. Go on to explain your commitment, which you hope they share, to providing the same spiritual growth opportunities to others in the community who have yet to be reached. Perhaps review some of the cases of those who have recently come into the church and how their lives have been positively affected because of church members who were willing to open the family of God to new family members.

In the conversation, focus on the Christ-ordained *mission* of the church (that is, to make disciples) and the contradictory view that the church exists only as a service to present members. William Temple, Archbishop of Canterbury, once said: "The church is the only organization that exists for the benefit of those who are not its members." God's people are called to be outwardly focused, seeking to bring others into a relationship with Jesus and to display God's kingdom on earth through works of love, peace, and justice.

Explain that you are considering an idea that will give the church greater outreach to the community, as identified in the purpose statement. But you realize that there is much history they have experienced in this church, and they probably find a sense of security in the church ministry and activities.

Ask for their ideas (see #86, The Soliciting Enhancements Rule) on how this possible change could be introduced without disrupting too much of the status quo. Sometimes it is easier for the person to talk about others in the church rather than themselves, even though their own position is reflected in those others.

Don't try to arrive at a commitment from people in one meeting. The bigger the change, and the larger the psychological impact, the longer they will need to think about it. Set up another meeting to continue the conversation and respond to any ideas or questions they may have.

When it appears that the person(s) is on board, ask for his or her continued support in public and private gatherings. Hopefully the new idea will be a both-and scenario rather than either-or.

#86 THE SOLICITING ENHANCEMENTS RULE

To get the support of people for your new idea, ask for help in improving it.

■ Introduction

A characteristic of human nature is that good goals are *my* goals, bad goals are *your* goals! Getting people to adopt a new idea that is not their new idea can be challenging for any leader. But if people feel they have had a part in developing the idea, then it becomes their idea and they are more likely not only to support it but also to advocate for it. So an important key to seeing a new idea adopted is to create ownership of the idea by people who have influence.

■ Explanation

How do you create goal ownership among members? One way is to distinguish between *strategy* and *tactics*. Strategy is the "what"; tactics are the "how." As a strategic leader, you should have a sense of the vision of your church. You are the one, as a conduit of God's heart and vision, who will take the primary role in leading the church.

But don't spend too much time on the "how" of getting there. Not only is micromanaging the tactics a poor management technique, but you also miss a great opportunity to create goal ownership. Broad involvement in the process will result in a higher level of support of the new idea. And goal ownership means they are "good goals"! For example, suppose you have the nice problem of inadequate parking on Sunday morning, and your strategy is to maximize ministry and outreach in your community. A necessary aspect of executing that strategy is having enough parking for people to worship. But rather than present your solution of enlarging the parking lot, ask the tactical question: "How could we solve our parking situation so more people can worship with us on Sunday morning?" You will probably get a variety of possible solutions, such as provide valet parking, expand the parking lot, begin a second service, buy a bus. Not all ideas may be tactically effective. But if you trust the judgment of your leaders, the good ideas will come to the surface. And best of all, there will be a high level of ownership as people analyze the problem and contribute to the solution. Remember, strategy is the *what*; tactics are the *how*. Generals focus on strategy for mission success.

This is not to say that you turn over all the how-to decisions to others. Usually pastors have more experience and exposure to tactical approaches than do church members. And effective tactics are an important part of an effective church. So it's a balance between the (desirable) process of involving people, and the (undesirable) process of micromanaging them.

■ What You Can Do about It

Begin with a clear and honest assessment of the change you are thinking about proposing. Is it a strategic issue (which you should be involved in) or a tactical matter (which you may want to leave to others)? For example, is starting a new-style worship service a strategic goal or a tactical one? It's probably a tactical concern, with the strategic issue being that of reaching new groups of people in your community.

The best place for a discussion on tactics is a group of five to eight people, or perhaps several groups of this size. Don't bring a group of twenty-five people together to discuss a topic if you want each person to contribute. Have three groups, instead. Prior to the discussion, appoint a recorder; or, better yet, record the meeting with everyone's understanding and permission. Then have the session transcribed. This gives you a record of who said what, and the various ideas and suggestions that came out of the meeting. Finally, refine the transcript into a concise report.

Tell the group that you will be distributing a summary of the meeting and ask them to share any additional ideas that have come to their mind since the meeting. Thank them for their involvement and ideas and ask for their support if and when the new idea comes before the larger church body.

#87 THE HOMEOSTASIS RULE

The longer a church has gone without growth,
the harder it is to begin new growth.

■ Introduction

Homeostasis is the tendency of churches, as well as other organizations and organisms, to seek stability and equilibrium. The practical implication is that congregations tend to prefer safety over risk, survival over mission, stability over change. When homeostasis—the lack of new growth—occurs for five or more years, it becomes increasingly difficult to begin a new pattern of growth.

■ Explanation

Some level of stability is, of course, necessary for any church to exist. Constant change can be endured for only a limited amount of time before people and churches need to rest. For example, when churches go through successive building programs, the people will want, and need, a time of rest. (Even God rested after "building" his creation!) One fund-raising campaign is good, a second is okay, but a congregation, in search of homeostasis, will resist a third.

However, extended homeostasis is not healthy. Churches are designed for mission, not maintenance. When a church seeks stability (homeostasis), unseen forces begin to destroy it from within:

- It becomes increasingly comfortable to remain stagnant. It's like most of us and exercise—if we stop for a while, it's increasingly difficult to get started again.
- A static church, by definition, is not growing. And a church that is not growing is in some stage of dying.
- The lack of mission focus creates an increasingly self-centered focus, and a church's time, attention, prayer, and budget are spent on itself.
- Depending on how long a church has clung to the status quo, there will be an increasing discomfort when change is introduced. Thus there may actually be some value in change simply for change's sake.

The best way to avoid extended homeostasis is to constantly hold up and pursue your mission. A healthy mission keeps a church focused beyond itself. It is only as churches change and grow by reaching out in mission to a lost world that they thrive. "Unless a grain of wheat falls into the earth and dies, it remains alone; but if it dies, it bears much fruit" (John 12:24 ESV).

We have found that when a church's growth stalls for more than five years, only 20 percent are able to return to their previous level of growth within the next five years. You can't steer a parked car.

■ What You Can Do about It

The key to avoiding homeostasis and stagnation is to continuously lay the groundwork for future accomplishment. The following ideas may get you thinking about how to keep your church going and growing:

- Graph the weekly and monthly worship attendance in your church. The best predictor of what's going to happen in the coming three years is what has happened in the last three years. Extend a dotted line on your graph to represent the continuation of the trend from the past several years.

- Hold an annual planning retreat to review the growth pattern of the church and its various ministry areas (youth, music, education, etc.). Set some realistic growth goals for each ministry area in the coming year and then identify people or groups who are willing to develop specific plans to achieve those goals.
- Encourage each ministry area to begin at least one new initiative in the coming year (while perhaps closing down a nonproductive function). Ministries and programs tend to lose their impact after seven to ten years. Thus new ministries keep a church moving forward rather than standing still.
- Make changes even if they appear small. Leaders often overestimate what can be accomplished in one year and underestimate what can be done in five years. Never dismiss the power of small changes. Five years from now you'll look back and discover that more has been accomplished than you dared to dream.
- Growing churches tend to use "episodic" planning—a continuous process of dreaming, strategizing, planning, and changing. Change isn't just a once every year (or every few years) activity. With regular updates and changes, you will avoid the congregational lethargy that accompanies homeostasis. The world changes rapidly; so should your ministry.

#88 THE DISCONTENTMENT RULE

To increase the likelihood of adopting a new idea, sow seeds of creative discontent.

■ Introduction

For many longtime members, one of the most appealing things about their church is its predictability. Things are the same yesterday, today, and forever. (Of course this may be one of the primary reasons the church is not growing.) But it is the desire to maintain this stability that causes some to resist change. "The solution," says Aubrey Malphurs, "is to help those people and their churches discover that everything is not all right."[3] Voluntary change happens only when there is sufficient discontent with the status quo.

■ Explanation

Creating and nurturing vision is one of the most important roles a pastor can have in a healthy, growing church. As you promote buy-in to your new idea, share the greater ministry God desires through your church and the greater number of people he wants to touch. Point out that simply to continue the present course will not, in all likelihood, realize such a dream.

There is a difference between *destructive* discontent and *constructive* discontent. Destructive discontent is a desire to leave the present for a more appealing past. Constructive discontent is a desire to leave the present for a more appealing future. Moses experienced both as he led the Israelites toward the Promised Land. During their time in Egypt, probably few Israelites had a desire to stay in the oppressive slavery under which they had lived for generations. When Moses gave the word to pack up and prepare to leave, the anticipation must have been almost palpable!

But it wasn't long before their constructive discontent was replaced by destructive discontent: "The whole congregation of the people of Israel grumbled against Moses and Aaron in the wilderness" (Exod. 16:2 ESV). "Who will give us meat to eat? We remember the fish which we used to eat free in Egypt, the cucumbers and the melons and the leeks and the onions and the garlic, but now our appetite is gone. There is nothing at all to look at except this manna" (Num. 11:4–6 NASB).

Obviously constructive discontent is far more productive and likely to move a congregation forward with anticipation and enthusiasm. Constructive discontent is the ability to see a need for improvement and the ability to see (or sometimes just desire) a way to make things better. Only when people see a problem will they be interested in finding a solution.

■ What You Can Do about It

Change is what it takes to get from here to there. Creative discontent is the longing to be there rather than here, and a desire to figure out how to get there. As a result, it is up to the change agent to create such a tantalizing picture of *there* that people are willing to leave *here*.

This is essentially the process of vision-casting. Here are some guidelines for communicating a vision to your congregation:

1. *Who we are.* Every church member should have a clear understanding of the purpose of Christ's greater church and how their congregation relates to it.
2. *Where we are now.* An honest description of the church's present position is important. Charts and graphs are helpful in describing where the church is in its life cycle.
3. *Where we are going.* Specific goals give a clear personification of the purpose. Purpose without goals is like a ship without a rudder.
4. *Why we are going there.* The bottom-line "business" of the church is helping people become Christlike. Christ told us to go and make disciples. It's that simple.

5. *What people can do.* The image of the body of Christ is one in which every part is functioning and contributing to the overall health of the body. This is the way it should be in each local church.

6. *What the rewards will be.* The rewards are the spiritual and emotional benefits of fulfilling the vision that God has for us. Imagine what it will be like when Jesus says, "Well done, good and faithful servant."

#89 THE LEADERS FIRST RULE

To successfully introduce change in a church, start with the leaders.

■ Introduction

The quickest way to identify leaders is to look behind them. If someone is following, the person is a leader. If no one is following, the person is not a leader. It's that simple. (This leadership test applies to pastors as well.) The best way to get a group of people to endorse a change proposal is to get the (formal and informal) church leaders to endorse the proposal. It makes the task of moving a group forward much easier when you can move the leaders forward. When you do, the rest will follow.

■ Explanation

"A wise leader," observes Doug Murren, "will subscribe to a basic 3-step process in presenting new directions to the church: (1) explain the idea to the core group, (2) collaborate with the committed workers, and (3) share with the entire congregation."[4] The diagram on page 231 visualizes the appropriate points and sequence for introducing a new idea to the people in a church.

Many churches have informal leaders who are influencers even though they may not have a formal position in the church. These people should obviously receive attention, and in the sequence on the illustration fit between Church Leadership Board and Other Boards.

■ What You Can Do about It

Enlarge the chart "Where Do They Stand" and list each person in each group from the "Circles of Leadership" illustration. In the second column of the chart note the

Circles of Leadership

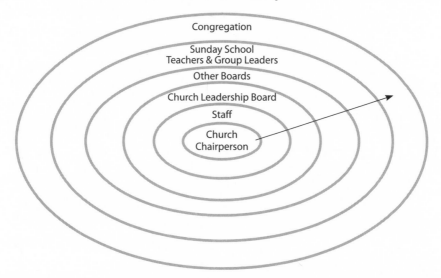

group they are in. Next, note when and where the person was introduced to the new idea. Finally, write any comments regarding the person's response to the idea.

Where Do They Stand?

Name	Group	Date	Response

Keep the chart current as you speak with your leaders about the new idea. Summarize their comments and responses and make notes to yourself on appropriate follow-up. Such a list will help you keep track of whom you have spoken with and their opinions, whom you need to speak to, and what steps you need to take for the successful adoption of your great new idea!

14

Ministry Rules for Revitalization

There are different reasons that churches get to the point of needing revitalization. Sometimes it is spiritual stagnation that deadens the passion for outreach or even for welcoming visitors. Other times it is institutionalization where the priority of people, time, and money has become substantially self-centered. It may be a church quarrel, split, or scandal that has distracted the church's focus from its priorities. Whatever the reason, it's no fun being in a church that needs renewal. And the longer a church goes in need of revitalization, the less likely it seems that it will happen. The words of Jesus to the church in Ephesus come to mind: "But I hold this against you, that you do not love as you did at first. Remember then how far you have fallen. Repent and live as you lived at first. Otherwise, if your heart remains unchanged, I shall come to you and remove your lampstand from its place" (Rev. 2:4–5 Phillips).

Revitalizing a church is not so simple that a few rules from a book will make it happen. Congregational renewal happens when there is spiritual renewal among church leaders and members. Such renewal, of course, requires the Holy Spirit's participation more than any other factor.

In this chapter we would like to suggest a few rules of thumb that can be part of the complex process of church revitalization. In fact, we believe that the ideas in this chapter will be helpful to any church, regardless of its spiritual temperature. For example, few who study the life, growth, and health of the local church would disagree with William McConnell's statement: "The revitalization process begins and ends with prayer. The part in the middle is also supported with prayer. Prayer is the glue that holds the church together during this difficult process."[1] Thus our first rule of thumb focuses on prayer.

#90 THE MONTHLY PRAYER RULE

Every church member should be prayed for at least once every month.

■ Introduction

How do you feel when someone prays for you or for someone close to you? Most people feel honored, valued, grateful, loved. Every member and regular attender in your church should have that feeling every month.

■ Explanation

Healthy churches are constant in prayer. Consider the apostle Paul's words to the Christians at Ephesus: "For this reason, because I have heard of your faith in the Lord Jesus and your love toward all the saints, I do not cease to give thanks for you, remembering you in my prayers" (Eph. 1:15–16 ESV). Notice Paul's comment about *not ceasing* to pray for those in the Ephesian church. Or consider Paul's words to the believers in the church at Rome: "Rejoice in hope, be patient in tribulation, be constant in prayer" (Rom. 12:12 ESV).

Sporadic prayer will not keep (or get) a church healthy. It must be an ongoing lifestyle. Yet few churches provide a systematic way for members to integrate regular prayer into their life or into the life of their congregation. Usually prayer requests are shared in small groups, children's or adult classes, and occasionally in larger church gatherings. But this hit-or-miss approach includes only those who take the initiative—or have the nerve—to make their prayer requests public. And once the event passes, the prayed-for, as well as the prayer requests, tend to be forgotten.

What if each member and family in your church were prayed for—and knew they were being prayed for—specifically *each month*? What spiritual energy would be generated!

■ What You Can Do about It

Here's an idea that could transform—and revitalize—your congregation: Contact each member/attendee each month and ask what special concerns they have for which the church could pray. Then petition God each month on their behalf. It will change your church! Here are a few thoughts on the logistical considerations behind setting up such a powerful ministry:

- The ministry should be able to solicit and receive monthly prayer requests from members, present these prayer requests to God, and track answers to prayer.
- Begin by creating a "mock-up" of a three-panel brochure that describes this new prayer ministry. Include an answer to the traditional questions of What? Why? When? How? Who? Once you have described the prayer ministry in a brochure, it will be easier to think through the dynamics of organizing such a systematic prayer process.
- Brainstorm a name for the prayer ministry. One church called theirs "I Thought You'd Never Ask." A creative name, but you can do better.
- As you develop your prayer system, consider issues such as these: Do you want a team of intercessors to pray for all the requests or do you want to invite a larger number of members and attendees to pray? How do you handle confidential prayer requests? Do you want to track people's prayer requests over a period of months, as well as answers to prayers? Do you want to have one person praying for the same family over a period of months or have a different person praying each month? What is the best way to invite members to be a part of the process? How are members contacted each month to obtain their prayer requests? How do people opt out if they no longer wish to participate? How do newcomers opt in during the year?
- Consider a monthlong focus on how to pray as you introduce the prayer emphasis. This could include a sermon series, adult Bible classes, children's classes, and small groups. Topics might include:

  different kinds of prayer

  how to pray for others

  are prayers always answered?

  what do we pray for?
- The task force should discuss how to manage the program from month to month. You may want to try a three-month test with some people willing to be "guinea pigs" and see what you learn.
- Set a date for launching the program. Remember, things usually take longer than you expect.

In 2 Corinthians 1:8–10, Paul describes his brush with death, and then in verse 11 says: "And you are helping us by praying for us. Then many people will give thanks because God has graciously answered so many prayers" (NLT). Praying for others is a great way to enhance the spiritual maturity of your corporate body and individual members.

#91 THE TIME FOR RENEWAL RULE

It takes four to seven years to completely renew a church.

■ Introduction

Revitalizing a church takes time. While pastors may hope (and in exceptional cases it has happened) that the Holy Spirit sweeps into the building and turns the church around on a dime, more often renewing a church calls for exercising one of the fruit of the Spirit—patience. Most church leaders overestimate the revitalization results that can be expected in one year and underestimate what can be seen in five. Actually, experience indicates that four to seven years is the average time range required for a compete church makeover.

■ Explanation

The time necessary to revitalize a church will be affected by many issues:

- *Age of the church*. The older the church, the more difficult (and, thus, longer) the revitalization process. The challenge increases dramatically once the church is over fifty years old.
- *Length of decline*. The longer the decline, the longer the revitalization will take. Decline of more than twenty years is like cancer that has moved to the lymph nodes; at that point, revitalization is much more difficult.
- *Pastor's intervention skills*. The characteristics of a pastor that are needed to revitalize a church are not unlike the characteristics needed of a successful church planter—both are endeavoring to fan a small spark into a roaring flame. High on our list are the following qualities:

    strong commitment to making disciples

    clear vision of a better tomorrow

    strength in initiating

    willingness to risk

    emotionally stable

    strong relational skills

    a good listener

    motivated by results

    able to influence others

enthusiastic

able to focus on details

a critical and objective thinker

Sounds like superman, doesn't it? Well, that's about what it takes!

- *Willingness of the congregation to change.* The decision by members to commit to revitalizing their own church—and the change that will inevitably accompany it—is not easy. For many it is akin to admitting failure. For all, it draws a line in the sand; people are either for it or against it. If a majority of the congregation is not willing to change, the pastor should consider investing his or her efforts elsewhere, since the harvest is great but the workers are few (Luke 10:2).
- *Ability of the congregation to change.* Sincere, well-meaning people may be willing to change but later discover that they are simply unable. "When you said loud music, Pastor, I didn't expect it to be *that* loud. And I don't even know the words! I'm sorry. I know this change is for the good of our church. But I just can't stay."
- *Location of the church.* Churches in larger towns or cities take less time for renewal—four to seven years. Churches in smaller towns or rural communities need longer for a complete turnaround—ten to fifteen years. This is due to the transiency rates of people in the surrounding community. The slower the rate of people relocating, the longer it takes to build a new vision and leadership in a congregation.

■ What You Can Do about It

Realize that revitalizing a church is one of the most difficult endeavors a pastor and/or church leader can undertake. In fact, one of the more common prescriptions for churches needing revitalization is to simply close the church down and then start a new one. It's just easier to have a baby than to raise the dead! While churches that need revitalizing are not necessarily all dead, neither are they newborns with vision and energy and contagious enthusiasm for life.

The first requirement in leading a turnaround church is a willingness to be present for the long haul—seven years at least. The rule of thumb for the time a pastor should be in a church (see #62, The Pastoral Tenure Rule) applies even more to revitalizing a church.

The good news is that the longer you stay at a church, the more people will join under your administration and the easier it will be to lead the church forward. People who have no history with the church, and only one pastor, are much more open to change and new ideas. And they are more willing to follow the only pastor they have known.

We suggest that you find at least three pastors who have successfully led turn-around churches and spend some serious time with them. If possible, follow them around for a week if they are still at their turned-around church. Ask questions like: What are the most important things to know in revitalizing a church? Where and how did you begin? When did you start to see progress? Did you have setbacks along the way? What were those setbacks, and how did you deal with them? What would you do differently?

Talk to new members who joined the church during the revitalization experience. Ask questions like: How did you hear about the church, and what attracted you to it? Did you have any misgivings at first? Do you still? What would you suggest to a church that wanted to be revitalized?

During the entire revitalization process, keep a journal. The experiences you will have in the next seven years are the essence of a great book, series of articles or lectures to benefit those who will follow you. There will always be the need for guidance on revitalizing churches.

#92   THE SUCCESSFUL MERGER RULE

The mathematics of church mergers is 1 + 1 = 1.

■ Introduction

These are not the best of times for churches in the Western world. The total number of congregations is in rather dramatic decline. Responding to this difficult situation, some churches are seeking revitalization through merger with another church. Others are merging simply to avoid death. Each year in the United States, between one and two thousand churches merge—about ½ percent of all Protestant congregations. Is merging two (or sometimes more) churches an option for revitalization?

■ Explanation

Why merge? Churches give many different reasons for merging:

- a desire to better use limited resources
- a changing neighborhood
- a desire to demonstrate Christian unity
- a hope for expanded ministry
- a way to address church needs

- geographical proximity
- perpetuate denominational presence
- desperation for survival
- a catastrophe or crisis in the church
- a weak church plant
- a need to reduce expenses
- hope for increased membership
- a need for more financial resources
- passion for specialized pastors
- a shortage of pastors

As a rule, merging churches doesn't work. Consolidating two sick churches does not bring life, it simply prolongs death. If a church with 50 worshipers and a church with 150 worshipers merge, 3 years later the reconfigured church will typically have 150 worshipers. In other words, there is usually a net loss in merging two congregations. Thus the rule of thumb for church mergers is 1 + 1 = 1.

Here are ten reasons that most church mergers fail:

1. The merger was motivated by the wrong reasons. Mergers that occur because of a desire to survive are prone to fail.
2. The differences in traditions, values, styles, cultures, priorities, and theology become obstacles—even with churches of the same denomination. Like many marriages, significant differences do not surface until after the merger.
3. The efficient use of property and facilities was not realized.
4. The expectations were too high. Dreams of higher attendance, more programs, and greater optimism are seldom met.
5. There is a sense of intrusion when one congregation moves into the other church's building. The "homesteaders" feel they gave up too much, while the host church gave up too little. The host church feels a sense of entitlement to the facilities, while the homesteaders seem like intruders.
6. The merger was emotionally premature. Church leaders often bring congregations to a point of decision and action before one or both groups are ready, not unlike a shotgun wedding.
7. Leaders lack the unique skills and/or experience required to merge.
8. There is conflict between the lay leaders of the two churches. Disagreements may occur in the greater issues of mission, vision, philosophy of ministry, or just day-to-day details of doing church.
9. There is an organizational mismatch in the committees, boards, and staff that are not properly aligned before the merger.

10. The "we versus them" syndrome arises, and the congregations never bond to become one church with one self-image.

While these observations almost always apply to merging two "sick" churches, there is recent evidence indicating that other kinds of mergers have greater potential for success:

- *Adoption,* when a larger church "adopts" a smaller church to create a satellite or multisite location. One of every three multisite campuses are now created through a church merger.
- *Missional merger,* when two or more healthy churches agree to form one church to reach more people and have more influence than either of the two could achieve separately.
- *Shared campus,* when two or more congregations (almost always of different denominations or identities) jointly own and use one facility but continue to meet separately.
- *Cluster,* when two or more churches form a joint organization and each provides a specialized ministry (for example, youth, special needs, older adults, singles).
- *Rebirth,* when two or more churches agree to close and then begin an entirely new church as one.
- *Partnership,* when two churches share resources, such as facilities, vehicles, and staff but do not give up their respective identities.

■ What You Can Do about It

If you are considering a merger, use the points below as a checklist to determine whether your future is gloomy or bright.

A merger works best when

- the merger is motivated by a strong sense of purpose, mission, and reaching new people.
- it is with churches that share common values, vision, theology, corporate culture, and philosophy of ministry.
- it results in the merged churches meeting in a new building, at a new location, with a new name.
- it is led by one pastor (not two). Ideally a new pastor is brought on who was not previously associated with either church.
- it is a product of clear communication among all people involved.
- it arises from a lengthy courtship and gradual cooperative activities between all churches involved.

- it is between churches of the same denomination or very similar theological traditions.
- the merger conversations early on address plans for church property, buildings, and facilities. The final "prenuptial agreement" describes clearly the eventual disposition of these physical resources.
- the merger agreement also describes the working arrangement between pastors, staff, and lay leaders.
- the merger results in one staff, budget, treasurer, treasury, and board.

Is a merger in your future? If so, give serious attention to these rules of thumb before you say, "I do."

#93 THE CHURCH CLOSURE RULE

Churches facing the greatest need for revitalization have declined by 5+ percent for the past ten years and now have fewer than fifty members.

■ Introduction

One of the most difficult decisions for any church leader to make is when to close a church. Yet it is estimated that ½ to 1 or 2 percent of all Protestant churches in the United States close each year. This means between three to five thousand churches close annually. There are some churches that not only would benefit from revitalization but that also are in desperate need of it.

■ Explanation

There are four types of churches that are most likely to close.

1. *New church plants.* As a group, new churches face a greater risk of closing than any other kind of church. One-third of all new churches die before their fourth year.[2] Obviously the first several years are critical. If a new church does survive past its fourth year—and two-thirds do—it is likely to last another sixty years.
2. *Churches that lose their enthusiasm.* When church stops being rewarding and starts being boring, people stop coming. That doesn't mean the role

of church leaders is to entertain pew sitters. The role of church leaders is to enable the Christ-following process to be a dynamic and rewarding one. The energy that drives a church into the future is enthusiasm for what God can do in people's lives. But some churches have just lost that enthusiasm.

3. *Churches with serious attendance loss.* A major loss of three-fourths or more of worship attendance over a two-year period is obviously critical. This can happen because of a church fight, leadership failure, catastrophe, or some other crisis. Such occurrences can destroy a church's will to live.

4. *Churches that are sealed off from outsiders.* Some churches actually never open up to those around them. They are started by a family and intended to be a family. Other churches have so little outreach success that they forget what newcomers look like. If a visitor eventually shows up, the church can't remember what to do. The leading cause of death among churches is a deterioration in the ability to reach and assimilate new members.

■ What You Can Do about It

It is a struggle for church leaders to choose between praying for a "revitalization miracle" on one hand and accepting the fact that the church has reached the end of its life cycle. Any discussion of whether your church is a candidate for revitalization must include a realistic assessment of the other alternative. A decision to close a church should not be made quickly, but the indicators below can help provide a way to evaluate the revitalization potential of a church:

1. *Public worship attendance.* The more people who are gathered in a public worship service, the more celebrative and attractive it is to participants and visitors. Fifty is a good breakeven rule of thumb. More than that makes it easier to have celebrative worship; fewer makes it harder. Of course newly planted churches are almost always under fifty, and they grow. But there is a huge difference between a church of twenty-five on the rise and excited about its future and a church of twenty-five on the decline and nostalgic for its past.

2. *Total giving units.* As noted earlier, it usually takes a minimum of ten to twelve faithful giving units to support a full-time pastor. It takes another ten to twelve units to provide for general church expenses. So if you're in a church on the upswing, passing twenty-five giving units is a sign that you have a bright future ahead. If you're on the downswing, dropping below twenty-five giving units is a warning of impending demise.

3. *Lay leadership pool.* As a rule of thumb, a church needs one leader for every ten members (junior high age and up), one leader for every six elementary children, and one leader for every two preschool or younger children. Fewer leaders will make it difficult to provide an attractive ministry.

4. *A signature ministry.* A church should have at least one "signature ministry"—a program or activity for which it is known in the community. Some churches are known for their outstanding children's ministry, others for their sports program, others for their community benevolence, others for their work with senior citizens. The lack of a signature ministry means your church could cease to exist and no one in the community would know or care. This means the only people who benefit from your church's existence are members, and this is not a very good reason to exist.

5. *Spiritual health of congregation.* Would you characterize your church as being at peace? Is there a pervading sense of joy and love? Or are people's relationships characterized by anger, bitterness, and resentment? The spiritual DNA of a church is hard to change, and a church that carries this destructive gene may not be worth perpetuating.

6. *Average membership tenure.* How long, on average, have people been in your church? Add the number of years each person has been attending and then divide it by the number of members/attendees. If the average tenure is longer than twenty years, it is a church that will have considerable difficulty reaching and assimilating any new people.

7. *The church's goals.* Is the focus of the congregation outward on new people or inward on members? Do leaders talk about mission, ministry, and purpose? Or do they talk about money, maintenance, and problems?

8. *Budget expenditures.* Where does the money go? Is it spent on outreach, advertising, and ministry? Or do these items even make the first cut when the budget is tight?

9. *Church rumors.* What's the talk behind closed doors? Is it instinctively positive about God and his work in the church? Or is the talk about problems in the present and pessimism for the future?

The decision to close a church should be approached cautiously, realizing that God is capable of renewing any church that is willing to change. But God has also included the eventuality of death in his overall creation of life.

#94   THE GROWTH-RESTRICTING OBSTACLES RULE

Five common barriers account for the lack
of growth in most churches.

■ Introduction

Consider the potted plant. It will grow and flourish in the soil, up to a point. But when the roots become constrained in the pot and can no longer hold sufficient nourishment, the hungry plant stops growing. If the plant is transplanted to a bigger pot, the barrier is removed and growth begins anew.

The same thing can happen to a church—it can become root-bound and growth is stunted. If this is the case, the prescription for revitalization is simply to identify and remove the barriers.

■ Explanation

A church can easily encounter one or more *growth-restricting obstacles*—internal or external barriers to growth. Here are five of the most common obstacles that keep otherwise healthy churches from fitness and vitality. If your church is in need of revitalization, check these possible obstacles to see if one or more may be a factor.

Obstacle #1: The pastor. Just as the pastor is a key part of the "mix" for a healthy church, he or she can also be a key part of the problem. There are three different ways in which a pastor can be an obstacle to the health and growth of a church:

1. No priority for outreach. Churches grow when they have a priority for reaching the unchurched. When the pastor doesn't, the church won't either.
2. No vision for outreach. Growing churches have pastors who believe God wants to reach lost people in their community. Without a vision, the people (and church) will perish.
3. No knowledge of outreach. Working harder is not the secret to growth; it's working smarter. Unfortunately, little is taught in seminaries or Bible schools about how to reach and assimilate new people.

Obstacle #2: The church members. We often find competent and skilled clergy in nongrowing churches because the problem is not in the pulpit, it's in the pews. Church members can keep a church from growing when there is:

1. No priority for outreach. "Sure, our church should reach out," they say. "But me? I've got three kids, a job, membership at the health club, and a lawn to mow. Someone else with more time should feel compelled."
2. A self-serving attitude. If members believe the priority of the pastor and the church should be to "feed the sheep," then the message newcomers hear is: "We like our church just the way it is, which is without you!"

Obstacle #3: Perceived irrelevance. A relevant church ministers to the issues and concerns of people in its community: health, finances, relationships, and/or employment. In contrast, stagnant churches plan their ministry and programs primarily for their own members. As a result, unchurched people are seldom even aware of such churches, let alone believe that they have anything relevant to say.

Obstacle #4: Wrong methods. Imagine a farmer driving into his beautiful ripe field of wheat with a corn picker. The harvest may be ripe, but the wrong methods yield nothing. Churches can also be surrounded by a ripe "harvest field" in their community, but wrong outreach methods will yield nothing.

Obstacle #5: No assimilation. New members do not automatically become active members. There must be an intentional plan to assimilate visitors and newcomers into a caring Christian community. Many declining churches have neither a caring community nor a plan for assimilation.

God wants your church to grow. He created it to grow. Sometimes it's just a matter of finding out why it's not growing and removing those obstacles.

■ What You Can Do about It

The first obstacle concerns the pastor, which means you'll need to take an honest look in the mirror. If you suspect that you may be the growth-restricting obstacle keeping your church from a new life cycle, the best thing to do is talk with a trusted confidant. Share your honest questions and seek out their honest opinions. Do you lack a personal *priority* for reaching lost people? Do you lack a *vision* for your church's future? Or, maybe you just lack the *knowledge* for leading a growing church.

It is also possible that the growth-restricting obstacle may be in the pews. Don't use this as an easy cop-out to avoid looking in the mirror. But there are some churches that it seems even Jesus can't help, mostly because they are self-centered and like it that way. The pastor is usually not the best person to tell the church that *they* are the problem. This task is best accomplished by an outside church consultant. It's like your general practitioner sending you to a specialist to determine whether there is a deeper problem.

Bill Easum, a noted church consultant in his own right, suggests a good consultant/coach should have at least five things:[3]

1. A track record of having done what he or she teaches and recommends.
2. Experience in working with your size church, your community context, and your church's mission orientation.
3. Recognition and credibility through previous church consultations, publishing, and personal endorsements.
4. Listening, synthesizing, and communication skills.
5. The ability to paint a realistic picture without alienating the leaders.

If you feel the problem is irrelevance (growth-restricting obstacle #3), it is best to let nonmembers tell you so. Here's an idea that we heard Rick Warren used at Saddleback Church recently. Tell your members that you want to survey people in your community at work, school, soccer, the doctor's office, anywhere. And explain that you need their help. Give each member five printed copies of a "60-Second Survey" and instructions for them to give the surveys to five people they encounter in the coming week. The survey should be anonymous, addressed to the church, and postage paid. Here are the survey questions:

1. What do you feel are the greatest spiritual or emotional needs of people in our community today?
2. Why do you think most people don't attend church?
3. If you had a spiritual question or problem, where would you look for an answer?
4. If you were looking for a church family, what would you look for?

Offer a free gift to anyone who completes a coupon with their name and address at the bottom of the survey. (Saddleback gave a free copy of *The Purpose Driven Life*.)

The cost of such a survey is just the printing, the return stamps, and the gift. The results will provide you with information that will help you evaluate community needs and the relevance of your ministry. Plus, you'll get your members involved in a creative way.

If you conclude that you are facing growth-restricting obstacles #4 or #5, you'll find lots of help throughout the pages of this book.

#95 THE HIGH MORALE RULE

Churches grow as they keep hope alive.

■ Introduction

Attitude is everything. Just as individuals' attitudes affect their personal outlook and behavior, churches' attitudes affect their corporate outlook and behavior. A church's attitude affects its congregational self-esteem. It affects the likelihood that members will invite friends and relatives to attend. Attitude affects the church's willingness to risk. And attitude affects the church's level of hope about the future. One of the crucial challenges facing a declining church is the loss of hope, which then becomes a self-fulfilling prophecy. Consequently, one of the major responsibilities of church leaders in such situations is to fan the flame of optimism, even in the face of major obstacles and challenges.

■ Explanation

Healthy churches believe that their best days are still ahead. Unhealthy churches recall their best days in the past. Healthy churches are optimistic about the future. Dying churches fear the future.

Steve Clapp asked more than 250,000 active members of churches in North America about their morale and enthusiasm for their church's future. He found, not surprisingly, that there were significant differences between churches with declining memberships and churches with growing memberships.[4]

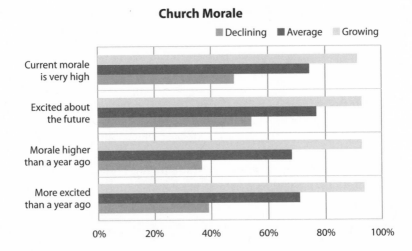

One of the first things we do in consulting with a church is to get a reading of the congregation's self-esteem and sense of hope. Does the church feel it brings something of value to its community? Do people have a sense of anticipation that the future will be better? It is possible to measure hope. Try the following:

• *Engage in active listening* (see #44, The Learning to Listen Rule). Active listening with key people and groups is one way to evaluate the morale of a church. Since pastors spend much of their time talking, attentive listening may be a difficult practice. Begin taking time to ask questions that will give insight into leaders' and members' overall morale or sense of hope: What are leaders saying about their church? Do they feel good about the church's future? Do they feel good about themselves? Listen carefully to their answers.

- *Engage in passive listening.* What do you hear others saying about the church? Is there a hopeful buzz of excitement about the future or a quiet silence of resignation? Do leaders complain that the majority of members are apathetic and do not care about the church? When new ideas are introduced in leadership meetings, do you hear comments like: "That won't work here" or "People won't support that"?

- *Listen to complaints.* Since all complaints are not related to morale, listen particularly for ones that focus on deeper issues. Are problems with finances a frequent topic of discussion? Usually concerns that reveal a general sense of frustration, or even anger, point to low morale and a lack of hope. The old adage that hurting people hurt people is true. Those who are most critical may harbor feelings of despair.

- *Pay attention to nonverbal language.* Do people exhibit a lack of pride in the facilities? Are people on time for events or habitually late? Is relatively little done to celebrate the positive achievements of the church? Is it difficult to recruit workers? Do many people feel there are cliques that exclude others? Is financial giving down? All of these may be nonverbal clues that morale is low.

- *Decode all your listening.* After all this, determine the answer to the question, What is the state of the church's morale?

■ What You Can Do about It

Hope and optimism about the future must begin with the pastor. If the pastor has a positive attitude, the people can catch it. If the pastor doesn't have it, it won't be caught. Do you, Pastor, believe there can be a bright new day for the church, or do you see nothing but problems ahead? (The main indicator for knowing that it is time to leave your pastorate is if you no longer have hope for your church.)

If you see a positive potential for your church, the next question is, Are you willing to actively pursue it? Colin Powell distinguishes between passive optimism and dynamic optimism. Passive optimism is simply a "don't worry, be happy" attitude. Dynamic optimists set and pursue goals and enlist others in the pursuit of these goals. Passive optimists hope the church will reach new people and grow. Dynamic optimists ask God specifically for his blessing of their new outreach initiatives in the coming year.

If you see a bright future and determine to act on it, the word *hope*, as an acrostic, can give you some ideas for raising the morale in your congregation.

> *H—Hearts beating for what God desires.* At the heart of every hopeful church is spiritual vitality. Preach a series on God's optimistic future for your church. Teach on passages that focus on faith in God. Highlight Scripture passages that illustrate how God gives hope to his people and church. Organize a series

of sermon-based small group discussions to process the sermons each week. When people gather into small groups to focus, study, and pray together, a new spirit of hope is frequently born in the congregation.

O—Outline a clear direction. Bless the past, as well as the future, by reminding people how God worked in your church in earlier years *and* how God is going to work in the future. Establish a vision for the future and begin aligning your talk, work, and ministry around that vision. A clear vision of the future is the best way to be rid of nostalgia for the past. Celebrate the positives in your church as you begin moving toward that new vision. Call attention to anything and everything positive that happens in the church. Regularly thank workers and leaders for the jobs they do. Highlight victories, no matter how small.

P—Pastoral leadership that inspires. Be positive. People watch everything a pastor does and says. The way you speak, preach, and teach sends clues about your own morale and hope for the future. Set a hopeful example in your language and tone of voice. Stop talking about problems and recast them as opportunities. Don't talk about past failures; begin focusing on what you have learned. Ask your leaders to try five new things this year. Tell them you expect some of the efforts to fail, but that failure is better than inactivity. Ignore the failures and praise the successes.

E—Evangelistic outreach that is effective. Turn the focus of your congregation away from themselves and to those outside your church who have clear needs. Consider replacing one worship service each month with a planned gathering to go into the community as God's helping hands to people in need. Ask members to call the church office throughout the month with anyone they know who would benefit from your church's "Good Samaritan Sunday." Develop an ongoing list of people who have needs and appoint a task force to coordinate the process of meeting those needs in Jesus's name.

#96 THE INTERVENTION OPPORTUNITY RULE

There are certain times in the life of a church where intervention is more likely to spark revitalization.

■ Introduction

A *window of opportunity* is "a short time period during which an otherwise unattainable opportunity exists. After the window of opportunity closes, the opportunity ceases to exist."[5] There are certain times in the life cycle of a church when revitalization is more likely to occur. Wise church leaders will know *when* those windows of opportunity open and *what* to do when they open. For churches in dire need of revitalization, missing the open window may mean missing the last opportunity.

■ Explanation

In our experience, there are certain events that can cause windows of opportunity for revitalization to open in a church. Keep in mind that none of these events *cause* revitalization, but they can create an environment where revitalization is more likely to occur.

- *Change of pastors.* As we pointed out in #62, The Pastoral Tenure Rule, rapid pastoral change usually diminishes the growth potential in a church. At the same time, a new pastor with a new vision and a new way of doing things—who stays for seven-plus years—can be the source of a new life cycle in the church.

- *A crisis.* It can be the proverbial cloud with a silver lining. What seems like the worst of events can turn out to be the spark that lights a fire of revival in the church. A common example is when severe damage or destruction occurs to the church building, which leads to rebirth. The same phenomenon can happen through other church crises as well.

- *Plant a daughter church.* It seems counterintuitive that a struggling church can be revitalized through planting a new church. Yet it happens consistently! In the process of organizing and establishing a new congregation, those in the sponsoring church discover that their own priorities have become self-centered and self-serving. Thus planting a daughter church can become the roots for revitalizing the mother church.

- *Closing the church, then reopening it.* Here's another apparently paradoxical idea—revitalize a church by closing it and then reopening it. Actually there are a surprising number of examples of this process across different denominations. In such cases, the building remains, but the old church is put to rest. Then, in the subsequent year, a church planter is brought in to start what is essentially a new church. The "old-timers" from the former church are invited to be a part of the new church, but they have no more influence or authority than a newcomer who is joining for the first time.

- *Spiritual renewal of the pastor.* The Holy Spirit can renew a pastor as much as anyone else! Sometimes, through divine intervention, a pastor will confront his or her own shortcomings, sinfulness, or personal issues that are creating an obstacle to the Spirit's work in the church. This renewal of God's Spirit in the life of the pastor can spread to the church and be a window of opportunity for revitalization.

- *Spiritual renewal of the laity.* Most revivals in the American church have begun through the laity. Sometimes pastors conclude erroneously that the spiritual renewal of the congregation is entirely dependent on them or on the speaker at the next revival meeting. The Holy Spirit alone, however, is quite capable of stirring the hearts and minds of a church. When this happens, it creates a wonderful window of opportunity. At the same time, there are more than a few churches who have "had revival," only to look essentially the same five years later.

- *Intervention by the denomination.* For certain denominationally affiliated churches, the regional or national office has the authority to intervene in a church that seems to have simply run out of gas. There are heartwarming stories of a church that was near death when a pastor from the denomination was brought in to close down the church. But through a combination of events, prayers, innovations, and recommitments, the church experienced a turnaround and today is a healthy, growing group of believers.

- *Hire a consultant.* There are few surprises to specialists who have researched and studied the life and death of churches. Because of their experience, consultants can see problems—and solutions—that others in the church may not see. And usually, when facing the immediate prospect of closing the church, leaders are much more receptive to adopting the necessary changes proposed by a knowledgeable consultant.

- *Relocate the church.* Some churches are simply in the wrong place for the ministry they are trying to conduct and constituency they are trying to reach. As we discuss in #73, The Relocation Rule, some churches simply need to move. While a move is no guarantee of revitalization, it presents a wide-open window of opportunity.

- *Start a new worship service.* One of the most controllable and most predictable intervention events is beginning a new worship service to reach a new target audience. Similar to when a church decides to plant a new church, many of the same positive dynamics are created when a church decides to start a new service. In so doing, church leaders are forced back to the questions, Why are we here? What is our purpose? The answers to such honest questions can stimulate church leaders to a recommitment of their mission, which almost always guarantees revitalization.

■ What You Can Do about It

Watch for the events that create windows of opportunity for revitalization in your church. Realize that they present chances for a turnaround. If and when such events occur, encourage church leaders to see them as opportunities for change, not simply challenges to endure.

Encourage conversation on the topic of "form versus essence" in your church. Forms are *how* you do things—when you meet, where you meet, what you do, and how you do it. In the best sense of the term, they are rituals. And every church has them. Ask your leaders to identify your church's forms.

Then discuss your church's essence. What are the nonnegotiables that comprise your very core? These are the *why* of what you do. Finally, consider whether there are things that should be in the forms side of the ledger that have slipped over into the essence side. A few examples of forms that have become essence in some churches include using the King James Version of the Bible, meeting at 11:00 a.m. on Sunday, holding Wednesday night prayer meetings, the way communion is conducted, or having Sunday school classes. Forms should be changeable. Essence should be constant. Such a discussion will move a conversation from "how we do things" to "why we do things." If there are no good, current answers to the "why" questions, it's time to start asking the "whether" questions.

15

Ministry Rules for Demographics

Demographics is defined as "the statistical characteristics of human population groups (such as age, income, education, etc.), used especially to identify markets."[1] Pastors do well to add "demographer" to their many other titles and abilities. Not only is the study of human population groups and subgroups fascinating, it has great relevance to pursuing the mission of God to make disciples.

Jesus was aware of demographics when he issued his final Great Commission: "Go and make disciples of all nations" (Matt. 28:19). Missiologists point out that the word *nations* in modern translations of Jesus's words is often misconstrued to mean nation-states, such as Britain, India, Peru, or Egypt. In reality, the term Jesus used was *panta ta ethne*. This referred not to political countries but to individual "people groups" within countries and cultures. A people group is "an ethno-linguistic group with a common self-identity that is shared by the various members."[2] People groups share not only a common language but a common sense of identity, history, and customs. So when Jesus told us to go and make disciples of all nations, he was saying to proclaim the gospel in every ethnic segment and cultural level of every society.

Understanding these segments of society—the people groups—is what demographics is all about. Here are a few rules of thumb.

#97   THE MINISTRY AREA RULE

Ninety percent of church attendees live within twenty miles of their church.

■ Introduction

Every church has a *ministry area*, defined as a reasonable driving distance from the church. Your ministry area is your Jerusalem, as when Jesus said, "You will be my witnesses in Jerusalem, and in all Judea and Samaria, and to the ends of the earth" (Acts 1:8). While we are called to take the good news beyond our immediate community, we are called to *begin* with our Jerusalem. The average church has a ministry area of no more than twenty miles (or twenty-five minutes, whichever is less) around its primary facility.

■ Explanation

How far away do people live from the church they attend? What is the ministry area boundary of most churches? Is there a difference in the distance that new members will travel versus the distance long-term members will travel? To find out, I (Gary) conducted research on 740 churches in numerous denominations located in 41 states. I focused particularly on people who had been in their church for less than two years. More than 1,100 people participated in the study, which included churches in towns with populations of 10,000 or greater, representing all sizes of churches.

The study found that 45 percent of church attendees live within 5 miles of the church they attend. Another 24 percent travel between 6 and 10 miles to get to their church. Thus more than two-thirds of the typical church's attendees travel less than 10 miles to church. Another 21 percent live 11 to 20 miles from their church, giving a combined 90 percent who travel 20 miles or less to church each Sunday. Just 10 percent of the entire study group was willing to drive more than 20 miles to church on any given Sunday.

An interesting observation from the study was that people who had recently committed their lives to faith in Christ lived even closer to their church than those with a more mature faith. Fully 100 percent of new converts in our study lived less than 20 miles from their church, with half living less than 5 miles away. (Of the remainder, 26 percent lived 6 to 10 miles away, while 24 percent lived 11 to 20 miles away.)

Exceptions to this ministry area rule are found in rural communities where people may drive a greater distance to their church, and among some people groups with a high ethnic identity. However, in 90 percent of churches in the United States, a 20-mile radius is their maximum ministry area.

■ What You Can Do about It

Understanding your church's ministry area provides several strategic insights for a more fruitful ministry. Consider the following suggestions:

- *Focus outreach initiatives on church members' friends and family who live within twenty miles of your church.* The Unchurched Friends Rule (#5) says that evangelistic receptivity will be greatest among church members' friends, neighbors, and relatives. Since 90 percent of your regular attendees probably live within twenty miles, a good number of people in your members' social networks will also live in your ministry area. By contrast, it is difficult for members to invite friends and relatives to events that meet beyond a reasonable driving distance.

- *Focus general community outreach events within your ministry area.* While it may be part of your "Judea and Samaria" strategy to reach out beyond your ministry area, realize that such events will not directly contribute to your own church's growth. Your goal in outreach is to reach people for Christ and the kingdom and see them actively involved in a fellowship of believers. But it is also true that you really have little or no control over the kind of church the people outside your ministry area will attend, if they attend one at all. By offering outreach events within your ministry area, you make it easy for your regular attendees to invite people in their social networks. And it is these people who are most receptive and can be most easily assimilated into your fellowship.

- *Follow up on visitors who live within twenty miles of your church.* It's a nice gesture to send an email or letter to those who visit your church from outside your ministry area. But the best investment of your limited resources is in the visitors who can return and become regular participants. Recognize distant visitors; emphasize nearby visitors.

- *Advertise within twenty miles of your church.* Advertising is one way to create awareness of your church's ministry in your community, but advertising outside of your own ministry area is not cost-effective. Advertising in the *Los Angeles Times* (if your church is in Pasadena, California) is poor stewardship, since it is delivered to far more people who live outside your ministry area than within it. Advertising in the *Pasadena Star News*, however, will provide excellent exposure. The same is true for advertising or broadcasting on cable TV and radio, purchasing mailing lists, or pursuing other direct marketing endeavors. Stay within your ministry area for the least cost and most effective results.

- *Form partnerships within your ministry area.* Missional partnerships with local schools, hospitals, parks departments, and city governments can be an effective way to connect with and serve those in the church community. However, the best results will come from partnerships that are located near your church's base of operation, that is, within your ministry area.

#98 THE TARGET GROUP RULE

Evangelism initiatives will be most effective when they are focused on specific people groups.

■ Introduction

"Everyone Welcome" is often seen on signs in front of churches. And of course everyone is welcome. However, churches that try to reach everyone may end up reaching no one—or at least very few. In contrast, churches that experience significant conversion growth have a well-defined target group and a well-conceived strategy to reach them.

■ Explanation

Target group evangelism is defined as "a strategy of outreach that identifies one or more segments of a surrounding community [people groups], and then researches, communicates with, and builds bridges to people in that group with the goal of reaching them for Christ and the church."[3]

At first, the idea of targeting people for evangelism might seem suspect, even wrong. But in actuality, the idea of proclaiming the gospel to a specific group of people is a principle right out of the New Testament. For example, when a Canaanite woman asked Jesus to heal her daughter, he replied that God had told him to focus on "the house of Israel" (see Matt. 15:22–28 ESV). While Jesus did heal the woman's daughter because of her faith, publicly he identified his ministry target—the Jews. Jesus gave similar instructions to his disciples when he sent them out to proclaim the message of the kingdom: "Do not go among the Gentiles or enter any town of the Samaritans. Go rather to the lost sheep of Israel" (Matt. 10:5–6). Later, as the first church was growing, Jesus appeared to Ananias and told him that Paul was "a chosen instrument of Mine, to bear

My name before the Gentiles" (Acts 9:15 NASB). Peter targeted his ministry to Jews (see Gal. 2:7).

Targeting specific people groups is a particularly important outreach strategy for small churches with limited dollars, people, and resources. Since they cannot be all things to all people, these churches must decide which people groups they can best reach. The larger your church becomes, the more you can broaden your ministry through programs, events, and even worship services that focus on additional target groups of people.

So how do you define your target? Rick Warren suggests four aspects:[4]

1. *Geographically*. This simply means identifying where the people live that you want to reach—your ministry area. This is your "evangelistic fishing pond."
2. *Demographically*. What kind of people live in your ministry area? Don't overdo demographic research. The only critical demographic facts you need to discover about the people in your community are age, marital status, income, education, and occupation.
3. *Culturally*. Within your community there are many subcultures, defined by people's values, interests, hurts, and fears. To reach any of these groups, you need to discover how they think. The more you know about your target audience, the easier it will be to connect with them.
4. *Spiritually*. What do those in your target area already know about the gospel? You might interview other pastors in the area to see if there is a consensus on the spiritual climate of your community.

One church cannot reach all people. Thus you should begin by asking, "What groups in our community do we feel a particular burden for?" This question expresses a humble desire to come alongside particular people groups as "missionaries," to identify with their pain and misfortune, and to be willing to commit to their immediate well-being, as well as to matters that impact their eternal destiny.

■ What You Can Do about It

Here are some ideas to help you find your specific target audience. First, know yourself and your congregation. Churches and pastors tend to attract people like themselves. This is a statement not so much about us as about them. When visitors attend a church activity, their first questions are: Is there anyone here like me? and Is this a place I will feel comfortable? People are more likely to return and develop relationships with others who are like them; it's just the nature of how people relate to each other.

The more you know about the people in your church, the more you can identify receptive people groups in your community. For example, What is your age? What is the age range in your congregation and the average age? What age groups is your church strong in? What do you personally like to read? What are people in your church reading? What music do you enjoy, and what music do they prefer? What is your educational level? What is the educational level of your members? What kind of people tend to follow your leadership? If God directs you toward those who are different from you and your congregation, be willing to invest time in learning their language and values to make them comfortable enough to stay.

You will then need to learn more about the people in your potential target audience. Where do they live? What is important to them? Where do they gather? What is a typical family? What hobbies do they pursue? What are their needs, struggles, and pains? How would you communicate with them?

Within your target group, look for those who are receptive and open to the gospel (see #2, The Receptivity Rule). In general, people tend to be most receptive when they are going through transitions in life, such as relocating or getting sick or losing a job or having other needs they do not commonly face. Within your larger target group, are there subgroups with such concerns who could be more receptive?

Narrow your list down to one or two people groups. Conduct additional research on those whom God has placed on your heart. Then design a ministry specifically aimed to meet a need of your target group. Begin working to reach this group for Christ and your church. (See #4, The Side-Door Ministry Rule, for more on starting side-door ministries.)

#99 THE ETHNIC IDENTITY RULE

Some churches will be more effective than others in reaching ethnic population groups.

■ Introduction

Several years ago the United States accepted more legal immigrants as permanent residents than all other countries in the world combined. America has been called a "melting pot" with a myriad of cultures and ethnicities. When immigrants arrive, they bring their culture with them.

Rather than a melting pot, however, a more accurate metaphor for the amalgamation of ethnicities in this country is the "stew pot"—a common container, blending different ingredients that each retain their own identities. For local churches, the implications of this cultural kaleidoscope are considerable. Effective outreach and ministry to changing people groups and a changing community can be a perplexing challenge indeed.

■ Explanation

Most churches have more than one cultural or ethnic people group within their ministry area. Realistically speaking, no church can reach every person in every ethnic group. In such a context, then, how can a church be a faithful steward and invest its limited resources for the greatest harvest?

There are two basic strategies for outreach to a target cultural or ethnic group in a community. One is the *assimilationist approach*. This is the traditional method of Anglo churches attempting to integrate ethnic minorities into their membership. The other approach to cross-cultural outreach and ministry is the *identificational approach*. This process affirms the development of distinct monoethnic church plants and missions and is an approach that is becoming increasingly popular and effective. You will need to study the people groups in your community to know which approach your church should use.

The assimilationist approach is most effective with people who have a low degree of ethnic consciousness. It is least effective among people with a high degree of ethnic consciousness. The various identificational models, on the other hand, are most effective among people with a moderate to high ethnic consciousness. *Ethnic consciousness* is the intensity of awareness and identification with one's distinct people group, based on race, religion, and/or national origin.

To help you identify the intensity of ethnic consciousness among a particular cultural group, and therefore determine the approach that will be most successful for your church, consider each index on the Ethnic Identity Scale[5] below. Circle a number (1 through 5) that most accurately describes the ethnic group in your ministry area. If the general trend of the responses is toward the left side of the scale, the assimilationist approach to reaching this ethnic group will generally be more productive. If the majority of characteristics trend toward the center or right end of the scale, the identificational approach to reaching this ethnic group will be more successful. If the total score is 75 or above, it is likely that a new church (or new worship service in an existing church) is needed to successfully reach this group.

Ethnic Identity Scale

Lesser social distance (attitude)	1 2 3 4 5	Greater social distance (attitude)
Little racial discrimination in the community	1 2 3 4 5	Persistence of racial discrimination in the community
Lack of pride in national heritage	1 2 3 4 5	Pride in national heritage
Light skin	1 2 3 4 5	Dark skin
Area with high degree of racial mixing	1 2 3 4 5	Area with low degree of racial mixing

Exogamous marriages common	1 2 3 4 5	Endogamous marriages common
The second, fourth, or later generation of the people group	1 2 3 4 5	The immigrant or the third generation of a people group
Anglicized last name	1 2 3 4 5	Pride in one's cultural name
Upward social mobility	1 2 3 4 5	Minimal upward social mobility
Dispersion of the people from a common geographic region	1 2 3 4 5	Concentration of the people in a geographic region
Absence of ethnic identity movements	1 2 3 4 5	Presence of ethnic identity movements
Low consciousness of one's national lineage	1 2 3 4 5	High consciousness of one's national lineage
Residence in a community of under 15 percent ethnic	1 2 3 4 5	Residence in a community over 50 percent ethnic

■ What You Can Do about It

If you decide there are ethnic people groups in your ministry area, determine whether you feel called to reach out to one or more of these groups. Identify those in your church who have a particular interest in reaching out to one or more of these groups. If there are at least three such people, ask them if they would be willing to form an exploratory task force. (If no one in the church shows interest in any group, you may want to wait until God gives someone the desire.)

If you have enough interest to form a task force, ask the group to specifically describe the ethnic group and evaluate their ethnic consciousness on the Ethnic Identity Scale. Unless the task force is intimately familiar with the ethnic group, they should discuss how to make an accurate assessment, including interviews with members of the group.

Once the Ethnic Identity Scale has been completed, calculate the total number of points and compare the results to the 75-point threshold to determine whether an assimilationist or identificational model would be most effective. Encourage the group to continue exploring the best ways to reach out to this people group using the appropriate methodology.

#100   THE RULE OF FOUR

Each person in a church is only four people away
from every other person in the world.

■ Introduction

Networking is a buzzword today, but the process has been going on for thousands of years. Most people conceive of networking as a process of searching for sales contacts or finding a new job. Yet that is a limited perspective. Networking is really a very large concept that applies directly to you and your church.

■ Explanation

The basic rule is highly predictable. For anyone you want to know in the world, someone you already know knows someone they know. Here's how The Rule of Four works. If you know 50 people, and each of them knows 50 more people, you have 2,500 friends of friends. If each of them knows 50 more people, you have 125,000 friends of friends of friends. And, if each of them knows 50 others you have more than 6 million friends of friends of friends of friends.

Networking is basically an exchange of information from one person to another. The important thing to remember is that it is not what you get from another person but what you can give them that makes relationships work. And the most important thing we can give people is knowledge of Jesus Christ and an opportunity to follow him as their Lord. As you can detect from the numbers above, even a small church has sufficient contacts to reach a lot of people with the gospel.

■ What You Can Do about It

Research shows that the most effective method of evangelism is simply conversation. The people in our churches have many contacts with whom they can share the gospel, but they must be taught and encouraged to build relationships with the non-churched.

Relationships are built one conversation at a time. Thus church leaders might empower The Rule of Four in their churches by doing the following:

1. Ask church members to identify their non-churched friends and family members. One way to do this is to ask each person in your church to make a list of all the friends, family members, and work associates they know who do not attend church. You and your church members will be surprised at how many people they already know as The Rule of Four comes into play.

2. Encourage church members to pray faithfully for one year for the people they have listed. Regularly remind people of their commitment to pray, and pray publicly for everyone's lists when appropriate.

3. Encourage members to spend time socializing with some of the people on their lists. As people spend time together, natural conversations take place, and these conversations can turn toward the spiritual issues of life. It is

in these spiritual conversations that real life change begins to occur, and hearts begin to turn toward Christ.

4. Offer one event each quarter when your members are encouraged to bring their non-churched friends or family. Picnics, concerts, Christmas Eve services, Easter services, baptisms, and alternative Halloween events are excellent opportunities.

5. Train your members to share their faith. Provide at least one or two classes or small groups each year when church members are shown how to engage their friends and family in conversations about Jesus Christ. One easy tool is the "feel-felt-found" outline (I know how you feel. I felt the same way. Then I found . . .).

As you put all of these things together, over time your people will reach out to their friends, who will share with their friends, who will share with their friends . . . Networking is the way to connect with lost people who need to hear of new life in Jesus Christ.

#101 THE ISOLATION RULE

People are losing friends—and there is something you can do about it!

■ Introduction

John Naisbitt accurately forecasted the phenomenon back in 1988, using the phrase "high tech—high touch."[6] His contention was that, as the personal isolation due to high technology grows in our society (drive-through restaurants, banking ATMs, internet shopping, downloadable movies, etc.), it is increasingly easy to live without much human interaction. The result is an increasing void in the high touch of human interaction. Online social networks are a ludicrous effort of high technology to cure itself: "Facebook is to friendship what fast food is to nutrition—a quick way to feel like we've gotten what we need. When compared with what we really need, what we get is insubstantial."[7]

■ Explanation

A few years ago I (Charles) was conversing with a marketing executive from Ford Motor Company. He posed the question: "If the church were a business, what product would we be selling?"

"Interesting question," I responded (my standard comment when I don't know the answer). "What do you think?"

"I think our product would be—or should be—relationships." He continued, "First, the church strengthens our relationship with God. Then we grow through relationships with others in the church. Finally, the church should help us grow in our relationships to those outside the church."

I like that. What better "product" could we offer in this increasingly high-tech culture, than high touch—with God and then others. It brings to mind how Christ placed a high priority on relationships when he responded to the question of what was the greatest commandment. He said, first, a loving relationship with God, then loving relationships with those around us.

Actually most churches already have their relationship "product" on the shelves. And most members are buying it and enjoying the benefits. For many people in churches today, the friendships they have in their Christian community are the only meaningful relationships they have. And since relationships are known to contribute to health and longevity, perhaps it is not a coincidence that Christians have been shown to be healthier, live longer, and be happier than non-Christians.[8] How sad, then, when the need for our product is so great in the unchurched marketplace and our ability to "sell" and "deliver" our product is so weak.

Think for a moment about the people who do not have church as a part of their life. Where do they find a place to really connect with others? Perhaps at work, but most such relationships are superficial. Perhaps with a neighbor or at a club, but this is not typical. People in our society are losing friends. In fact, Americans are more socially isolated today than we were barely two decades ago. Recently *Time* magazine noted, "The latest evidence of [our social isolation] comes from a topflight team of sociologists who, after comparing national surveys in 1985 and 2004, report a one-third drop in the number of people with whom the average American can discuss 'important matters.'"[9]

Robert Putnam, in his landmark book *Bowling Alone,* observes: "Faith communities, in which people worship together, are arguably the single most important repository of social capital in America."[10] He goes on to elaborate for an entire chapter on the connection between religion and relationships, observing how people who attend church are much more likely to entertain at home; attend club meetings; belong to sports groups, professional academic societies, school service groups, youth groups, service clubs, and hobby or garden clubs; be part of literary, art, discussion, and study groups; join school fraternities and sororities, farm organizations, political clubs, nationality groups, and other miscellaneous groups.

Perhaps it's time to revisit the description of our product. Maybe we really are—or should be—in the business of "selling" relationships.

■ What You Can Do about It

There are excellent Christian books, videos, and study courses on the topic of friendships. Start a Sunday adult class to learn more about it. Encourage your small groups to explore the topic. It makes a great study for teens. Help members develop skills for nurturing relationships, not only with existing friends and family but with new people.

Start new groups (see #32, The New Groups Rule). Groups are the very best place for new relationships to flourish. Make a point to open the groups—and intentionally "market" the groups—to unchurched people.

In all your groups, realize that there are different levels of relationships. Encourage and train group leaders in the skills of moving beyond superficial relationships to nurture deeper relationships among members.

Confession is good for the soul. It is also good for nurturing deeper relationships. Consider how this important dynamic of Christian living can be integrated into your church's ministry.

The most genuine manifestation of friendship is love. Jesus said, "My command is this: Love each other as I have loved you. Greater love has no one than this: to lay down one's life for one's friends" (John 15:12–13). Teach people in your church how to love. (For more thoughts on love, see chapter 7.)

Notes

Chapter 1 Ministry Rules for Evangelism and Outreach

1. Howard Snyder, *The Community of the King* (Downers Grove, IL: InterVarsity, 1977), 91.

2. Dean R. Hogue, *Converts, Dropouts, and Returnees: A Study of Religious Change among Catholics* (New York: Pilgrim Press, 1981), 211.

3. "The Holmes-Rahe Social Readjustment Scale" is reprinted by permission of the publisher of T. Holmes and R. Rahe, "The Social Readjustment Scale," *The Journal of Psychosomatic Research* 2, 213–18. Copyright 1966 by Elsevier Science, Inc.

4. Charles Arn, *Heartbeat: How to Turn Passion into Ministry in Your Church* (Longwood, FL: Xulon Press, 2011), 14.

5. Gary McIntosh, *Beyond the First Visit* (Grand Rapids: Baker, 2006), 22.

6. "Emergent Dialogue," *Denver Seminary* (fall 2004): 14.

7. See the book *Side Doors* by Charles Arn (Indianapolis: Wesley Publishing, 2013) for a complete guide to building new side doors in your church.

8. Flavil Yeakley, "Research and the Growing Church," *Church Growth: America* 7, no. 1 (1989): 4.

Chapter 2 Ministry Rules for Visitors

1. Andrew Sullivan, "Forget the Church, Follow Jesus," *Newsweek*, April 12, 2012, 26.

Chapter 3 Ministry Rules for Worship

1. John Stott, *Between Two Worlds* (Grand Rapids: Eerdmans, 1982).

2. "How John Piper Prepares a Sermon," http://www.sermoncentral.com/pastors-preaching-articles/john-piper-how-john-piper-prepares-a-sermon-942.asp, June 3, 2011.

3. Quoted in Charles Arn, *How to Start a New Service* (Grand Rapids: Baker, 1997), back cover.

4. James White, *Opening the Front Door: Worship and Church Growth* (Nashville: Convention Press, 1992), 29.

5. Arn, *How to Start a New Service*.

6. J. Howard Griffith, "Membership Growth Insights from a Sabbatical," *Net Results*, October 1994, 14.

7. Paul Anderson, "Balancing Tradition and Innovation," in *Word and Worship*, vol. 1 of *Leadership Handbook of Practical Theology*, gen. ed. James Berkely (Grand Rapids: Baker, 1992), 239.

8. James Emory White, *Relevant Preaching: What They Didn't Teach You in Seminary* (Grand Rapids: Baker, 2011), quoted from: http://www.preaching.com/resources/articles/11653970/.

Chapter 4 Ministry Rules for Connecting with and Assimilating Newcomers

1. Charles Arn, "The Friendship Factor," *Church Growth: America* 7, no. 3 (1989): 13.
2. John Chandler, "3 Minutes," *RASNET*, April 16, 2009, www.rasnet.org.
3. Lions Club, http://www.lionsclubs.org/EN/common/pdfs/me21.pdf.
4. Rick Warren, "Meeting People's Four Deepest Needs," *Ministry Toolbox* 366 (November 26, 2008): 1–2.

Chapter 5 Ministry Rules for Small Groups

1. Lynchburg Area Newcomers Club, http://www.lynchburgareanewcomers.com.
2. Charlottesville Newcomers Club, http://charlottesvillenewcomersclub.org.
3. Newcomers Club, http://www.newcomersclub.com.
4. Lyle Schaller, "Making 'Outsiders' into 'Insiders,'" *Church Growth: America* 7, no. 2 (1989): 4.

Chapter 6 Ministry Rules for Christian Education

1. Richard Myers, "Sunday School and Church Growth," *Church Growth: America* 4, no. 4 (1988): 8.
2. Ibid.
3. Win Arn and Charles Arn, *Growth: A New Vision for the Sunday School* (Pasadena, CA: Church Growth Press, 1980), 108.
4. See Ken Hemphill, *The Bonsai Theory of Church Growth* (Nashville: Broadman, 1991), for more on this phenomenon.
5. D. Campbell Wykoff, *Theory and Design of Christian Education* (Philadelphia: Westminster, 1961), 22.
6. H. W. Byrne, *Christian Education for the Local Church* (Grand Rapids: Zondervan, 1975), 56.
7. Carl Dudley and Lyle Schaller are two authors who have addressed the Rule of Forty in their writings. For further information see Carl Dudley, *Making the Small Church Effective* (Nashville: Abingdon, 1978).

Chapter 7 Ministry Rules for Love and Caring

1. Robert Arnett, *India Unveiled* (Columbus, GA: Atman Press, 2006), 155.
2. Christian Schwartz, *A Guide to Eight Essential Qualities of Healthy Churches* (Emmelsbuell, Germany: NCD International, 1996).
3. Win Arn, Carroll Nyquist, and Charles Arn, *Who Cares about Love?* (Pasadena, CA: Church Growth Press, 1992), 118.
4. Dietrich Bonhoeffer, *Life Together* (Minneapolis: Augsburg-Fortress Press, 1996), 98.
5. Dennis Wiggs, "Send Birthday Cards," FWBPastor.com, http://fwbpastor.com/?p=696.
6. Roger Peterson, opening presentation, annual conference of Fellowship of Short-Term Mission Leaders (Atlanta, October 11, 2006).
7. Chuck Gailey and Howard Culbertson, *Discovering Missions* (Kansas City: Beacon Hill Press, 2007), chapter 9.

Chapter 8 Ministry Rules for Volunteer Involvement

1. Lee Sparks, "The State of Volunteer Ministry," *REV!* (January/February 2009): 52.

2. Flavil Yeakley, "Growth and Assimilation," *Church Growth: America* 7, no. 2 (1997): 17.

3. Pam Heaton, "Every Church Needs a Profiler," www.BuildingChurchLeaders.com.

4. Rick Warren, "Explosive Growth: Unleash the Creativity of Your Congregation," *Ministry Toolbox* (March 2, 2005): 193.

Chapter 10 Ministry Rules for Staff and Leadership

1. Hendrik Kraemer, *A Theology of the Laity* (Philadelphia: Westminster, 1958), 52.

2. http://pastoralcareinc.com/WhyPastoralCare/Statistics.php; http://jmm.aaa.net.au/articles/2049.htm.

3. Paul Stanley, *Connecting: The Mentoring Relationships You Need to Succeed in Life* (Colorado Springs: NavPress, 1992), 40.

4. Dr. G. Brian Jones, "Mentoring Examples in the Bible," http://www.faithmentoringandmore.com/html/articles/idea_6.htm.

5. George Barna, *The Second Coming of the Church* (Nashville: Word, 1998), 5.

6. "Study Shows Why Protestant Clergy Change Jobs—Promotions Are a More Common Cause than God's Call," GreyMatter Research, September 7, 2005, http://www.greymatter-research.com/index_files/Job_Changes.htm.

7. Roger Parrott, *Lasting Strategies for Rising Leaders* (Colorado Springs: David C. Cook, 2009), 19.

8. Rick Warren, *The Purpose Driven Life* (Grand Rapids: Zondervan, 2002), 17.

Chapter 11 Ministry Rules for Facilities

1. Richard J. Krejcir, "Statistics on Pastors," Schaeffer Institute, http://www.intothyword.org/articles_view.asp?articleid=36562&columnid=.

2. Alice Mann, *Raising the Roof: The Pastoral-to-Program Size Transition* (Bethesda, MD: Alban Institute, 2001), 20.

3. Marlis McCollum, "The 80% Rule: Fact or Fiction?" *Congregations*, Alban Institute (winter 2006): 1.

4. Walter Bruggeman, *The Land* (Philadelphia: Fortress Press, 1977), 5.

5. Dudley, *Making the Small Church Effective*, 53.

Chapter 12 Ministry Rules for Finances

1. John C. LaRue Jr., "Church Staffing Levels and Expenses," *Your Church* (November–December, 1993): 48.

2. Elmer Towns, *Towns' Sunday School Encyclopedia: A Practical Guide for Sunday School Workers* (Wheaton: Tyndale, 1993), 95–96.

3. Victor Frankl, *Man's Search for Meaning* (Boston: Beacon Press, 1959), 73.

4. Donald McGavran, "How to Grow a Church" (Church Growth, 1979), 16mm film.

5. Charles Arn, *Growth: A New Vision for the Sunday School* (Pasadena, CA: Church Growth Press, 1991), 129.

Chapter 13 Ministry Rules for Change

1. *A Church for the 21st Century* (Monrovia, CA: Church Growth, Inc., 1966), video.

2. First Church of the Nazarene, Pasadena, CA, "Questions & Answers Concerning Multiple Worship Service Options," 1996.

3. Aubrey Malphurs, *Pouring New Wine into Old Wineskins* (Grand Rapids: Baker, 1993), 80.

4. Doug Murren, "The Process of Change," *Worship Leader* 12, no. 3 (September/October 1995): 30.

Chapter 14 Ministry Rules for Revitalization

1. William T. McConnell, *Renew Your Congregation: Healing the Sick, Raising the Dead* (Columbia, SC: The Columbia Partnership, 2007), 13.

2. Ed Stetzer, "Church Plant Survivability and Health Study" (The Center for Missional Research, North American Mission Board, 2007), 13.

3. Bill Easum, "The Importance of a Church Consultant/Coach," *Religious Product News*, www.religiousproductnews.com/articles/2011-May/eNewsletter/The-Importance-of-a-Church-Consultant-Coach.htm.

4. Steve Clapp. "Congregational Morale and Church Growth," http://www.newlifeministries-nlm.org/online/nlm_report_6.htm.

5. http://www.investopedia.com/terms/w/window-of-opportunity.asp#axzz1p8BbxiiR.

Chapter 15 Ministry Rules for Demographics

1. Merriam Webster, http://www.merriam-webster.com/dictionary/demographics.

2. http://www.globalfrontiermissions.org/unreached.html.

3. Win Arn, "Target Group Evangelism—Unlocking a Secret to Growth," *The Win Arn Growth Report* 30 (1991): 1.

4. Rick Warren, "Targeting for Evangelism," *Pastor.com* 254 (April 12, 2006): 1.

5. This scale was adapted from "Finding Ethnic America" by Tetsunao Yamamori in *The Pastor's Church Growth Handbook*, ed. Win Arn (Pasadena, CA: Church Growth Press, 1979), 182.

6. John Naisbitt, *Megatrends: Ten New Directions Transforming Our Lives* (New York: Warner, 1988).

7. Arleen Spenceley, "Facebook Is Going Public," *Tampa Bay Times*, February 12, 2012.

8. For a variety of studies correlating Christianity with health benefits, see http://www.creationtips.com/newsclips.htm.

9. Robert Putnam, "You Gotta Have Friends: A Study Finds That Americans Are Getting Lonelier," *Time*, July 3, 2006, 25.

10. Robert D. Putnam, *Bowling Alone* (New York: Simon and Schuster, 2000), 63.

Gary L. McIntosh (PhD, Fuller Theological Seminary) is professor of Christian ministry and leadership at Talbot School of Theology, and president of the Church Growth Network. He leads seminars and has written twenty books, including *Biblical Church Growth*, *Beyond the First Visit*, and *Taking Your Church to the Next Level*. He lives in Temecula, California.

Charles Arn (EdD, University of Southern California) is professor of outreach and Christian ministry at Wesley Seminary, Indiana Wesleyan University, and president of Church Growth, Inc. He has thirty-four years of experience in leading training events for churches and denominations throughout North America and the world. He lives in Glendora, California.

Your church's bright future
STARTS NOW.

It's easy to feel discouraged by shrinking attendance and slow spiritual growth in your church. But the first step to turning things around is hope. God can and does restore churches to new life, even as he restores individuals. Church health expert Gary McIntosh offers hope by showing the first things you need to do to make a new start for your church.

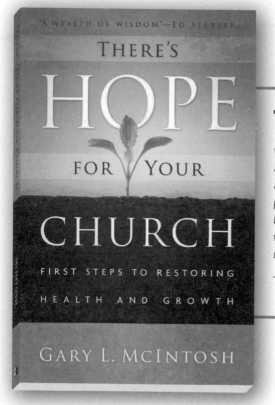

There's Hope for Your Church provides a wealth of wisdom for anyone seeking to turn around a declining or plateaued church. This book gives you hope and will show you the way to revitalize your church."

—Ed Stetzer, author of Viral Churches

Does your church put out the WELCOME mat or the DO NOT DISTURB sign?

We all like to think that our church is the friendliest one in town. But do visitors see it that way? Church consultant Gary L. McIntosh invites you to take another look at your church through the eyes of a first-time guest to identify the things that might be holding them back from a second visit.

This book offers sound advice on assessing and improving the ways in which your church attracts people, welcomes them, does follow-up, and brings them into the church family. It gives suggestions for making a welcoming attitude part of the very fabric of your church.

*When it comes to congregational outreach the fundamentals are inviting, welcoming, and following up with guests. **Beyond the First Visit** is an essential training tool on how to implement these fundamentals."*

—Dr. John W. Ellas, Center for Church Growth

BakerBooks
Relevant. Intelligent. Engaging.

Available wherever books and ebooks are sold.
Like us on 🅵 • Follow us on 🅱 ReadBakerBooks • Baker Books blog: relligent.com